Embracing Truth in Times of Adversity

Embracing Truth in Times of Adversity

Learning How to Listen and Trust Divine Guidance

Marjorie Daun Timberlake-Linton

iUniverse, Inc.
Bloomington

Embracing Truth in Times of Adversity
Learning How to Listen and Trust Divine Guidance

iUniverse books may be ordered through booksellers or by contacting:

iUniverse
1663 Liberty Drive
Bloomington, IN 47403
www.iuniverse.com
1-800-Authors (1-800-288-4677)

ISBN: 978-1-4620-1748-5 (sc)
ISBN: 978-1-4620-1749-2 (dj)
ISBN: 978-1-4620-1750-8 (ebk)

Library of Congress Control Number: 2011906882

Printed in the United States of America

iUniverse rev. date: 06/25/2011

Dedicated to my parents, the late Victor and Doris Timberlake, whose truth is the replica of a lighted candle and a continuous flame . . . also to my niece, Alexis Raine—an offspring from that "truth".

CONTENTS

Part III

Part IV

Acknowledgments

I would like to acknowledge and thank God for my mother and my father, the late Victor and Doris Timberlake, who constantly lived and demonstrated a life of prayer and encouraged me through the process to trust in God.

Throughout my childhood and after, I witnessed constant and unwavering faith in God enacted through every need, heartache, and challenge. As a result my childhood years were fruitfully shaped and I learned to embody good discipline and outstanding morals that my mother and father instilled in me.

My parent's profound faith had a great impact on my life, and it never ceased to inspire and uplift me in times of doubt. The source of their faith was an anchor from within, coursing throughout veins, arteries, and cartilage, never failing to withstand even the most threatening and raging storms of life. From this vantage point of light, I learned to acknowledge God in all my ways, put Him first, and trust and surrender to His presence during the most heartbreaking times of my life.

I treasure my siblings enormously, and I thank God for the bond we share physically, emotionally, and spiritually, and for their unconditional love and support in all things.

It was a wonderful and liberating moment when I discovered my spiritual home—Unity of Jamaica. The welcome I received from this loving community was like a breath of fresh air. Here, at this blessed place, I felt nurtured and uplifted, filled with new vigor and a mighty zest for living. It was evident that divine order was established, a new chapter of my life and a subsequent transition to greater heights imminent. The rich and practical teachings of the Unity movement have impacted my life in a very grand way. Not only have they helped to awaken my divine capabilities, but I am also constantly learning each day how to rightfully execute principles of truth.

My experience as a ministerial student at the Unity School of Christianity during the years 2000 and 2002 was exceptional; a once in a lifetime experience, the worth of a treasure! I consider myself very blessed to have afforded this privilege. From this place of gratitude I would like to acknowledge the faculty and staff of Unity School of Christianity for their patience and understanding; the management and staff of Silent Unity for their unconditional love and support; and most of all the class of 2002 for helping to unleash the caged spirit within me.

I desire to express special appreciation to my early spiritual guides, the late Reverends Enid Bailey and Steve Samms from Unity of Jamaica who both were intuitive enough to look beyond the appearances, discover something of potential within me, and help to bring it into expression. I am ever so grateful for their vote of confidence, which greatly helped to foster a sense of self-worth within me.

I also offer special thanks to Rev. Maxine Martin for her friendship, and for allowing me the freedom to express and to pursue my spiritual path. I acknowledge a host of light-bearers: my friends, confidants, and cheerleaders of Unity of Jamaica for helping to define my spirituality as we contemplated and processed our truths together.

Also worthy of mention are the board of directors and the congregation of Unity of St. Croix for allowing me into their lives as their first full time minister. My experience was no doubt a challenge, yet not a bit less than rewarding. In retrospect I consider the experience as a stepping—stone that afforded me ultimate growth as I strived to find my balance.

I am happy to express my profound appreciation and thanks to the present and past board of directors and to all the supporters of Unity on the Rock Prayer Ministry for their encouragement and support. Through all the ups and downs, trials and errors, I was forced to retreat, take stock, reevaluate my mission and my intention, and ultimately stretch far beyond my comfort zone in an effort to find my niche.

Last but not least, I am grateful for my very special friend, my unending support, my critic and my advisor, Eugeino, who constantly infuriated me by pushing my buttons and challenging me. Nevertheless, he unrelentingly proved his devotion and utmost belief in my ability to deliver and accomplish my goals, standing by me through it all.

Preface

Having been brought up in a closely-knit family structure, my spirituality was shaped to a large extent by my parents, who were ardent Christians. After many years of soul searching however, it became evident that my spiritual journey, unlike the rest of my siblings, would take a detour.

My parents taught me at an early age how to utilize my faith in handling challenging situations and I learnt to rely on God as sustainer and giver of all good things.

Since I was endowed with a very enquiring mind, I had many questions and I yearned for a greater understanding of "truth." I was subsequently divinely guided to Unity, an organization founded over one hundred years ago by Charles and Myrtle Fillmore, who both demonstrated physical healing of life threatening illnesses by simply changing their original concept of God in relation to themselves.

Their outstanding demonstration led to the publishing of Unity literature, a prayer ministry and a school of Christianity. Today, there are many Unity ministries worldwide, and the prayer ministry, "Silent Unity," is one of the largest of its kind in the world. Unity is described by Charles Fillmore as, "A link in the great educational movement inaugurated by Jesus Christ; our objective is to discern the truth in Christianity and prove it."

The teachings of Unity are timeless. It continues to bless me day by day as I discover the truth about myself. Through the process of acknowledging my powerlessness, I am learning how to transcend worldly consciousness, thus experiencing the fullness of life exemplified by Jesus, our way-shower. It is from this premise that I have been inspired to write this book, attempting to demonstrate that life is a journey of the soul, the destination of which is "self" discovery.

Practical Truth Teachings

The teachings of Unity are based primarily on the teachings of Jesus, and are referred to as "practical Christianity." Unity believes that everyone is a child of God, and within each individual is a spark of divinity. By acclaiming our divine birthright, ultimately by the understanding and practice of the principles of truth, each person is able to live a happy, peaceful, successful, and spiritually fulfilled life.

Perhaps the quality of Unity that I admire most is that it does not proselytize; it allows each person the freedom to choose his or her own path. Each individual is therefore drawn to his or her own place of worship by divine appointment. Willing participants are encouraged to discover their divine power within them, but no one is coerced into acceptance. Although each person as an individual has free choice, in the long run each person has to give an account for himself or herself.

In many instances, Unity is often misunderstood and mistaken for other religions. The pamphlet, "A Unity View of New Age and New Thought" helps to clarify this misconception, as it states, "Clearly Unity is a Christian religion in that it is based on the life and the teachings of Jesus Christ." Originally, Charles Fillmore simply called it "practical Christianity."

Unity is firmly Bible based and interprets the Bible metaphysically, meaning, "*Beyond the Physical.*" In this case, it refers to the reading of the Bible for its allegorical or underlying meanings. Unity declares that the truth taught is not new, nor do they claim special revelations of new religious principles; Unity teaches humankind to use and prove the eternal Truth taught by the Master Jesus and therefore describes its methodology as "more of a teaching than a creed, and more an attitude than a teaching"

The teachings of Unity are centered on the message of Jesus that the kingdom of God is within (Luke 17:21). Many people, however, have been brought up to believe in an autocratic God, living somewhere up in the sky, which punishes us when we are bad and rewards us when we are good. Many people also believe we need to plead to and placate God. This does not stand to reason when we read the creation story in chapters 1 and 2 in the book of Genesis. In Genesis 1:27 "So God created man in His own image, in the image of God created He him; male and female created He them," and verse 31: "And God saw everything that He had made, and, behold, it was very good." If humankind is created in God's image and likeness, and if everything that God created is good, then humankind should be able to work in harmony with the universal law, or what we know as a principle, to create our desired good. Unity acknowledges God as substance, the source of everything; the source of all power, authority, and strength.

Basic Truth Principles

There are many guiding Truth principles, but Unity outlines five basic ones as a guideline to living the abundant life as taught by the Master teacher, Jesus. The first is that *"God is absolute and unchanging good"*; everywhere equally present, present in all circumstances—even in the most heartbreaking situations in life—whether we call them good or bad. Because God is good, He is capable of restoring all things to newness of life and purpose. In order for us to experience the goodness of God, however, we need to acknowledge our powerlessness. We of ourselves can do nothing, but with God we can do anything. God will work in and through us to bring forth absolute good.

The second principle and perhaps the most profound teaching of Unity is that *"Christ Spirit lives within each individual."* In other words we have been blessed with divine potential, and by living the perfected life demonstrated to us by the Master Jesus we are able to realize and express the Christ nature within us. This is substantiated by Colossians 1:27: "To whom God would make known what is the riches of the glory of this mystery among the Gentiles; which is Christ in you, the hope of glory."

Unity also believes in the creative power of thought, which brings us to the third basic principle. *"Thoughts held in mind create after their kind."* Consequently, whatever we concentrate on will expand. We should therefore focus only on the good we wish to create in our world. The mind of God is all-good, all encompassing, and all-pervading. By applying the principles of God-Mind, Jesus demonstrated to us how we too can live the abundant life and do even greater works than he did (John 14:12).

"Whatsoever things are true, whatsoever things are honest, whatsoever things are just, whatsoever things are pure, whatsoever things are lovely, whatsoever things are of good report; if there be any virtue if there be any praise, think on these things" (Philippians 4:8).

Prayer and meditation are important tools by which we gain access to the kingdom of God, and the fourth principle therefore states that "*the mind is the connecting link to God.*" Prayer and meditation help to bring our attention to God, who in all knowledge and wisdom gives us the desires of our hearts. We can only hear from God, however, when our minds are unencumbered, fixed on Him.

The fifth basic truth principle of Unity is to *"practice the truth that we know."* In order to demonstrate Good, one should not only know the truth, but one should also practice the truth that one knows. Practicing the truth involves doing the will of God, which not only aligns us with the mind of God, but also demonstrates our faith and brings into manifestation the perfect will of God concerning us.

Heaven and Hell

Unity believes that heaven and hell are not a physical place of existence, but rather a state of consciousness that can be experienced right here on earth. We experience both states from time to time, depending on the way we think and the way we live our lives. "And I will give unto thee the keys of the kingdom of heaven: and whatsoever thou shall bind on earth shall be bound in heaven: and whatsoever thou shall lose on earth shall be loosed in heaven" (Matthew 16:19). The good news is that we can chose to live the perfected life by changing our thinking at any moment. "Be ye transformed by the renewing of your mind, that ye may prove what is that good, and acceptable, and perfect, will of God" (Romans 12:2).

Our reluctance to let go of things that do not serve us will undoubtedly delay our good. In the book of Mark chapter 10, the rich young ruler was reluctant to cooperate with the universal laws of God, and because he was self-serving, he was unwilling to facilitate his healing and demonstrate Good. Jesus gave him the formula, which was to sell all his reliance on materiality and give it all to the poor.

These practical teachings of Unity are simple but they are profound. Jesus worked them all daily by putting God first in all things, trusting in God's omnipotence, omnipresence and omniscience and by doing the will of God. He subsequently demonstrated Good in all walks of life.

Introduction

God is our every existence. In Him we live, move, and have our being. "All things were made by Him and without Him was nothing made that was made" (John 1:3). God is therefore the unfailing, limitless, invincible capacity to accomplish good, and humankind is therefore inherently good and has the innate potential to create good using the universal laws of God.

Life is a process that takes us in a full circle from circumference to center of our being, or from sense consciousness to spiritual consciousness. Most of our distress in life is due to a belief in the myth of separation, manifesting in a mixed state of consciousness. As this feeling of separation is not our true state of being (like the Israelites during the Babylonian captivity), we yearn to go back to our true and natural state of being (Jerusalem, a state of peace and tranquility).

No one is exempt. Because of free will, we all embark on individual journeys with individual encounters. Sometimes we get distracted, consequently finding ourselves in unfamiliar territories. The journey back home to the center is executed through trust and ultimate surrender achieved through the practice of prayer and meditation.

All things are possible with God, but for miracles to appear we first need to surrender to the process by embracing the Truth. Author Paul Ferrini says in the book *The Silence of the Heart*, "To live a surrendered life is to be present moment to moment with our experience. It is to accept our experience without judging it. Or if we judge it to forgive ourselves for defending, for pushing away."

I have found the Bible to be a very powerful guide and a most necessary tool for living. It is called the "Living Bible" because all the teachings are authentic, alive, and relevant to life as it is lived today. Those of us who take time to read the Bible will find hidden truths revealed from within that relate to outer experiences. When read with understanding, the messages of the Bible are purely moral, psychological, inspiring, and comforting. The chapters in this book relate to human experiences on a whole, and relate to the teachings of the Bible.

The Bible contains the sum total of our experiences as an evolutionary race. Author Charles Fillmore and cofounder of Unity states "The Bible is the story of man's generation, degeneration, and regeneration." The first few chapters in the book of Genesis relate to the progression from spiritual man to manifest man. This is followed by the fall of man and man's search to find the lost Eden.

It is my belief that although some of the teachings of the Bible can be interpreted literally, most of its interpretations are beyond the physical and are revealed through desire coupled with deep levels of concentration and contemplation. "And ye shall seek me and find me, when ye shall search for me with all your heart" (Jeremiah 29:13).

The reading of the Bible helps us to renew our minds and find peace through inner transformation. Mind is the essence of its teachings, and humans subjected to trials and errors always have the opportunity to be transformed by the renewing of the mind. Ultimately, the Bible exposes the fragility of human nature, as well as the divinity of the human soul. It exposes our humanity through trials from all walks of life, and at the same time gives us hope.

"Truth" within each individual can be discerned through individual awareness, and although many people may have different concepts of truth, it is nevertheless a universal message from the heart. There is no doubt that living life from the highest perspective of the "self" greatly improves one's quality of life.

In the book of John, Jesus used many "I am" statements with very positive connotations. From a metaphysical perspective the "I am" represents the Christ Spirit within. It is often used by human beings both negatively and positively, but we should be careful how we use it, as whatever we attach to it becomes a reality. Saying the words "I am sick" for instance, is actually claiming sickness as an experience. Conversely, affirming "I am healthy" will also attract health and wholeness as our experience. The "I am" or Christ within us cannot be sick, afraid, poor, or weak. To attach negation to the "I am" is therefore to take the name of the Lord in vain. Discrediting our Christ potential will land us in the dark, but there is always an opportunity to take responsibility and regroup, because the forgiving love of God sets us free from all mistakes of the past and present.

I am able to write this book and attest to the power of God only because I have lived and proven the truth principles laid down for us by our master teacher, Jesus the Christ, over and over again. The main objective of this book is to therefore confirm the greatness of God with the appropriation of individual experiences and inspiring stories, further validating them through the lenses of biblical teachings and other religious writings. As the teachings of the Unity and the writings of the cofounders Charles and Myrtle Fillmore have shaped and formed my spirituality to a large extent, I have consequently made many references from many of their written materials.

Using the Bible as well as other Scriptural references, this book attests to the authenticity of prayer, supported by personal stories of overcoming experiences. Although these stories are individual experiences, they are by no means isolated or restricted to any particular individual. Rather, they point to the commonality of the whole human experience. We all have our individual stories, but they are intricately interwoven into one grand design, ultimately pointing to our similarities and hence our connectedness. Sharing our stories not only validates the teachings of the Bible and other scriptures, it also accentuates our similarities as a race. Being interdependent and interrelated, we are mirrors for each other, and sharing our stories reinforces our commonality.

Ultimately, we all learn from each other just as much as we are also capable of teaching each other. With a spirit of humility we become empty vessels, teachable, ultimately receiving the abundance of the universe—success and contentment in all affairs, and a peace that surpasses all understanding.

My intention is to help build a bridge over which we can cross, thereby realizing our oneness with God and with each other; to encourage the hopelessly despondent, the lonely, the lost, the forsaken, and the helpless by proving the authenticity of the omnipresent, omnipotent, and omniscient God. May all who read this book find it meaningful; May they all be greatly blessed, and may they all be mightily inspired and motivated to pursue and experience the depth of the Spirit.

PART I

1

Embarking on the Journey . . .

There can never be a new way of life without first negating an old one. The Bible portrays humankind on a journey, where old ways of thinking and being may be transformed to new ways of thinking and being; hence the Old Testament and the New Testament. The Old Testament is centered on God as Principle, the law of cause and effect, whereas the New Testament extends beyond the law, through Jesus Christ, by whose grace we are redeemed. In other words, we can be saved from erroneous beliefs and adverse situations through grace, or through the consciousness of the Christ spirit within whenever we deny error, affirm truth, and live our lives from that perspective.

The New Testament portrays a resurrected consciousness, demonstrated by Jesus, whose death and subsequent resurrection paved the way to eternal life. Jesus tells us that we too can do what He did, and we can also do greater things too by having that resurrected consciousness of Jesus. We therefore can redeem our lives and achieve conscious union with God through the denial of our innermost self.

Our Divine Nature

We are spiritual beings . . . one with God and one with each other. The presence of God is everywhere, equally present, within and without every human being, as well as within every living thing. Nevertheless, as individuals our experiences are invariably different. Consequently, we all experience different states of consciousness. "In my father's house there are many mansions" (John 14:2). God accepts us all, no matter who we are, where we are in consciousness, whether we err or whether we fail to practice the truth.

Truth, which is very simple, is within each individual, but it is often obscured because of willfulness, as the human mind tends to analyze and judge, often invalidating the truth. Consequently, we often question the unknown, conceptualizing and formulating, but arriving nowhere. By ourselves, we cannot accomplish anything.

> "In the beginning was the Word, and the word was with God and the Word was God. All things were made by Him; and without Him was not anything made that was made. In Him was life; and life was the light of all men" (John 1:1-3).

We are all connected to the divine Spirit; it courses throughout our entire being, and although we have different personalities, our individuality remains the same—authentic, and the very existence of our being reflected in the nature of the indwelling Christ. Although we may not be consciously aware of it, there is no denying that we all reflect the nature of the "Christ". "To whom God would make known what is the riches of the glory of this mystery among the gentiles; which is Christ in you, the hope of glory" (Colossians 1:27).

Although our individual circumstances are different, the desired manifestation, goal, or destination for all mankind is typically the same even though we may not all acknowledge this. The ultimate goal for us on the spiritual path is to experience a resurrected self. Ultimately, through the realization of the resurrected Christ consciousness within, we experience everlasting life. This is our gift from God. "For God so loved the world that He gave His only begotten son, that whosoever believeth on Him should not perish but have everlasting life" (John 3:16).

Metaphysically, the Bible portrays the evolution of human consciousness. It is viewed as a compass for living, alive with relevant truths applicable to the sum total of all our experiences on earth. Each story and each character represents different aspects of our lives with a subsequent message for us all. We will find relevant truths within the Bible applicable to every aspect of our lives when we engage in the daily reading of God's Word, spend quiet moments in prayer and meditation, and live lives of truth.

A New Consciousness

In the Old Testament, the first covenant was marked by the Mosaic Law that basically said if you obey God, you are blessed, and if you disobey God, you are cursed. After over one hundred and twenty years of Judaism, the new covenant, Christianity, and subsequently the New Testament was born. With the new covenant and the New Testament came Jesus Christ and old thoughts became personified in Jesus. Consequently, the spiritual journey for humankind involves a transition from the Adam consciousness to Christ consciousness, or from law to grace.

Despite all this revelation, however, many people from generation to generation still believe in an autocratic God who lives up in the sky and punishes us when we are bad and rewards us when we are good. There are many people like myself, however, who by applying simple logic and reason have repudiated the authenticity of this teaching from the premise of a loving and good God depicted throughout the entire Bible.

In the book of Genesis, God created everything that was good, including humankind, who He created in His image and after His likeness, ultimately giving us dominion over everything he made. (Gen. 1:27-28; 31) This by no means sounds like a stern and autocratic God.

The hardships that we experience in life are due to personal will, which results in lack of spiritual understanding. Like the prodigal son who strayed from his good because of willfulness, and like the Israelites who got distracted due to sense consciousness, we too often fall short and as a consequence fail to maintain our good.

Because God is good and His love for us is unconditional, we have the choice at any moment to be reconnected with our divine selves simply by changing our thinking (old thoughts must die, as symbolical in the death of the old folks prior to reaching the Promised Land).

We all fall short both collectively and individually, making all manner of mistakes, but nevertheless we all have the opportunity to correct them and start all over again. In order to aspire to the desired goal of a resurrected consciousness, we need to die to, change, or release old ways of thinking and being that do not serve us. This is a continuous process.

The Secret of Eternal Life

In our effort to achieve that perfected state of consciousness, we unconsciously make several journeys toward the Promised Land of achieving the spiritual in our lifetime, failing miserably at times and starting all over again. The apostle Paul says "I die daily" (I Cor.15: 31). As we strive to arrive at our perfected state, sooner or later we arrive at that place in consciousness where the only thing that matters most is our relationship with our Divine self, which in and of itself is the perfect gift of surrender and the manifestation of every good thing.

It is not always easy to let go of old habits, things, or people that seem to hinder our spiritual progress. In Mark chapter 10, although the rich young ruler had observed the commandments that God gave to Moses, Jesus emphasized that mere observation of the law alone did not merit eternal life. Jesus told the rich young ruler that he lacked one thing. Interestingly, Jesus did not name that one thing, but added that in order for the young ruler to inherit eternal life he needed to sell all his possessions and give to the poor. God is the one Presence and Power in our lives and in the world, and He is the only source of every good thing. As co-creators with God, we must do our part and take responsibility for our desires to be fulfilled. We must act. When Jesus told the rich young ruler to sell all that he had and give to the poor, I believe that Jesus was referring to the young man's attitude, and his dependency on outer things.

Jesus did not tell the rich young ruler just to give his earthly possessions to the poor. He told him to sell them first, and then give what was sold to the poor. Why would Jesus advise him to sell them if they were actual things? If they were, He could have told him from the beginning to give them straight to the poor. One can only imagine that Jesus was referring to the young man's state of consciousness, which obviously lacked a sense of humility.

Jesus knew that self-sufficiency, egotism, self-righteousness, pride, and dependence on materiality were the young man's hindrances. All these negative things pointed to his ego that stood in his way. This was that "one thing" that he lacked according to Jesus. Instead of focusing on the power of God within him he focused on himself. To sell his possessions was to release all his mental baggage and self-sufficiency, after which he would experience a resurrected state of being . . . . the presence and power of God within him, the source of all good things. "Blessed are the poor in spirit: for theirs the kingdom of heaven" (Matthew 5:3).

Unfortunately, releasing his self sufficiency or selling his possessions was a difficult task for him, so the young man went away sorrowful and obviously lost his blessings. "Whosoever shall not receive the kingdom of God as a little child will not enter therein" (Mark 10:15).

In His healing ministry, Jesus performed various types of healing depending on the consciousness of those afflicted. When great faith was demonstrated, Jesus would simply speak the Word and it would be done according to one's belief. In other cases He would simply give instructions, allowing the opportunity for introspection as he did with the rich young ruler, while in other cases He used physical touch. Jesus is our way-shower, but ultimately we have to do the work for ourselves and let go of negation and affirm and practice the truth. We need to acknowledge God as the only Presence and Power in the world by letting go of our egos and living our highest truths from within.

Willfulness Causes Spiritual Dissention

Willfulness consequently takes us into deep waters, and like Job, our good works are delayed because we have more questions than answers. Due to willfulness the human mind often seeks difficult and complex solutions to easy and non-complicated problems, resulting in mental disconnection from our divine selves. This manifests as mental confusion and distraction as demonstrated by the "fall of man" in the book of Genesis. Author and cofounder of Unity, Charles Fillmore says in his book, *The Mysteries of Genesis,* "Man fell because he did not keep his mind on the source of life. He departed from spiritual consciousness and saw both good and evil. If he had held to the one good, good is the only thing that he could have manifested."

When our thoughts are chaotic and confusing we often miss out on experiencing the presence of God within us, and we subsequently find ourselves in a far country like the prodigal son, mentally separated from what is rightfully ours. "For God is not the author of confusion, but of peace, as in all churches of the saints". (I Corinthians 14:33). David, God's beloved reminds us that the only way out of this dilemma is to become still, by releasing all negative thoughts and activities. "Be still and know that I am God" (Psalm 46:10).

This wonderful promise from God is the sheer simplicity of the equation, but sometimes we complicate simplicity and subsequently delay our good. Such was the case with Naaman, captain of the host of the king of Syria, stricken with leprosy, who was told to wash in the river Jordan seven times. Because of pride, Naaman discounted the simplicity of this advice as the possible cure for his ailment. Why should a man of his social standard wash in such an ordinary river when there were more important rivers available to him?

Sometimes we become fixed in sense consciousness and in our humanity become our own providence, as Naaman did, envisioning healing from one angle only, through the touch of Elisha and the spoken word of God. Healing, however requires a great amount of faith, humility, and obedience that comes in all shapes and forms. Sometimes it may involve going to see a doctor; in other cases it might just involve something simple like engaging in daily exercises and eating nutritious foods. Sometimes it might just involve being still, and surrendering to the presence and power of God and sometimes it might just involve immersing ourselves in constant prayer and fasting.

When our backs are against the wall, however, and we have no other place to turn, we eventually surrender to the will of God and prove what is perfect and good. Having no other place to turn and realizing that he had nothing to lose after all, Naaman eventually consented to washing in the river Jordan, and he was subsequently healed of leprosy.

Obviously Naaman's healing required much more than mere physical touch or the use of the spoken word. He required a deep spiritual and physical cleansing, which according to Elisha the prophet could only be accomplished by washing seven times in the river Jordan.

When we believe God's promises and act according to his Word, we will accomplish our goals and our lives will become meaningful. The woman with the issue of blood was instantly healed by merely touching the hem of Jesus' garment. Because of the Centurion's faith and humility, his daughter was healed before he knew it. Of the ten lepers healed, only one who went back to thank Jesus seemed to have maintained his healing.

Some things are beyond our ability to comprehend. All we need to do is have a desire for a higher sense of awareness, and God will reveal what is necessary to be revealed. "I have many things to say unto you, but you cannot bear them now. Howbeit when the spirit of truth is come he will guide you into all truth" (John 16:12-13). What we need to know will be revealed at the right time, whenever we are prepared and ready to receive illumination. "The secret things belong unto the Lord our God: but those things which are revealed belong unto us and unto our children forever that we may do all the words of this law" (Deut. 29:29).
"It is not for you to know the times or the seasons which the father hath put in His own power" (Acts 1:7).

Experience Teaches Wisdom

Most lessons in life are predicated on experiences. During our human experiences we all have the tendency to fall short and make mistakes, mentally suffering the consequences. Each mistake we make is due to a belief in separation from our Christ nature, and attracts a related consequence because of the law of cause and effect. Yet we also have the opportunity to take responsibility and be redeemed by the grace of God. Consequently, we can begin again and again and again. The choice is ultimately ours. "Choose you this day whom ye will serve" (Joshua 24:15).

Although we are individuals, we all have individual choices and experiences, and from a humanistic standpoint we all make mistakes and fall short of living the perfected life.

Nevertheless, no matter where we are or how severe our circumstances God is always present, and the moment we become consciously aware of His presence, we undeniably prove that God is absolute good, everywhere equally present.

Although we are one in spirit, as individuals our journeys may take different paths. We may encounter many different challenges along the way, but through them all we learn that survival depends on our ability to release, let go, and let God. We experience victory only when we take ourselves out of the way and trust God's divine will for our lives. "He must increase, but I must decrease" (John 3:30).

There is no more of God in any one person, but God reveals Himself to us according to our level of receptivity. "When He, the spirit of truth is come, he will guide you into all truth" (John 16:13). To be truly cognizant of the power of God is to be conscious, and to be conscious is to be present to this moment, living constantly in the awareness of the Father. To live in the present moment is to behold God in everything and in all aspects of life, to acknowledge Him in all our ways, and to live a life of non-resistance. God is in every experience, and we have the privilege of experiencing His presence when we surrender to His will and purpose for our lives.

Jesus reminds us in Matthew 6:20 that "things" do not last. Thieves will break in and steal them and dust and rust will corrupt them. In order to experience the kingdom of God, the rich young ruler needed to release his attachment to outer things, outer distractions. "Seek ye first the kingdom of God and his righteousness and all these things will be added unto you" (Matthew 6:33).

Surrendering to God's Will

Surrendering to God's will is not about living a non-productive life; it is about acknowledging God as the essence of everything; it is about being rather than doing. It is a state of being when thoughts and feelings become united. In a metaphysical sense, it was necessary for Jacob experience this state of being as he arrived in the land of the people of the east. On his arrival he came upon a field with three flocks of sheep lying by it and a well from which the flocks were watered. There was however, a great stone upon the mouth of the well. As Jacob spoke with the shepherds, he sensed the distress of the sheep in the midday heat and suggested that it was time for them to be watered and fed. The shepherds, however, worked according to the divine plan, and even though the flocks appeared thirsty, the time was not right. "We cannot until all the flocks are gathered together and the stone is rolled away from the well. Then we water the sheep" (Gen. 29:7-8).

According to author Charles Fillmore in the *Metaphysical Bible Dictionary,* sheep metaphysically represent "the natural and pure thoughts that flow into man's consciousness from spirit." Jacob, still in transition, was not yet ready for his transformation. Consequently, he had to wait until his thoughts and feelings were in sync with each other and ultimately with God. It was only when this was accomplished that the stone of negation would be removed and the light of God revealed, resulting in guidance and spiritual understanding.

Nothing happens before its time, and there is a divine process to everything in life. Whenever we are on a spiritual journey, we invariably reach a crossroad when we become ready to release old habits and transform them into the love and light of God. Letting go of the old is a gradual process. Sometimes it takes a period of time for our thoughts to be gathered together (acknowledged), watered (cleansed), and released (healed).

There are certain steps involved in the process of surrender:

1. Taking responsibility
2. Acknowledging your powerlessness
3. Transforming your thinking
4. Letting go and letting God

When the state of surrender is achieved, one realizes God as the resolution to all challenges, the answer to all desires, and the silent partner in every situation; nothing can be accomplished without Him. "Before they will call I will answer, and while they yet speak I will hear" (Isaiah 65:24). In his book *The Universe Is Calling,* author Eric Butterworth writes, "Whatever you are seeking to pray about there is an answer that is at once a pattern and a plan for its unfoldment. You do not make this answer. It exists within the depths of your subconscious mind, even before you have the awareness of need."

The ensuing chapters of this book contain many perspectives of Truth teachings derived from the Bible and interpreted from an individual perspective with the help of the teachings of Unity. These insights and interpretations are tools that are helpful in overcoming many obstacles.

Many of them I have tried and proven. Many of them I am still trying; it is a continuous process that never stops. Consequently, the sky is the limit to our spiritual growth and development. The opportunities to rise higher and higher often manifest themselves in greater or lesser ways depending on our level of receptivity. Ultimately, the choice is ours. There is no depth to the Truth that lies within us. Consequently, we are always on the journey of self-discovery.

2

The Preparation

> "I am now in the presence of pure being, and immersed in the Holy Spirit of life, love and wisdom. I acknowledge Thy Presence and Thy power, O blessed Spirit; in Thy divine wisdom now erase my mortal limitations and from Thy pure substance of love brings into manifestation my world, according to Thy perfect law."
>
> Charles Fillmore

Christian growth is an interior process that involves an inner growth and transformation of the heart, the soul, and the mind. It includes attitudes and opportunities seasoned with the love and nurturing of those who act as our guardians.

The journey of the spiritual aspirant is often adorned with many trials and setbacks, but nevertheless with wonderful and unlimited possibilities that only God can give. This is the gift of grace. Grace equips us with hope, the spirit of understanding and the power of perseverance. Ultimately we unfold like a flower and grow toward the light.

During His outstanding childhood Jesus demonstrated this inner growth process and inner transformation. He had a mission to complete, and His earthly parents gave him unwavering support by allowing Him the opportunity and space to stretch and grow beyond limit. His earthly parents, Mary and Joseph, were tirelessly devoted to God and trusted

Him with abandon. They were undoubtedly instrumental in doing their part to the outworking of God's divine purpose for Jesus. He was to become the Savior of the world, so He grew in wisdom and in stature beyond His years.

As the preparation of the soil is important to the feasibility of the crop, likewise the starting point of home plays a very important role in the advancement and development of one's future endeavors. Whatever a child learns in his childhood years stays with him throughout his lifetime and prepares him well for the unforeseeable future.

Looking back over the years of my childhood, I am grateful for my parents, whose unrelenting faith in God molded and shaped my life in no uncertain fashion and resulted in an aftermath of praise and thanksgiving to the One presence and one power in my life and in the world—God, the good, the omnipotent.

Life during my childhood years was nothing spectacular. In retrospect, however, I would never trade it for anything else in the world. My family and I lived a very simple life, partially unaffected by the demands of society, highly adventurous, but unequivocally spiritual nonetheless.

As a cultivator of the land, my father had no fixed income since everything depended on the harvest. There were times when the harvest was scanty, but my mother never lost faith. Even in the appearance of lack, there was an air of expectancy. There was many a time when there was nothing visible for us to eat, but my mother never lost faith. She would simply go down on her knees and pray, and it never failed that somehow, miraculously, someone would appear with provisions to save the day. We subsequently learned to be content whether there was much or little, because we knew that God was our provider.

My parents were born prayer warriors. Their rich prayer consciousness anchored them safely through many storms. Children live what they learn, so it is no wonder that I am deeply affected by my parent's prayer habits. Prayer subsequently has become the cornerstone of my life, and I cannot imagine my life without the consciousness of it.

My spirituality was shaped from an early age. Under the guidance of my parents I quickly learned the importance of taking responsibility. Their unrelenting spirit of truth prepared me for many future endeavors, eventful and uneventful, which I attracted both consciously and unconsciously. Under their spiritual guidance and support I learned that there are many facets to life, but by trusting God's divine plan of good for my life I learnt to endure and overcome many seeming obstacles in my way.

Living in the country did not afford us the luxuries and amenities that city life offers, nor did we have the privilege of frolicking around in malls or amusement parks. Instead, we made use of and enjoyed what nature offered us freely and naturally—the sun; the moon; the stars; the hills; the valleys; lush vegetation and shrubbery; giant trees firmly rooted, towering high up in the sky (some as old as our ancestors); fruit trees of every description (some often laden with ripe and juicy fruits within our very reach); and to top it all, flowing rivers and streams both large and small, carefully designed to cool us down and add a spark of serenity in the midday sun. Overall, everything seemed to be a great conspiracy to bless us in the moment by providing food, shelter, shade, light, and even water to quench our thirst and refresh our spirits. Such things were the source of zeal and enthusiasm we often experienced, whether or not we were aware of the lavishness and generosity of the universe.

Our way of survival while we grew up in the country was a cultivated art. Without the use of modern amenities we were forced to rely on our inner resources, putting our skills and creativity to the test. Our talents and skills literally shone through relentlessly, as we often outclassed even ourselves, producing and directing all manner of cultural activities. We believed that our fun was unmatched, and we were extremely happy even through perilous times and challenging situations.

I also learned that self-reliance is the product of belief, and that belief is anchored and upheld by faith. The importance of a lasting relationship with God and relying on the Word of God ultimately constitutes the sole purpose for living; anything else is unimportant. Ralph Waldo Emerson states in his book *Self Reliance,* "To believe your own thought, to believe what is true for you in your private heart, is true for all men—that is genius. Speak your latent conviction, and it shall be the universal sense; for always the inmost in due times becomes the outmost."

We were daring and adventurous to say the least, often overriding barriers way out of bounds, venturing into deep waters way up to our necks, often putting our very lives at risk. Even though we were often warned of ensuing dangers, we took the risks anyway; we were prepared to suffer the consequences of broken bones and limbs, bruises to our bodies, as well as severe punishment, the ultimate of which was being grounded for weeks. Nevertheless, the fun we experienced was worth it.

I loved to follow my bigger sister around, but this often proved very unwise and detrimental. Being a tomboy, she was very good at getting into trouble, but also very skilled in avoiding the whip. I was not as skillful in my escape as she was, so I would be severely punished. By the time my sister got home my father's anger would subside, but my mother, in her fairness, often insisted that my sister got her share of punishment as well. This seldom happened. My sister always got away Scot-free.

Mother often left the spanking for father to do—which he seldom did—and whenever he did, our mother had to come to our rescue. Despite his cool disposition, whenever he approached us with his hands behind his back it spelled trouble.

I was the sixth child out of nine, with two boys after me followed by a girl ten years my junior. My two brothers often teamed up against me and constantly teased and provoked me, which resulted in constant fights. In order to survive I resorted to aggression, using mostly my fingernails as my weapon. Needless to say, my father often chastised me, because being the oldest of the three meant I was required to exercise restraint.

Before my baby sister arrived on the scene, I was the object of attention. I was told that I was cute, and I often paraded in front my sibling's friends, much to my sister's annoyance. They were even more annoyed when my mother sometimes sent me along with them on their dates. Their boyfriends didn't seem to mind at all, but my sisters were often infuriated. Nevertheless, I felt very important.

Growing up in the country of Jamaica was quite a privilege for me, as I often felt a wealth of inter-dependence, a connectedness with nature and freedom that was unparalleled. There was no limit to the fun and enjoyment to be experienced climbing hills, treading steep and rustic valleys, and swimming in crystal-clear rivers that seem to meander endlessly across the terrain. This wonderful and freeing experience naturally sets the tone for the ultimate unleashing of one's creativity in its entirety.

At night, as there were no street lamps to guide us, we walked in the dark daunted by fear, yet with a calm assurance that we were protected by an unexplained presence somewhere around us as well as within us. We often felt this presence as a deep and penetrating light, not visible to the physical eyes, yet all pervading and most undoubtedly powerful. It penetrated our very being to the fullest degree as we surrendered in its presence. Although we could scarcely fathom the dynamics of this presence, in an uncanny way we felt secure and at one with it. This was the only light that we knew during the night, and we relied on its protecting and guiding presence. At times, when we seemed engulfed with anxiety and fear, we somehow miraculously found strength to overcome such unfounded weaknesses.

As our recreational activities were centered on outdoor sports and activities, we became gruesomely attuned to the whisper of the universe. At nights the stillness of the moment could be felt like rapture, so intense that it penetrated the very core of our beings. We could almost hear our own heartbeats. The moon and the stars in their glory executed the demands of the moment, casting their silvery beams upon our path, guiding us along the way. As fearful as we were at times, we had to admit that the ambience of the countryside during the nighttime was undoubtedly captivating, filled with magnificence and pure wonder.

The scene at night was spectacular, as creatures and insects of every description paraded in our presence: fireflies, butterflies, moths, bees, frogs, grasshoppers, and even mosquitoes, just to name a few. They surrounded us from virtually every angle—before us, above us and around us—in all their glory, each with its individual mission. They all meandered in the dark, unique and independent, each communicating its own language, but nonetheless in collective solidarity with each other, and subsequently in perfect harmony with the universe. The splendid array of lights made it feel like a magic kingdom, as we felt infused with a strange combination of fear and tranquility, suspense and mystique.

As fearful as we were of the dark, our mother always seemed unaffected. She was a true Trojan rising to the occasion at all times, always ready to tackle the seemingly insurmountable.

She was a captain in charge of her ship, always miraculously steering in the right direction. In an effort to decrease our fears and anxieties, boost our self-confidence, and encourage humility, Mother often took pleasure in telling us stories about ghosts, maidens, mermaids, and princes. Mother's stories were very rich in morals and often had a deep spiritual message. We were encouraged to be compassionate, honest, brave, humble, appreciative, never failing to give thanks to God. She would laugh at our folly when in pure ignorance we believed some of the stories about ghosts, many that she herself composed just to get our attention.

My favorite story was called "The King of the Sea." There was once a maiden, she told us, who went fishing. She caught one single fish. The fish bargained with the maiden to spare its life in exchange for the granting of three wishes. This sounded wonderful, so the maiden agreed. There were so many things she wanted in life! Her first wish was to have riches. The second wish was to own a home, and the third, to own land. The fish kept its promise and all the maiden's wishes were subsequently granted. Soon, however, she began to develop an air of importance.

One morning as she lay in bed, the sun grazed through her bedroom window and greatly disturbed her rest. How annoyed she was! She wanted to enjoy her home without the penetrating glare of the sun. On impulse she hurried out of bed. She had to make yet another wish to the king of the sea. She had to ask him to get the sun out of her face in the mornings as she lay in bed!

Upon her arrival at the sea she noticed something odd. The sea was not the same. It looked troubled. "O king of the sea," she said, "I have just one more wish. Please take the sunlight out of my face in the mornings so that I can rest more comfortably in my bed." "Okay," said the king of the sea. "Your wish is granted." The maiden hurried back home, and to her surprise she found herself right back where she was in the beginning with the same old home, no land or riches.

This maiden was allowed only three wishes and she became greedy asking for a fourth one. This story reminds us that humility, gratitude and spiritual contentment are all necessary tools live a happy and successful life. Jesus reminds us that although things in life are helpful to our well being we should not allow them to control our world. "Take heed, and beware of covetousness: for a man's life consisteth not in the abundance of the things which he possesseth." (Luke 12:15).

Sometimes the more riches and things we pursue the less we achieve. Our mother frequently reminded us that material things of the world should not be the focus of our existence. We should focus our attention on the divine presence within us and know that all our needs will be supplied.

Undoubtedly, my siblings and I grew up with a rich legacy, a sincere and rightful approach to life and a profound strength of character. Of the many things I admire about my mother, perhaps one that takes precedence is her outstanding prayer habit. She always found time to sit alone and pray, on bended knees, whether or not there was a need—morning, noon, or night. No matter where she was, at home or abroad, no matter what went on around her, she never started her day or retired at night without first going on her knees in prayer. Her ritual of going on bended knees portrayed a deep sense of humility, unquestionable faith, and a relentless spirit, all of which I greatly admired and tried desperately to emulate.

I did not understand the dynamics of what really took place then. I only knew that Mother believed in something almost outlandish; something far beyond the reaches of the mind; something beyond the realization of the five senses, yet something real and tangible. In fact, she proved that although God could not be seen with the physical eye, or even thought of with the intellect alone; God could be felt and loved.

Whatever strength my mother generated from prayer was displayed in her general disposition. She always seemed unaffected by limitation, always content with what she had, never failing to demonstrate from healing to supply, often at the opportune moment. Although she had nine children to feed and no visible form of supply, one could never tell if my mother was flustered, as her calm demeanor erased any signs of concern. Her positive attitude gave us a sense of comfort and security. To us she was the epitome spiritual peace and contentment, the symbol of a lighted candle dispelling any evidence of darkness.

Looking back, I do not believe that her act of praying on bended knees in itself was the key to my mother's constant demonstrations, but evidently this discipline reinforced her faith in God, who is unseen, within and without, and everywhere equally present. The important thing is that she believed in a power higher than herself, God the good, and that was all she needed. She lived each moment without a murmur, content and secure with cultivated hope and trust.

As children we were often in awe of our mother's remarkable acts of faith. We thought she had magical powers. She was our mediator and our protector and we felt safe and secure with her as she frequently offered prayers of intercession on our behalves. She was doctor, lawyer, friend, and advisor to us, and we trusted in her intuitive spirit until the day she died. In the wake of impending dangers or life threatening situations, she gathered us together like a mother hen and calmed our fears with her prayers. She always had the right remedy for every situation that faced us, whether it was the spoken word or a special concoction of herbs. It didn't matter which one it was, all that mattered is that it was ministered with faith and love, and it never failed to work!

Not to be forgotten is my father, who also had a profound effect on my life. His calm and endearing demeanor could easily be misjudged. When we went way beyond our limits, he could be very firm. Seldom ruffled and easy-going, my father lived his life in absolute reverence to God and man. He was comical, full of joy and laughter, a real charmer, father and friend to all and sundry. He had an ear for listening, and he was lovingly called "Uncle Vic."

As deacon of the church my father ministered with pride and devotion, always going to church on Sunday mornings, come rain or come shine. He officiated in the absence of the minister who trusted him with abandon. My father was chief cook and bottle-washer of the church. On many occasions during inclement weather conditions he would often be the only one in church, but he didn't mind. He held service anyway.

Living in the countryside of Jamaica was a very rich and rewarding experience. We lived in a very close–knit community where everyone looked out for each other. We learned to respect our elders, or else we would be subjected to severe punishment. The public school that we attended was very edifying morally, spiritually, and intellectually, fully preparing us for our chosen career paths. In order to enter into a high school, we had to do very well on an entrance examination. This was a very competitive examination, as the space in the high schools was limited; consequently, the pass mark was very high. Those of us who were awarded scholarships were considered very bright and lucky. I was awarded a half scholarship, which meant that my pass mark was satisfactory, but not high enough to qualify me for an expense-free tuition, so my parents had to pay a part of my tuition expenses. This was a big stretch for them, but they were willing to make sacrifices for our education. This was a privilege, and my family and I were overjoyed.

Due to financial restrictions, however, my parents could not afford boarding accommodation for me, so I had to ride the country bus mornings and evenings to and from school. There were three busses that traveled that route daily, and when you missed them, you were in big trouble. Transportation after certain hours was limited. My mother was not very open in demonstrating her affection, but nevertheless she loved us fiercely. This was publicly apparent in the face of grave danger. I was to prove her undying love for me one day when I missed the last bus back home from school after attending an after-school event.

When I missed the bus home that evening I became frantic. I tried to settle my frazzled nerves, but anxiety got in the way. I finally resorted to my best defense—prayer. I immersed myself in the act of prayer and I prayed, "Please God, let someone come to help me!" Not long after, my prayer was answered when a truck driver and his wife, who passed our home daily, came to my rescue.

Unfortunately, things did not go as easily as I expected. The truck developed mechanical problems, leaving us stranded in the middle of the night. We waited for hours—way past midnight—until help finally came.

I certainly felt loved when I eventually arrived home that night. My mother was very happy at my return, and she held me closely, tears streaming down her face, and she praised God for my safe return. Afterwards, I discovered that mother had sent out a search party to find me, and when they returned later that night, dreading to report their fruitless search, they were surprised and relieved to find me at home, comfortably tucked in and fast asleep. What a relief that was for everyone!

My mother's acts of faith were very inspiring, and she never failed to demonstrate them despite the adversity of the situation. Her acts of faith had a great impact on me, and I was moved with great admiration for her depth of faith and her ability to demonstrate. One day there was absolutely no food in the house, nor was there money to purchase food. If my mother was stressed about the situation, we could not tell. She appeared unaffected. She went about her daily chores as if all was well; like she knew something that we didn't. During the course of that day, as was her custom, I later observed her on her knees in prayer.

Later that day, while dusting and cleaning, a miracle took place. My mother found an envelope neatly tucked away under a book. Inside it was enough money for us to buy food not just for one day, but for many days. This remarkable demonstration remains a mystery to me to this day. No one knows how that envelope appeared or from whence it came.

My mother was highly motivated and very competitive. She never settled for mediocrity. She taught us how to stand firm even in the face of adversity and how to be the best at whatever we did. We were compelled to make our lights shine. Whenever we messed up she would always illustrate her points with little stories, and we often got the message—loud and clear.

She was never selfish. She instilled in us outstanding values, one of which was to remember those less fortunate than we were. She taught us how to share what we had with others, and she demonstrated this by sharing her blessings with our neighbors and friends. She often cared for the underprivileged, taking in the homeless, giving them food and clothing, encouraging them through crisis, and sending them to school.

This ability of my mother's to create something out of nothing truly touched my spirit in an unforgettable way. She always managed to, in a sense, multiply the loaves and fish, proving the inexhaustible supply of God's substance. Miraculously, we were never hungry and we were always immaculately dressed. Most of all, we were happy.

Mother was also very resourceful and creative. She would dissemble our old clothes, window curtains, and bedspreads and reassemble them, making them look completely new. This was particularly effective at Christmas time when funds appeared low. She would use her creative ability to transform the entire house, making it look brand new. Anyone coming to our home for the first time could not tell that the furnishings and accessories were not brand new.

As a parent my mother played an active role in the school's extracurricular activities, generously offering her skills and talents. We were known in the community for our talent as elocutionists, and we were always chosen to represent the church and the school in elocution competitions. Mother did not accept mediocrity; she demanded a very high standard. Consequently, each night we would stand in front of her bed and rehearse our lines until we perfected them, at least according to her standard. We were of humble means, but we were very rich in spirit, and my mother taught us always to be our best at whatever we did.

Of most importance was our education. As we had no electricity our mother tirelessly assisted us with our homework by lamplight each night. Despite our meager means, she made sure that we were ready for school mentally, emotionally, and physically. Outsiders often assumed that life was very good for us, and that we were quite comfortable economically. Little did they know that my mother's faith in God was practically the very source of everything we had.

As stern as she was, Mother was young at heart, free-spirited and playful, always ready to indulge us in our fantasies. Being readily accommodating, she never failed to identify with our needs. We cherished her guiding principles and wallowed in her leniency when she allowed us the freedom to explore our world. My mother trusted us with abandon; one of her guiding principles was, "honesty is the best policy," and she always encouraged us to share our concerns, our fears, and our wildest dreams with her.

As kids, we welcomed the freedom our mother entrusted to us, and it was very difficult to violate her trust. When temptations arose as we grew older, we made it a point of duty to stay within our boundaries, obeying her requests and never overriding them. Overall, we tried our best to be as honest and open with her as possible. If ever we were tempted, we would always remember her leniency and reconsider our intentions.

Her deep trust in us mimicked her deep belief in God. She knew that God would guide and protect us, so there was never the need to overprotect us. We welcomed her leniency and her way of interceding on our behalf at times, always managing to sway our father into allowing us a little freedom. "Let the children go. They will be all right," she often implored.

Mother loved nice clothes. She would help us to dress up on special occasions like when we went out on dates. She loved it when we looked smashing. She would use her creativity to transform our old clothes into brand new creations, and she would often deny herself so that we could have the best of what was available.

We also welcomed the times when we were ill, as her nurturing, comforting, and compassionate spirit gave us all the attention we craved. She fussed over us like a mother hen, not leaving us for a moment until she saw signs of recovery. She felt good when our appetites were unaffected. This was her way of gauging the severity of our illness. When they weren't up to par, she would appease us with the delicacies we often craved when we were well. If we were unaffected by her generosity, then she would really be concerned. Overall, we felt truly loved and cared for.

Despite our economic situation and having nine children to support, one day my mother saw a need to fill and courageously took the task of adopting a little five-year-old girl named Sandra. She treated Sandra as her own and likewise did Sandra. We all welcomed Sandra as a part of the family and later my mother received her blessings as Sandra was of great assistance during her illness.

As my father's income was unpredictable, our Christmas shopping was often done a day or two before Christmas. As a result, our Christmas tree, which was the local myrtle, was never decorated until Christmas Eve. We did not care, though; this was the norm for us, and the joy we experienced decorating our Christmas tree was unequaled. That feeling of glee has remained with me even to this day, and I still feel that Christmas trees should not be decorated before Christmas Eve.

Sleep was usually very short-lived for us on Christmas Eve night, as we were impatient for our good fortune from Santa Claus. We refused to go to bed because we wanted desperately to see Santa arrive. Santa was magical and mysterious, and we knew he would bring us many gifts. He strangely knew exactly what we wanted and exactly when to appear—when we were asleep! No matter how long we waited, we never ever got a chance to see Santa. Although the suspense was very intense and calculating, it did nothing but add a spark of excitement to our celebration. Christmas would not be the same without that air of suspense and excitement.

After weeks of anticipation, the calendar moving slowly, the most important day of the year would finally arrive, accompanied by an array of tinsel, plastic, and wrapping paper. This was a feeling of sheer jubilation. At the crack of dawn on Christmas Day we would hurry out of bed, anxious to see the goodies that Santa brought us. Under the tree would be gifts of all sorts—ribbons, socks, inexpensive toys, books, pens, crayons and the like. Although they were all inexpensive gifts, each item was beautifully and individually wrapped, giving the impression of abundance.

What we looked forward to most of all was our Christmas attire that was always carefully selected and fitted us perfectly. I remember going shopping with my mother once prior to Christmas, and she bought me a very pretty dress. On Christmas morning my pretty dress was nicely wrapped and placed under the Christmas tree, supposedly from Santa. In my childish curiosity I wondered how could Santa have given me the same dress that my mother had bought me, but my curiosity got quickly wrapped up in the exuberance of Christmas and all other inconsequential details were quickly forgotten. In that moment, all that mattered was the joy of Christmas celebration and my gifts from Santa.

We also looked forward to attending church on Christmas Sunday when we would proudly model our carefully selected attire for the congregation. We felt special, loved, and really cared for by our parents.

Our Christmas meal was usually very lavish. My brother, who was the eldest child, would come home for Christmas with a ham and a turkey. This of course was a special treat for us, as we only had this privilege at Christmas time. My mother, who was never selfish, would invite the neighbors to join us for Christmas dinner, and we felt that our Christmas celebration was the best in the whole world. Our celebration was very festive. For us kids this was a time of magic when everything was transformed. There was fun, laughter, and togetherness and we never lost sight of the true meaning of Christmas—the birth of Christ. Overall this was a time of joy and goodwill for us all as our hope and faith were renewed in Christ Jesus.

Our home was the center of attraction during the summer holidays, so our relatives and friends looked forward to the holidays when they would come to visit, let their hair down, and have nice clean, unadulterated fun. Being young at heart, my mother welcomed everyone in our home and took pleasure in entertaining at a moment's notice.

There was never a dull moment during the holidays. Our fun consisted of many and varied activities: hide and seek, moonlight hops, bush-cooking, dance parties, and even river bathing to name a few. Every day was an activity, even if it was simply to congregate at our home and appease each other with jokes. It was a very refreshing and enjoyable time for us all. We felt very blessed indeed.

People viewed my mother as a beacon of light in our community, and there was a generous outpouring of love and respect from everyone she encountered. Despite her leniency and accommodating spirit, there were rules and regulations to be obeyed. Respect and discipline were a natural part of the order, and interestingly, no one stepped out of line. “There is a time for everything” was one of her mottos.

Mother loved to sing. She would sing when she was cleaning house, when she was happy, or when there was a need. This seemed to be her way of communicating with God at a very deep level. Her favorite hymn was, “What a Friend We Have in Jesus,” which she would sing with such intensity that one could actually feel the presence of God in our home.

There was absolutely no room for doubt in my mother’s domain. My mother knew that that her supply came from the one and only source, God, the good, the omnipotent. She had a great resolve that somehow we would never go hungry, and miraculously we never did! I later learned from my mother that her secret power lied in her ability to surrender to the all-powerful, all-knowing and all-present power of God within her.

During my childhood years I was very quiet and reserved, often withdrawn, but I felt very spiritually connected to my mother. We communicated not with many words, but rather in the silence. I watched her closely and as young as I was, I could understand the depth of her faith. Her frequent demonstrations proved that God is omnipresent, omnipotent, and omniscient, and most of all, our constant and abundant supply. As I grew older I found comfort in this knowledge and I continued to emulate her. With an enquiring mind I was determined to be like my mother and experience the power of God in my life.

My earlier belief was that God punishes us when we are bad and rewards us when we are good. I also believed that I had to plead and placate God in order to receive my good. As I grew older, however, my search for God took on a new dimension of reason. I subsequently began to question these ideas that were passed down to me, with an inner knowing that something didn't quite add up. "If God is my father and my mother" I reasoned, "then I must be a part of Him, but if He is only up in the sky, then how can I identify with Him?

In my quest to experience God, my enquiring mind revealed to me that God was not only up in the sky, but also everywhere equally present within me and within every living thing at the same time. Nevertheless, in order for me to experience Him, I had to learn the art of communing with Him, and that meant I had to abandon all my earthly opinions and human judgment and listen to Him from the silence of my soul.

Unlike most of my siblings, I never did get baptized in the local church, as was expected of me by my parents. My mother, who nevertheless sensed my spirituality, gave me the freedom to pursue my own path, but it was obvious that she hoped one day I would demonstrate my faith through the ritual of water baptism in the local church. This never came to pass, and although I took many detours along the way, my spirituality remained intact. So my search to find my "self" continued.

3

Living in God's Presence

"When thou passeth through the waters I will be with the: and through the rivers they shall not overflow thee: when thou walkest through the fire thou shall not be burned, neither shall the flame kindle upon thee."

Isaiah 43:2

Children live what they learn, so my mother's prayer habits had a tremendous impact on me, and I began practicing the presence of God at the tender age of ten. On one occasion I remember being accused of misplacing something that my mother needed. I was moved to tears, and I frantically searched for the missing item. As I searched for the missing item, I began to pray, singing a little song that I learned at the Sunday school I attended:

"The best book to read is the Bible,
The best book to read is the Bible,
If you read it every day
It will help you on your way,
The best book to read is the Bible."

I sang this little song so earnestly, and I truly believed that God would reveal the missing item. Miraculously, within a short space of time, the missing item was recovered. I was greatly encouraged from this simple demonstration of God' omnipresence and I was utterly convinced He hears and answers us always! These simple but profound demonstrations helped to shape my spirituality, and like my mother I subsequently developed the good habit of turning to God for help and strength in times of need. I learned how to attune to the Spirit by the spoken word, in song, or simply just praying silently from my heart. Whatever form it took, the answers were always forthcoming.

My prayer habit gradually intensified, and so did my desire to serve God. By the age of thirteen, as soon as I started high school, prayer became my defense, my daily sustenance, my shield, my rock, and my hiding place. Traveling on a market bus from the countryside of Jamaica each day to and from school was sometimes fun, but there were also many anxious moments. Many times the narrow, winding, and treacherous roads were no matches for the country busses, being heavily laden with market supplies; they often gave way to the effects of overload, sometimes even turning right over. During those anxious moments I often thought of my mother, and instantly my faith would be restored. It often seemed quite miraculous how we survived many mishaps along the way.

I subsequently learned never to leave home without immersing myself in the comfort and safety of prayer. Prayer became my anchor, and during challenging moments I affirmed, "God is with me." My mother also acted as a beacon of light for me, and often during my difficulties I would envision her on bended knees in prayer. My fears would instantly subside and everything would be all right. I had great confidence that her faith in God was enough to carry me through any difficult situation.

My childhood quest for "Truth" continued, and despite my budding spirituality and consistent prayer habits, still there were areas of conflict to deal with. Being vain and self centered and thinking that I was special and that the whole world revolved around me brought me dire consequences. I later became the target of persecution, suffering greatly for my self-indulgence, and chastised by my peers as well as my siblings.

As a result, my teenage years were very trying and lonesome, and as I grew older I became more moody and detached, often feeling sorry for myself. Having felt unduly persecuted, inwardly, I began to deny the compliments that I received, secretly wishing that others would stop complimenting me, especially in front of my peers. It was during these lonesome years that I really connected with God as my ever present help and companion.

As I emulated my mother's prayer habits, I gradually became more "self" conscious, ready to take responsibility for my actions. Those who took time to understand me realized that behind the mask of conceit was someone caring, loving, and compassionate, willing to be used by God. After helping my mother to recover from a dizzy spell one day, she afterward told me, "You have so much love inside of you!" With that wonderful compliment I felt empowered and encouraged. I thought a little light was shining from within me, and I secretly prayed that God would continue to use me according to His will and purpose for my life.

When we learn to acknowledge our human weaknesses, the light of the Christ within will be revealed. The unconscious mind holds our shadows and the light, our strengths and our weaknesses. When we try to deny the shadows, however, they will multiply and reveal themselves in unhealthy unexpected ways.

We should acknowledge where we are in consciousness—our fears, doubts, and anxieties and try to transform them into the light of the Christ so that we may become more gentle and loving—not judging or blaming—with a simple act of surrender. When we take that bold step into the world of the unconscious, we will come to know ourselves in a deeper way;

we will be healthier, richer, and a tremendous asset to our world.

One of my favorite Bible stories showing the omnipresence of God is Peter's imprisonment and his subsequent escape in the book of Acts. Being filled with the Holy Spirit, Peter was advised to speak to all the people and tell them of God's omnipresence not only with the Jews, but with all people. During that encounter, the Holy Spirit was made manifest among them all, and the people were astounded. He consequently commanded that they be baptized in the name of the Lord.

In retaliation, King Herod killed James and arrested Peter. Peter was bound with chains and heavily guarded. As he slept between two soldiers one evening, something miraculous happened. An angel of the Lord visited him, struck him on the side, and woke him saying, "Arise quickly." His chains suddenly fell from his hands, and he was safely led out of the heavily guarded prison.

By then Peter felt dazed, but when he came to himself he realized that the Lord had sent his angel to deliver him out of Herod's and the Jewish people's hands. When he showed up at his brethren's home, they were filled with wonder, but Peter calmed their anxieties and explained to them how the Lord had saved him.

We may not all experience a dramatic event like Peter did, but most of us can testify about many miraculous events in our lives when we have been delivered from dire circumstances through God's providence.

I had my fair share of worldly experiences after graduating from high school nevertheless, my spirituality was still intact. As I grew older, I continued to immerse myself in the study of God's Word and practiced the presence of God more and more. I was open and receptive to the goodness of God, and gradually my experiences became more meaningful and insightful. I felt very close to God indeed, and He never failed to prove His presence was near. God is always with us in the midst of crisis or confusion, and He always delivers us from our fears when we put our trust in Him.

During the summer of 1998 I proved this reality of God's protecting presence as I travelled from Kingston, to the north coast of Jamaica.

As I drove along the narrow winding roads alone with my thoughts centered on God, I literally felt empowered by the Holy Spirit. I reflected on my blessings and my growing ability to discern the truth and as I listened to comforting and inspiring music from the radio, I felt protected, peaceful, highly favored, and free.

Suddenly there was a slight drizzle, and I reduced my speed as I approached a hill. As I cautiously made it to the brow of the hill, I unexpectedly encountered a parked car with a flat tire just ahead of me. In an effort to make a detour, I gently depressed the brakes on the car, but unfortunately the car gave way to the wet road and I lost control, swerving to the right and overturning the car onto the embankment.

This all happened so quickly that I could scarcely comprehend what had actually happened. As soon as I was able to gather my thoughts together, I became frozen with fear; I realized that I was actually lying in the car on my right side, and that the car was also on its right side! I incoherently mumbled the word "help," fearing that any slight movement would send the car—and me—crashing down to the bottom of the cliff.

The sound of my voice was so weak that it was almost impossible for anyone to hear me. Fortunately, however, the driver of the parked car witnessed the entire episode and he quickly came to offer his assistance, very expertly guiding me to safety. First, he told me to switch off the ignition. Then he told me to slowly unwind the window on the other side of the car. He then asked me to hand him the keys, after which he slowly took my hand in his and gently pulled me to safety. The passersby were all curious, and those who witnessed the ordeal deemed it miraculous, as there was not a single scratch on my body. Someone had observed my *Daily Word* magazine, printed and published by Unity, on the seat of my car, and they exclaimed, "It is no wonder that you are safe. You have been traveling with God as your companion."

Once I was safely on the roadside, the reality of the situation began to take effect on me, and I shuddered when I observed the cliff below. The position of the car on the embankment and my close call to what could have been the end of my life here on earth was not easy to grasp. Everyone was bewildered to realize that it was only a small stump that had actually stopped the car from falling off cliff. This was certainly a miracle—God's—grace in action, and I could only thank Him, hoping that through that divine demonstration at least one person would concede to the goodness of God, and that the glory of God would be revealed.

God never fails to protect us whenever we are connected to Him through prayer, and He will always send His angels to help us through our difficulties. The help and moral support I received from the passersby that day was truly overwhelming and humbling.

After a while, with my car still in the embankment, traffic piled up tremendously, and people had to wait for hours before the traffic cleared. I was touched by the understanding and patience they displayed, as they were more concerned about my safety and the safety of the car still on the embankment rather than their lost time in traffic.

The next hurdle was to pull my car from the embankment to safety. This was a big challenge. There were no guarantees. One wrong move and the car would end up in the bottom of the cliff! I looked over the side of the cliff and offered a silent prayer from my heart. I thanked God that I was alive and surrendered to the outcome.

Finally, with a rope tied to his truck, a very skilled truck driver pulled my car from the embankment and back onto the road with what seemed like no great effort at all. We all continued to witness the extended miracle, as the car made it from the embankment without one single scratch.

Everyone was astonished and relieved. The experience left me exhausted and overwhelmed, but none-the-less my joy was full to overflow. The presence of God was surely with me. Feeling deeply humbled, I continued to thank God for His manifold blessings and for the opportunity to behold Him in the many faces I encountered that day.

It was very difficult for me to continue driving after that mishap, but with the insistence and encouragement of the people around me, I eventually mustered the courage. With the help of God, I finally made it safely to my destination. Before retiring that night, I meditated and contemplated the significance of what had transpired that day, and I could not help but identify a number of gifts. First of all, I acknowledged the gift of life God spoke of in John 3:16: "For God so loved the world that He gave us His only begotten son that whosoever believeth on Him should not perish but have everlasting life."

Secondly, there was the realization of unity of spirit—oneness with God and with each other. No matter whom we are or where we are from, we are all connected spiritually, and our initial response in times of crisis or need is to reach out and help each other. It was a pure, humbling moment when I felt everyone's heart reaching out to me in my pain, in my fear, and in my victory. I beheld the Christ in every face on that day, and we all became one in spirit.

The apostle Paul tells us in Romans 8:28, "All things work together for good." As I pondered the good in that situation, I came to the realization that God had a divine purpose for my life, and He had used this mishap to prove to all the people present that day that with Him, all things truly are possible.

Finally, on reiterating all that transpired that day, it was comforting to remember that prior to my adventure that morning my last thoughts were focused on God with an affirmation, "Lord I thank you for all your abundance, which is mine." Through this mishap that day, His abundance had become manifest, and His goodness was demonstrated to hundreds of people who had witnessed the happening.

4

Spiritual Gifts and the Call to serve

"Not that we are sufficient of ourselves to think anything as of ourselves, but our sufficiency is of God who hath made us able ministers of the New Testament" (2 Corinthians 2:5).

"But the manifestation of the Spirit is given to every man to profit withal. For to one is given by the spirit the word of wisdom; to another the word of knowledge by the same Spirit; to another faith by the same Spirit; to another the gifts of healing by the same Spirit; to another the working of miracles; to another prophesy; to another discerning of spirits; to another divers kinds of tongues; to another the interpretation of tongues; But all these worketh that one and the selfsame spirit, dividing to every man severally as he will. "For as the body is one, and hath many members, and all the members of that one body being many are one body: so also is Christ" (1 Corinthians 12:7-11).

Because my spirituality was shaped by the spiritual discipline of my parents, my desire to serve became evident at a very young age. Due to the working of their faith, I constantly witnessed many miracles in their lives, which subsequently encouraged me to cultivate a deep relationship with God by living a life of prayer.

My parents were ardent church-goers. Together they made a fantastic team, never missing Church on a Sunday morning. As children we had to follow suit. We had to go to church every Sunday morning unless we were too ill to attend. As I strived to attain a spiritual consciousness, I endeavored to put God first at all times. Because of my desire to serve, I know that God was the guiding force in my life. Despite my young and tender age of ten or twelve, I continued on my spiritual path, and it wasn't long before I understood my divine purpose.

One of the early signs of my call to serve happened during my adolescent years, when I took the responsibility to pray for divine order during an altercation at the church that I attended with my family. A male member of the church, who was married, had an extra-marital relationship with a young girl, impregnating her. This created a lot of controversy among the members of the church, many of whom wanted the man to be ostracized. I was touched by his situation, and I felt a great deal of compassion for the man. I acknowledge his error, but I didn't believe ruling him out of the church was the answer. Being just a minor, I wondered what I could do about the situation without making myself visible.

I prayed about it, and the Holy Spirit imprinted upon my heart the way that I could help make a difference in the situation. Thinking of the punishment as quite unjust from a Christ standard, I was prompted to write an anonymous letter to the minister of the church in defense of the gentleman, reminding him of the double standards under which we all live. I further reminded him that from a biblical standpoint, there is none righteous other than God, and therefore we have all fallen short. I also reminded him that God forgives, and because He forgives we all have the opportunity to repent and begin again.

I continued my letter to the minister by making reference to the story in the Bible about the woman caught in adultery, whose accusers wanted her stoned to death. I reminded him that Jesus did not condemn her, but instead He allowed her an opportunity to repent and receive salvation. When Jesus charged those present, who thought they were without sin, to cast the first stone at the woman, no one could. They all realized that they had all sinned in different ways. I ended my letter with the Lord's Prayer in Matthew chapter 6, emphasizing verse 12: "Forgive us our debts as we forgive our debtors."

I really do not know if my letter was acknowledged, but to my surprise the situation was later resolved amicably, and after repentance the gentleman was later reinstated in the church. I rejoiced and gave God thanks for the outcome, never disclosing my inner involvement to anyone, not even my parents.

This was the beginning of my call to serve. There was always a yearning within me to console others and help to bring comfort to the helpless and the sick. Because of my quiet nature, however, I was often overlooked, invalidated, and misjudged. Nevertheless, there was undoubtedly another side to me, one that performed in the most unexpected and sometimes uncanny ways. Often times, after rising to the occasion, I enjoyed observing the surprised reactions from people, whose overall impression of me up to that point had been much more subdued. With time, however, they all began to witness the butterfly in me take flight; and they were all amazed.

I have always had a great desire within me to fully validate and prove my hidden talent, but I felt somewhat hindered and overshadowed by my own lack of confidence; and so I stayed within the confines of my comfort zone, not daring to betray myself and expose my insecurities.

According to the law of mind-action, I was never given an opportunity because my unconscious feelings of insufficiency spoke more than words. Although I believed with all my heart that I was blessed with a divine potential to accomplish good, nevertheless doubts lingered in my mind, short circuiting all my attempts to deliver. In a state of desperation to prove my self-worth my heart kept crying out, "Give me a chance to prove that I can!"

During one particular job interview, I was asked to share one thing that I would like to accomplish most in life. My response was "to be validated." That was the truth. As unassuming as I appeared, there was a butterfly in me just waiting to emerge. "Not by might, not by power, but by my spirit says the Lord of hosts" (Zechariah 4:6).

My hidden ability finally came to light some time ago, when I once worked part-time canvassing for a solar company in Florida. This was a very challenging job, as some of the areas I was assigned to were not the nicest or safest places in the world. There were times when I experienced great fear, apprehension, and doubt, but with the help of my indwelling Christ Spirit, I was able to face my fears squarely, and subdue and finally conquer them.

Everyone was surprised at the end of the assignment when I was awarded the top canvasser of my area. The supervisor who was in awe of my hidden ability remarked, "Marjorie, you do what you do so quietly, and yet so effectively." I felt proud and ecstatic, especially as I was the only female on the team.

My gifts, which had been somewhat obscured, became increasingly evident. The more I opened myself to receive the truth, the more enlightened I seemed to have become. My world became increasingly interesting and challenging. The more I read, the more processed and beheld the mystery of the divine.

Because of my enquiring mind, I never accepted what I read unless I was able to prove it by experience, or unless it seemed reasonable. There were some areas of truth that were beyond my ability to fathom, so I reasoned that such knowledge was not yet for me to know. And so I prayed for divine understanding and wisdom, and it was just a matter of time before my relationship with God began to take on a new dimension. "I have many things to say unto you but you cannot bear them now" (John 16:12).

God's call does not come by any stereotype method. It varies with each individual, and although the purpose is the same for everyone, each individual journey is different.

God is our creator. We are created in His image and likeness; we therefore are co-creators with God, the developers of the gifts that God has bestowed upon us. God has lovingly graced us with these spiritual gifts to build up His kingdom, and we are responsible for utilizing our own gifts. Some people may have more than one gift, but a gift is not a gift until it is developed and utilized to the glory of God. As long as we hold back our gifts, we are not complete. "Behold I give you power to tread on serpents and scorpions and all over the power of the enemy, and nothing shall by any mean hurt you. Notwithstanding in this rejoice not, that the spirits are subject unto you: but rather rejoice because your names are written in heaven" (Luke 10:19-20).

Legend has it that one day Michelangelo was walking down the road, pushing a big slab of stone. A curious neighbor, who sat lazily on his porch watching him, asked why he labored so hard over that old piece of stone. Michelangelo replied, "Because there is an angel in that rock who wants to come out." We also have many angels or gifts within us and like Michael Angelo we all have the task of releasing the angels or gifts within us. Our struggles and challenges are the raw materials which we use to shape and carve our world of good.

Spiritual gifts are motivated by love and they draw us closer. Our responsibility is to identify the gifts that God has given us and use them for the glory of God. God gives us gifts not for selfish gains, but for us to use for the good of the whole.

The Holy Spirit initiates spiritual gifts. They are not something we earn or strive to earn; they are designed for all of God's people to use to lift each other up. Spiritual gifts flow naturally. James 1:17 states, "Every good and perfect gift is from above."

There have been many schools of thought pertaining to spiritual gifts; how many there are, how many each person has, or how they are cultivated. What is important, however, is that we recognize them and use them to the glory of God.

Spiritual gifts are many and varied. They may be classified as follows:

1. Serving others—the ability to help others in all walks of life.
2. Teaching—the ability to share God's truth with others.
3. Encouraging others—the ability to remind others of their divinity.
4. Wisdom—the ability to obtain insight and to apply knowledge.
5. Working miracles—the ability to help people meet a human need through the recognition of the presence of God within them.
6. Prophesy—the ability to discern and convey a specific message from God.
7. Speaking in tongues—This is the ability to speak in an unknown language that someone who hears it can translate.
8. Showing kindness and hospitality—the ability to nurture and care for others.
9. Faith—this is the ability to believe in the adequacy of God in all circumstances.
10. Giving—the ability to share time, talent, and treasure for God's work.
11. Healing—this gift allows individuals to act as an instrument of God's healing grace in mind, body, and spirit.

12. Discernment—the ability to see beyond the appearances to the truth of God's good.
13. Administration—the ability to organize direct and lead.

Although there are various gifts, all work together for the good of the whole. There is a story about a monastery that had fallen upon hard times. As a result of anti-monastic persecution in the seventeenth and eighteenth centuries and the rise of secularism in the nineteenth, all the branch houses were lost and everything was so decimated that there were only five monks left in the decaying mother house; the abbot and four others, all over seventy years of age. This was obviously a dying order.

In the nearby woods was a little hut that a rabbi from a nearby town often visited for a hermitage. As a result of their prayer habits, the monks had become a bit intuitive, so they could always tell when the rabbi was around. Agonized by his dying order the abbot of the monastery decided to pay the rabbi a little visit. Perhaps he could give him some encouragement and advise him about how to save his order.

Off he went to see the rabbi, who welcomed him with a warm hug. The abbot poured out his heart to the rabbi who, after listening intently, commiserated with him. "It is the same thing everywhere," he said. "The spirit has gone out of the people. I am experiencing the same decline in my town."

Together both of them wept. They read parts of the Torah together and spoke of deep things. They had a very good time, but eventually the time came for the abbot to leave. Just before leaving, he asked the rabbi, "Isn't there one little piece of advice you can give me about how to save my dying order?" "No, I am so sorry," replied the rabbi. "I have no advice to give at all, except to tell you that one of you is the messiah."

When the abbot returned to the monastery, the other monks gathered around him, anxiously awaiting some good news.

"He couldn't help," the abbot told them sadly. "But before I left, he did say something strange. He said, "One of you is the messiah."

During the following weeks the old monks pondered this message from the rabbi, and each wondered who that person could be. *It might very well be the abbot himself,* they thought. *He has led us over the years. Then again, it might very well be Brother Thomas. He is a holy man, full of light. It couldn't it be Brother Eldred,* they thought. *He gets heady at times. He is such a thorn in people's sides, although when it comes down to it, he is always right. Maybe the rabbi did mean Brother Eldred. Surely it wouldn't be Brother Phillip. Phillip is so passive; and really a 'nobody.' But he does have the gift of always being there for you whenever you need him. He just magically appears by your side. Maybe Phillip is the messiah.* Of course, they all thought it wasn't them. *He couldn't possibly have meant me,* they thought. *I am too ordinary. Yet, suppose he meant me? Oh no! God, not me! I couldn't be that much for you could I?*

The monks all contemplated this matter, and they began to treat each other and themselves with utmost respect on the off chance that one of them might be the messiah.

Because the areas surrounding the monastery were so beautiful, people often came to picnic, relax, and meditate. They now began to observe and admire the respect that the monks showed each other. The entire atmosphere of the monastery was permeated with the wonderful energy of the woods. They were captivated by it. This made them want to return again and again and again. Each time they brought their friends, and their friends brought their friends. Soon the entire place was buzzing with excitement.

The younger men who spoke with the monks were impressed with the energy they generated. One young man enquired how he might become a monk, and then another, and another.

Within a few years, the monastery had once again become a thriving order; and thanks to the rabbi's gift of spiritual insight and wisdom.

When the call comes to serve, there is no mistaking it. The call comes from the depth of one's being, and manifests as a deep and intense desire to serve. A true call to ministry involves an irresistible, overwhelming craving, a raging thirst for telling others what God has done for our souls.

We all have what it takes, and we all have been called to serve in different capacities, but like Moses, in the bible, not everyone is willing and ready to take responsibility. Remember, though, that God has a divine plan for our lives, as He did for Moses, who was divinely rescued from the river by Pharaoh's daughter.

Moses grew up in an affluent environment, enjoying the best of everything, but the experience of material gain was not the ultimate plan for Moses. Moses showed his true desire to serve when he was moved with compassion for a Hebrew slave who was treated with cruelty by an Egyptian. One day, Moses acted from sense-consciousness and killed the Egyptian slave. For this unmerciful act, Moses was consequently exiled from Egypt and from Pharaoh's court.

During his exile, Moses had time to reflect on his past while he tended sheep in the wilderness, and he found himself in transition, trying to make sense of it all. Subconsciously, Moses was ready for reconciliation. He had an intense desire to serve, and he eventually surrendered his past when he heard God's call through a burning bush. Moses turned toward the burning bush, and he came face to face with himself and with God.

God instructed Moses to go on a divine mission, to rescue the Israelites from bondage in Egypt, but Moses shunned this responsibility, doubting his divine potential. Moses was eventually convinced that he was worthy of fulfilling God's mission to save the Israelites when God demonstrated His divine power within him, as well as, reassuring him that his brother Aaron, would accompany him as his spokesperson.

Moses finally went on his mission, and further along the journey received the law, known as the "Ten Commandments," which he passed on to the Israelites.

According to Charles Fillmore in the *Metaphysical Bible Dictionary,* the name "Moses" is a Hebrew name that means "drawing out." The birth of Moses represents man's development in consciousness of the law of his being, from the negative side. In a metaphysical or deeper spiritual sense, the "law" is that we are a perfect expression of God, and one observes the law when one lives righteously.

We are children of light made whole and perfect, all created with a divine purpose to accomplish good. We obey the law when we understand that we are an expression of God and act from a consciousness of love. We break the law when we deny our divine potential. This is what it means to "let our lights shine" (Matthew 5:16).

The consciousness of Moses is within each of us. We were all born with a divine purpose, but because of doubt and fear, we tend to shun our responsibilities. Pharaoh's daughter is that part of us that pulls us out of obscurity into the light, and Pharaoh represents the ego within us that tries to dominate and stop our spiritual growth. The "I am" within us is our true gift, our divine Christ presence that gives us the power and authority to recognize, accept and demonstrate our spiritual gifts thereby living a spiritually fulfilled life.

5

A Deep Relationship with God

"And thou shalt love the lord thy God with all thine heart, and with all thy soul, and with all thy might" (Deuteronomy 6:5).

My love to thee

The hours I've spent with thee dear Lord,
Are pearls of priceless worth to me.
My soul my being, merge in sweet accord,
In love for thee, in love for Thee.

Each hour a pearl, each pearl a prayer,
Binding thy presence close to me;
I only know that thou art there
And I am lost in Thee.

O glorious joys that thrill and bless
O visions sweet of love divine!
My soul in rapturous bliss can ill express
That thou art mine, O Lord
That thou art mine.

Myrtle Fillmore
Adapted from "The Rosary"

To have a good relationship with God is to spend quality time with Him. It means to trust Him with all our heart, no matter what faces us in life. As His children, made in His image and after His likeness God expects us to listen to Him and to do His will. He expects us to have a relationship with Him as Beloved to beloved. Author Alice Steadman writes in her book, *Who's the Matter with Me?* "To see God, be what He is, Divine Love, Light, and Truth. He is not dictator, bossy or a critic. To be heavenly, try to be all the qualities that God is and consider people more important than things, be giving of self and praise all that He has made and grow in wisdom and understanding."

When we live outside of the consciousness of God we live in negation making things and people the object of our existence. We consequently experience hardships, loneliness, and frustration only because we do not have a deep relationship with God.

God is absolute good—constant, eternal, and unchanging. Therefore, we also have the potential to be good. Our goal in life should be to experience Him in a profound way by having a deep relationship with Him. First, we acknowledge Him as creator and sustainer of all life, the giver of all good things. Next, we acknowledge that we are made in His image and after His likeness. When this realization is achieved, all that we need is added unto us. "Seek ye first The Kingdom of God and His righteousness; and all these things will be added unto you" (Matthew 6: 33).

No matter what we are going through the presence of God is always with us. In order to experience His presence, we should stay connected to Him with daily periods of prayer and meditation, reading His holy Word, exercising obedience, and by living life from a loving, truthful, compassionate, and humble perspective. "I am the vine, ye are the branches; he that abideth in me and 'I', in him, the same bringeth forth much fruit: for without me ye can do nothing" (John 15:5).

The Bible is a compilation of inspired writings, and these writings are often convictions of the reality of God's power and presence in our lives and in the world. The authors of the Bible have relentlessly proven without a shadow of a doubt, the existence of a creator who is closer to us than breathing, and nearer than our hands and feet.

God related not only to the people of ancient times, but God relates to us, to all mankind according to His perfect plan and according to our level of receptivity. In other words, we do need to have a personal relationship with Him in order to feel His presence.

The human body is the temple of God (1 Cor. 6: 19), and having a deep relationship with God means having a deep relationship with ourselves. We can therefore only experience God when we are true to ourselves; when we live a life of integrity and truth. "Be not deceived, God is not mocked: for whatsoever a man soweth, that shall he also reap" (Galatians 6:7).

God is our higher Self; His thoughts are higher than our thoughts and His ways higher than our ways (Isaiah 55:9). He therefore knows our needs even before we do. He is both Father and Mother to us, and we should trust Him as we trust our earthly parents. God never slumbers or sleeps. He will never leave us or forsake us. He is with us always. To feel His presence is to know Him, and to know Him is to spend quality time with Him. "And you shall seek me and find me when you search for me with all your heart" (Jeremiah 29:13).

When we have a relationship with God, we do not have to face our trials alone. When we are connected to God in prayer, he will give us strength and courage to cope with pain and sorrow in times of trouble, and we will gain insight and understanding into the laws of life. He is always there to support us with wise and loving council. "God is faithful, who will not suffer you to be tempted above that ye are able, but will with the temptation also make a way to escape, that ye may be able to bear it" (1 Corinthians 10:13).

Having a relationship with God is more about being rather than doing. In the Bible, Mary demonstrated this attitude as she chose to sit at the feet of Jesus all day long, in contrast to her sister Martha, who was always busy doing other things. Jesus told Martha, who complained that Mary was not helping with the work, "Martha, Martha, you are troubled about many things but Mary has chosen the better part." When we sit in communion with God, the possibilities are endless. Wonderful ideas are revealed to us, and we live a richer and much more fulfilling life.

In his introduction of the book *The Cloud of Unknowing* and the *Book of Privy Counseling*, William Johnston paraphrased the unknown author of that book saying, "God can be loved but he cannot be thought." God is Spirit and His Spirit within us is life that is eternal. When we open ourselves to the experience of God, abandon all earthly thoughts, and focus only on this presence within us, we will be inspired to take action. God is our father and our mother, and He loves us despite our human shortcomings. He knows our needs even before we ask Him; therefore, there is no need to beg, beseech, or placate Him.

We experience God when our hearts and minds are in a state of surrender–in the stillness. In Matthew chapter 6, while teaching His disciples how to pray, Jesus instructed them first to go into their closet, shut the door, and then pray to their Father in secret. "The Father, who hears us in secret, will reward us openly."

We meet God in a secret place by entering the holiest of holy; the door through which we enter is our heart. Here, neither doubt nor fear can enter, as reality reigns supreme. When we become conscious of the great omnipresence of God, light, joy, peace, and satisfaction of His Spirit abide within our consciousness.

All knowledge comes from within. When one sits gently in meditation and abandons all to the totality of 'self,' all that is necessary to be revealed will be revealed. "I have many things to say unto you, but you cannot bear them now. Howbeit when the spirit of truth is come he will guide you into all truth" (John 16:33).

In the book *The Cloud of Unknowing,* William Johnston makes reference to the mystic Dionysius, who states that man can know God by way of reason as well as by mystical contemplation. He states,

> "But there is yet a higher way of knowing God, which takes place through ignorance. Such knowledge is not found in books nor can it be obtained by human effort, for it is a divine gift. Man can however prepare himself to receive it; and this he does by prayer and purification."

Once you enter into the silence of your own heart nothing can stand in your way, because nothing else matters but the sweet communion with Spirit. Once you have experienced this immense joy, there is no turning back. You will not want to live without it. Your whole life hangs on the presence of God; you rely on it for your daily sustenance in all things. You make time for Him. You live a life of non-resistance, acknowledging each and every moment, living in the flow of life's abundance. In this existence, there is beauty, praise, sincerity, and oneness with all creation.

*God'swillforusisabsolutegood.*Helovesusun-unconditionally and He will open doors that otherwise seemed closed, and we can always begin again and again and again. When challenges become overwhelming we only need to focus our attention on Him, and soon there will be a wonderful victory—as the words of a popular song state, "the hotter the battle, the sweeter the victory." When communion with God is constant and sincere, miracles will become a part of the natural order; when we trust and surrender to His promises He will make everything right. He will be a source of healing, reconciliation, and joyful self-expression.

We should not seek God only for the loaves and the fish, nor should we be attached to the result of our prayers. God is the ultimate experience and the ultimate gift. In God there is completeness in everything. We should therefore go to God out of a genuine desire to feel and experience totality of "Self".

The five thousand that were fed in the Gospels were only excited and interested in Jesus because He fed them. They wanted to make him their king. When they wouldn't leave Jesus alone, He told them, in John 6:26, "You seek me now, not because you saw the miracles, but because you did eat of the loaves and were filled. Labor not for the meat, which perisheth, but for that meat which endureth unto everlasting life, which the son of man shall give unto you: for him hath God the Father sealed" (John 6:26).

God has provided for our needs, and there is no need to toil and sweat to get our desired good.

> "Take no thought for your life, what ye shall eat, or what ye shall drink; nor yet for your body, what ye shall put on. Behold the fowls of the air: for they sow not, neither do they reap, nor gather into barns; yet your heavenly father feedeth them": "Consider the lilies of the field, how they grow; they toil not, neither do they spin": "Wherefore if God so clothe the grass of the field which today is and tomorrow is cast into the oven, shall He not much more clothe you, O ye of little faith?" (Matthew 6: 25-26, 28, 30).

Nevertheless, in our humanity we sometimes find it difficult to concentrate on God when we are bombarded with cares of this world. Remember, God is the answer to all our cares, our aspirations, and our desires, and despite our helplessness and feelings of desolation, God is always available and within our reach. We must ultimately cultivate trust, and we must believe. Jesus comforts us with these words in John 6:35: "I am the bread of life. He that cometh to me shall never hunger; and He that believeth on me shall never thirst."

The story of Job in the Bible demonstrates what it means to have a deep relationship with God despite our trials. In ancient times, Job was described as a very righteous man. He had a very good relationship with God. He feared God and turned away from evil. Job was blessed with a happy family and material wealth. Job turned a deaf ear to negation and pursued God the best way he knew.

Despite all his good virtues, however, trouble suddenly knocked at Job's door and his faith was severely tested. Without warning, Job lost everything he owned, including his family. To make matters worse, he was also stricken with disease. In Job's eyes, he felt he was righteous, and therefore he could not rationalize his present suffering.

Job continued to acknowledge God, but although he knew that God was with him, his effort to find God seemed strangely short-circuited, and the more he tried to find God in his distress, the further away God seemed. "Where is God? Why won't God take away this perpetual pain?" Job searched and searched for the answer, but there were more questions than answers. In trying hard to rationalize his dilemma, Job eventually had a long discourse with God. Job tried to find answers by seeking God from every imaginary angle, but he just could not find his center of being.

Like Job, the beginning of our spiritual journeys is usually very encouraging; everything unfolds perfectly, and we demonstrate our Good in an instant. The more we engage in spiritual activities the more we are blessed and the more eager we become to work towards the perfect life.

There comes a time however, when life's challenges get the better of us and it seems that the answers to our prayers get less and even harder to accomplish. This does not mean God has stopped working His miracles in us and through us; this only means we need to try harder. We simply need to rise higher in consciousness. If miracles were to continue at the same level each time, we would simply become complacent, neglecting our spiritual work, becoming stagnant, and achieving nothing. When we focus on the lessons and not on the challenges, we ultimately become stronger, more convicted and assured that God is the only power within us, and that *we can do all things through Christ, who strengthens us.*

Finally, Job reached the end of his rope, and in desperation he surrendered. The struggle seemed to have ended when the light of truth gradually dawned on him, and slowly Job began to get a glimpse of the bigger picture. What an awakening experience that was for him! He could now see with the eyes of spirit!

Most of us do try to cultivate that right relationship with God when things are going right for us, but when our faith is severely tested like Job, we seem to falter. The reality is that we do not always have sunshine in our lives. There will also be rain, snow, earthquakes, storms, and sudden destruction all around us—not to hurt or harm us, but to cleanse and heal, effecting balance and harmony in the world and in our lives.

God is good all the time and He never makes a mistake. He works even the worst case scenarios to our advantage, in most cases drawing our attention to His divine presence within us. If we were to have everything the way we want it at all times, there would be no need for God. Our responsibility, therefore, is to praise God despite our misfortune and know that God will turn things around into a blessing.

When Job stopped struggling and became open to the lessons he needed to learn, he was then able to discern the truth—that he had the answer to all life's challenges right within him. All he had to do was to stop the struggle and cooperate with the power of God within him.

Consumed in his challenges, Job continued to look in all different directions, and his challenges multiplied simply because he connected with them at a physical level, concentrating on them, rather than on the presence and power of God within him. His friends were not any better. All they did was blame him instead of encourage him. When no answer was forthcoming, Job found himself at a dead end, but the struggle to find release suddenly ended when he realized that his apparent woes were due to his own ignorance.

To have a relationship with God is to trust Him even during the most heartbreaking times in life, to know that He cares and wants the best for us, and to deny error thinking and affirm Good. The more we dwell on negation, the more negation we will experience.

Job really did have a relationship with God, but at an outer level. Although he acknowledged God, he still focused on his trials, and he was consequently unable to experience God or His good. It wasn't until he changed the direction of his thoughts that he was able to look beyond the appearances to the truth that the answer was God within him.

In the aftermath of Job's triumph, God's wrath kindled against Job's friends because they did not offer the right advice to Job. In fact, they tried to blame him for all that happened instead of encouraging him to look within. Job prayed for them, however, and he was blessed much more than he had been before.

Metaphysically, Job's friends represented his own limited thoughts. We sometimes become critical of ourselves or of others for choices we make, but we will not find true freedom until we take responsibility, release, let go, and let God.

Despite many trying experiences, I try to cultivate a true relationship with God, thanks to my mother, who exemplified a life of prayer. She taught me how to trust God, who constantly blesses His children with abundant good. Whether my mother saw God as a stern or autocratic God, or whether she believed that He lived up in the sky didn't matter. What really mattered is that she acknowledged Him in good times as well as in bad times, constantly proving His omnipresence, omnipotence, and His omniscience.

God is everywhere, equally present and equally present within each individual. He is our companion, friend, guide, counselor, judge, juror, great physician, and protector. Let us take him at His word and share our deepest fear and our darkest secrets with him. He will save us from all our troubles and free us from all fear.

Let us build our relationship with God as we-:

1. Put God first. Seek Him constantly. Pray and meditate often and spend quality time with Him. Don't take it for granted that God understands your desires. Talk to Him as friend to friend. Tell Him everything. Ask for His wisdom and help.
2. Prove our allegiance to Him with action. Be doers of the Word and not hearers only. Acknowledge God inside and out.
3. Give thanks and praise to God continually, even when things do not seem to be going right. Trust the divine presence within you. God knows and understands everything. He will work it out for you.
4. Let go and let God. Step out in faith and be willing to let go of a bad habit. Concentrate on God and He will replace your cravings with His love. With His love, you have everything.
5. Trust God with all your heart. He will carry your burdens for you.

6

Love Thy Neighbor

> "Thou shall love thy neighbor as thyself"
> Leviticus 19:18

Having a deep relationship with God extends to having deep relationships with humanity as well, and love is undoubtedly the main key to a happy, successful, and fulfilling life. Practicing unconditional love, however, is not always easy, as unfortunately we live in a society programmed to the wiles of the self: self-adoration, self-gratification, self-attainment, and self-protection. But living unto the "self" is more destructive than constructive.

God loves us unconditionally, regardless of our mistakes of the past or present, and so He expects us also to love one another as He loves us. "For if you love them which love you what reward have you? Do not even the publicans the same?" (Matthew 5:46).

When we live only from the human perspective or from sense consciousness, it is sometimes difficult to love those who cause us mental pain and frustration. We can try to love them by living from the consciousness of the Christ, loving and forgiving those who have wronged us, even as Christ has done unto us despite our many faults.

We are all one in Christ, and Jesus constantly stressed the need for mankind to live in peace and harmony. Having a good relationship with God means having a good relationship with everyone—not just our families, friends, and the ones who treat us well, but everyone—regardless of our differences, regardless of those who may have done us wrong. "Owe no man anything, but to love one another: for love is the fulfilling of the law" (Romans 13:8). If we live unto self, there is nothing to gain. We all need each other just like the body needs the cooperation of all the internal cells in order to function effectively.

There is a bigger picture to our existence, and Don Miguel Ruiz conceptualizes this in his book *Beyond Fear* when he states, "Individuality is a false concept. We are not individuals. We are a little piece of the chain called life." He continues to say, "We are not individuals. We are 'One'. That One is ultimately all universes together. This is the big mystery. This is God."

The first thing we ought to do to reverse self-gratification is to be conscious of our choices and then take responsibility for them. In Luke chapter 10, in response to a question that a lawyer asked as to how he may inherit eternal life, Jesus reminded him of the law of Moses that states, "Love the Lord thy God with all thy heart, and with all thy soul, and with all thy strength, and with all thy mind, and love your neighbor as yourself."

Not being sure who his neighbor was, however, Jesus then gave clarification by telling him a parable.

> A certain man traveled on the road from Jerusalem to Jericho and fell among thieves who robbed him, beat him, and left him to die. Many people, who came along, including a priest and a Levite, passed the wounded man on the other side.
>
> Then came a Samaritan, and although the Jews scorned the Samaritans, regarding them as an inferior race, this Samaritan went beyond the call of

> duty, and risking his own life, stopped to help the wounded man. After extending love and compassion, he took the wounded man to a nearby inn for further treatment.
>
> Not only did the Samaritan spend the night attending to the man's needs, but he also paid the innkeeper for the service rendered, promising to pay the balance on his return.

Jesus ended this parable by asking the lawyer who was a neighbor to the wounded man. "The Samaritan," the lawyer replied. Jesus then commissioned him to go and do likewise.

The Samaritan in the parable saw beyond the appearances; race, color, religion, and social standing did not stand in his way. Instead, he saw a human being in pain, one who needed help. He did not think of the prejudice or the injustice that existed between the Jews and the Samaritans. Instead, he saw his reflection in the wounded man through the eyes of Jesus. He did just what Jesus would have done; he exercised compassion and extended kindness. "Inasmuch as you did it not unto the least of these, you did it not unto me" (Matthew 25:45).

This parable represents the wiles of humanity in all walks of life. We all play the parts of Samaritan, Jew, Gentile, and Publican. Each day we all have a choice to bless others and to be blessed in return, or to live selfishly, ultimately losing our blessings. "He that loveth not, knoweth not God, for God is love" (1 John 4:8).

Although there might be cultural differences among us, love is that main ingredient that unites us all. We observe the law when we are true to ourselves and to others. "Love worketh no ill to his neighbor: therefore love is the fulfilling of the law" (Romans 13:10). We are all branches of the same vine, and God is equally present in each one of us. No one is perfect except the Father in heaven. Therefore, we should never be too quick to judge or persecute our fellowman.

We all have fallen short at one time or another and we are all subjected to the law of cause and effect. In loving one another we will cultivate the habit of rightful thinking and being, regardless of the circumstances, and we will ultimately experience the kingdom of God within us and a peace that surpasses all understanding.

If we truly love God, we will be kind and compassionate, honest, gentle, and forgiving to all. This will certainly be reflected in our lives and in the world. It is not easy to exercise this attitude at all times, but we can try. "If a man say 'I love God' and hates his brother, he is a liar, for he that loveth not his brother whom he hath seen, how can he love God whom he hath not seen?" (1 John: 20).

Listed below are a few steps to help us cultivate a good relationship with our neighbor:

1. Remember that God loves us all. His presence in everyone equally present. Love not just who loves you, but love everyone you meet.
2. Seek out the good in all persons and situations.
3. Smile as much as you can with everyone you meet.
4. Give a helping hand to a stranger. Give a compliment.
5. Encourage someone through a difficult period.
6. Give freely and joyfully of yourself, your time, your talent, and your treasure. Your blessings will multiply.
7. Let your light shine. Think thoughts that are good, pure, honest, just, and beautiful. Let everyone who knows you see a difference in you.
8. Practice forgiveness of self and others constantly.

7

"Be Attitudes"

When our relationship with God is sincere and meaningful we ultimately cultivate good relationship with ourselves and with others. As a result we develop positive states of mind that help us to advance spiritually, enhancing the quality of our lives. God's laws are perfect and just, and when we consciously observe them we radiate the light, love, peace of God and the abundant life exemplified by Jesus. The rightful attitudes of living that we need to employ were outlined by Jesus during His Sermon on the Mount in Mathew chapter 6 and are called, beatitudes, or "Be Attitudes."

Jesus specified that he did not come to destroy the laws, but to fulfill them. The fulfillment of the law is much more than the fulfillment of scriptural prophesies. It relates to the way of life demonstrated by Jesus that brings peace and fulfillment to the covenant relationship with God. The laws that Moses revealed are truly relevant in our lives, but living only from the consciousness of the law is not enough for us to experience wholeness and completion. When we honor God by putting Him first, living from within and without, our minds will become filters through which the creative energy of God shapes and forms our world.

As Jesus delivered His message during the Sermon on the Mount, the people listened with great expectancy. They were interested in the miracles that Jesus had performed. Many came to hear a politically inclined and rebellious master, one who would offer instant solutions to their challenges in life. Jesus, however, came with another agenda. Instead of words of rebellion, He spoke the Truth with such love and assurance that the people were instantly transformed.

Jesus began His sermon with the topic of light. "You are the light of the world. A city that is set on a hill cannot be hid" (Matthew 5:14). In other words, as children of God we need to live our lives by example. Others will follow us if they can see the influence that God has on our lives.

A story is told of a woman in a far country who prayed she might be able to take her family from the valley where her home stood to the high mountains of God. As she prayed, an angel appeared and said, "Before God is ready to take you and your family, you must set your house in order. There may be others who might want to stop there after you are gone."

So the woman put her house in order. She became cleanly, kind, and forgiving. Then she said to the angel "May I go now that my house is in order?" "No," said the angel, "Your garden is full of weeds; someone may want to watch a while in the garden while you are gone." So the woman weeded her garden and tended it for many years. She uprooted bad habits in herself and pruned poisonous growths of hates and grudges.

Then she said, "Can I now lead my family to the mountains of God?" The angel shook his head. "There is a beggar outside your door; until you have fed him you cannot say all is done." So the woman fed the beggar and served all her friends and neighbors, and all rejoiced because of her help.

Then she thought she was ready, but the angel asked to do one thing more. "There is someone coming on the road who is also seeking God, but they do not have your faith and courage. Give them courage and faith, and then ask to see the mountains of God."

So the woman helped the weak and discouraged wherever she found them. "And now," she asked the angel, "may I take my family in?" The son who was healed of drink through her love, the husband bound to her by silken cords of love and service, the daughter saved by a mother's prayers, even the grateful neighbors came in. The angel opened the window of the little house, and lo! It was on the mountaintop of God.

Jesus also told us that the kingdom of God is not a physical place, nor can we use a map to discover it. "Neither shall they say, Lo here! or lo there ! for behold, the kingdom of God is within you" (Luke 17: 21).

This story tells us that God is everywhere, equally present. In fact, we can experience the mountaintop wherever we are, but during the process we should constantly engage in prayer and meditation, and look for opportunities in which to serve God.

Jesus expounded on the subject of light by emphasizing the importance of cultivating the right attitudes. In order to let our lights shine, He gave us some guiding principles, or "be attitudes."

1. Blessed are the poor in spirit, for theirs the kingdom of heaven.

Being 'poor in spirit' comes from the awareness of our innermost self. It means to have a non-possessive attitude toward everything, and at the same time a sense of unity with everything. To be poor in spirit involves a simplification of one's lifestyle. There is no need to be self-conscious, to impress, or even to be envious of others. It is to be inwardly content, whether there is much or little, whether conditions are chaotic or orderly. The apostle Paul identified with this blessed attitude when he stated, "I have learned, in whatever state I am, therewith to be content" (Philippians 4).

It is by awakening to the presence and activity of the Holy Spirit that we become aware of the resurrection of the Christ Spirit within us. To be poor in spirit is to exercise a sense of humility, knowing we of ourselves can do nothing. To arrive at this level of consciousness, we need to deny our innermost self by detaching from the habitual functioning of our intellect and will.

When we acknowledge our spiritual poverty, we open the doorway to the kingdom of God. To be poor-spirited is to be emptied of the little self. *It was the habit of Principal Cairns, the Scottish theologian, to say to those following, "You first" I follow.* Once, upon approaching the platform, a great outburst of applause greeted him. Confused, he kindly stepped aside and allowed the person after him, who he assumed the crowd was clapping for, to go in first, and he began to applaud the man as well. He never dreamed the applause was for him. His action displayed a sense of humility, which made him a blessed man indeed, unlike the action of the worldly man who often displays arrogance, independence, and self-reliance. In his humility, the blessed man acknowledges God as His only source, creator, and sustainer of all life, and affirms, "I of my-self can do nothing, but with God I can do anything."

2. Blessed are those who mourn, for they shall be comforted.

No one wants to mourn, but we must understand that it is not the sorrow itself that is blessed, but rather the comfort that comes from God as a result of mourning. The psalmist reinforced this sentiment in Psalm 30:5: "Weeping may endure for a night, but joy cometh in the morning."

It is difficult to minister to someone in sorrow unless we too have experienced sorrow, and our lives are incomplete if we do not experience sorrow, as there can be no comfort unless there is grief. In order to grow spiritually, we have to give up certain aspects of our lives, and that sometimes bring sorrow, but acknowledging our shortcomings and mourning our mistakes sometimes multiplies our blessings.

The boastful Pharisee who thought he was worthy lost his blessings because of his ego, unlike the penitent publican, who in his humility confessed that he was a sinner and not worthy (Luke18:9-14). The Prodigal son who sorrowfully acknowledged that he had messed up was also generously reinstated into his Father's kingdom; Job who was sorrowful over his delay in acknowledging his "Christ Self" confessed, "I abhor myself and repent in dust and ashes" (Job 42:5).

3. Blessed are the meek, for they shall inherit the earth.

Meekness, undoubtedly, is not a sign of weakness. In fact, it is a sign of spiritual strength. The attitude of meekness is often displayed by a Christ-centered person. The meek are always ready to surrender to the will of God, always ready to put others first, and do not insist on their rights. The meek person is humble in nature and claims nothing for himself. The truth is that void of the little "self" we all have within us the aptitude of meekness.

Meekness is a virtue that has far reaching effects. 1 Peter 3:4 says "The ornament of a meek and quiet spirit is, in the sight of God, of great price." Moses demonstrated meekness, but he was nevertheless chosen by God to free the Israelites from bondage. "Now the man Moses was very meek, above all the men who were upon the face of the earth" (Numbers 12:3).

4. Blessed are those who hunger and thirst after righteousness, for they shall be filled.

God is the source of everything; therefore, whatever we seek in the material world is in essence God, whom we seek. God does not withhold any good thing from us. It is His good pleasure to give us the desires of our hearts, but we must acknowledge

Him first. When we acknowledge God as creator, source, and giver of all things, and focus on His presence within us, we will demonstrate abundant good according to God's will and purpose for our lives.

Having the consciousness of God should be our aim, and instead of hungering for food, drink, and the pursuit of happiness, we should strive for a consciousness of God. "For the kingdom of God is not meat and drink; but righteous, and peace, and joy in the Holy Ghost" (Romans 14:17).

5. Blessed are the merciful, for they shall obtain mercy.

> ""And it came to pass as Jesus sat at meat in the house, behold, many publicans and sinners came and sat down with Him and His disciples. And when the Pharisees saw it they said unto His disciples, Why eateth your Master with publicans and sinners?' But when Jesus heard that, He said unto them, 'they that be whole need not a physician, but they that are sick. But go ye and learn what that meaneth, I will have mercy and not sacrifice: for I am not come to call the righteous but sinners to repentance'" (Matthew 9:10-13).

According to author and cofounder of Unity, Charles Fillmore, in his book, *The Revealing Word,* mercy is "Christ-like treatment toward the suffering." The important point in desiring to be merciful is to exercise righteous adjustment that results in overcoming.

Jesus often shows us that righteousness is more than a moral conduct. He warned the Pharisees that righteousness was not only about performing the correct ritual sacrifice it was about living a life of mercy. Jesus constantly exercised mercy doing things to the disapproval of most of His followers. He healed on the Sabbath; He ate with tax collectors and sinners;

He spoke against dietary laws, but Jesus had a motive. His purpose was to demonstrate that mercy is a Christian virtue, and we receive it when we give it under all circumstances.

6. Blessed are the pure in heart, for they shall see God.

> "Keep thy heart with all diligence; for out of it are the issues of life" (Proverbs 4:23).

> "The quality of our lives is a reflection of our hearts, and to be pure in heart requires moral integrity; as it is within us, so it is without us. For as he thinketh in his heart so is he" (Proverbs 23:7).

A pure heart is a heart free of malice, resentment, pride or prejudice; it is a heart of compassion, love, and forgiveness. With a pure heart there are no hidden agendas. A pure heart is a heart of self-transparency; it is a heart that sees his brother as his very own; it is a heart accepting and considerate despite all outer conditions.

A pure heart should reflect the nature of the Christ within. God, who is not the author of confusion, cannot exist in a hostile heart. Therefore, we should endeavor to purify our thoughts and our minds daily. "Keep thy heart with all diligence; for out of it are the issues of life" (Proverbs 4:23.) Our aim should therefore be to free our-selves from self-gratification and unforgiving thoughts.

> "He that hath clean hands, and a pure heart, who hath not lifted up his soul unto vanity, nor sworn deceitfully, shall receive the blessing from the Lord, and righteousness from the God of his salvation" (Psalms 24:4-5).

God is always available to forgive us our trespasses and assist us with our needs, and like David who had sinned against

Him, we too can find His forgiving love and comfort when we pray, "Create in me a clean heart, O my God" (Psalm 51:10).

7. Blessed are the peacemakers, for they shall be called children of God.

Living life with a peaceful attitude requires discipline and prayer. No matter what faces us in life, we can always turn within for strength and guidance. God is our refuge and our strength in times of trouble; we only need to turn within and draw from that place of peace and serenity. God is love, peace, joy, and harmony, and as His children we should initiate peace and resolve conflict with ourselves and with others.

There are times when inner conflict seems to drain our resources, and we live in constant warfare within our souls, but when we learn to lean into the everlasting arms of God, we will experience a peace that surpasses all understanding.

A peaceful spirit calms the soul. Jesus often implored the people to turn the other cheek instead of reacting to strife. While this is generally not an easy task, substituting thoughts of anger with thoughts of the Christ often works wonders. It is surprising how this rule gives power over the enemy, who is considered to be our own thoughts. King Solomon conceded to this thought in the book of Proverbs, "If thine enemy be hungry, give him bread to eat; and if he be thirsty, give him water to drink: for thou shall heap coals of fire upon his head, and the Lord shall reward thee" (Proverbs 25:21-22).

Actually, in truth, the enemy is regarded as our own adverse thoughts. In reality, no one can mentally hurt us or cause us harm unless we take it on and allow it to pierce through our minds. No one can hurt the real part of us, the part made in God's image and after His likeness, or the Christ of us. The peace of God will always rule in our hearts when we dwell in that peaceful state of being in that state of "I am". We need to clothe ourselves daily in the armor of God to withstand the wiles of the carnal mind.

8. **Blessed are they who are persecuted for righteousness sake—when men shall revile you and persecute you and say all manner of evil against you falsely for my sake. Rejoice and be exceeding glad, for great is your reward in heaven.**

Most of us have been persecuted at one time or another, but persecution works both ways—inner and outer. Realistically, who persecutes us but ourselves? Jesus said in Matthew 10:36, "A man's foes are they of his own household."

Sometimes we face many trials while we are on the spiritual path, and we tend to persecute ourselves for not measuring up, feeling of guilty and shameful for our mistakes. However, living the ideal life as outlined by Jesus comes with many trials and errors. Ultimately, we should learn to take responsibility by making the right choices. "Chose this day whom thou shalt serve" (Joshua 24:15).

Outer persecution, however, sometimes subjects us to peer-pressure, and we become unpopular with the crowd for making the right choices. We may even lose our friends, and sometimes people may criticize us, judge us, and invalidate our authenticity, saying evil things against us. But when we turn a deaf ear to all negativity and focus on the presence and power of God within us, we will experience harmony and peace in our lives.

All these attitudes of being outlined by Jesus are attainable for all with the help of the indwelling Christ. They are simple, practical, and most of all, accessible to all. We do not have to wait for some distant time in the future or wait until we have accomplished some long-awaited goal in life. Though in our own eyes we may think of ourselves as ordinary and imperfect, God equipped us with the necessary tools to work in His vineyard. Let us use our hands, our eyes, and our feet to the glory of God. "Let your light so shine in the world, that all may see your good works and give glory to your father which is in heaven" (Mathew 5:16).

8

The Dynamics of Prayer

"Prayer is the key to the morning and the bolt of the evening . . ."

Anonymous

"Daniel would rather spend a night with the lions than miss a day in prayer."

Anonymous

Prayer is an inner journey, the ultimate destination of self-discovery rather than a desired manifestation. Prayer can be viewed as a prosperity bank whose withdrawals are dependent on the deposits. Therefore the more time we invest in prayer the more we have to draw from.

Ultimately, we discover that there is nothing to discover, nothing to receive, nothing to demonstrate, and nothing to win or gain, only the realization of the power and presence of God. God is the ultimate knowledge, the source of all things that already are, and we have already received His abundant good, being made in His image and after His likeness.

Prayer is a fundamental gesture of belief, faith, dependence, and connectedness. It is an act of communication between the mind of God and the mind of man. Someone once said, "Prayer is like a passage way between the physical and the spiritual worlds; the spiritual world being our true home, hence our longing to be reunited with it." Despite our challenges, we can never be separated from God. He is always within our very grasp, and there is no place where we are where He is not. In Him we live, move, and have our being.

There is but one mind in the universe—the mind of God. Humankind connects with the mind of God through prayer. As co-creators with God, our potential is unlimited and good. Disobedience to the laws of God, however, causes mixed states of consciousness, but God is always loving and forgiving when we surrender to His presence and power and acknowledge Him in all our ways.

All prayers are always answered. They might not be answered the way we expect, but God is our father and our mother, and He knows our needs even before we ask him. "Before they call I will answers, and while they are yet speaking, I will hear" (Isaiah 65:24).

Thoughts Are Prayers

Prayer is anything we do on a conscious level. It is the highest form of concentration, a total involvement of both thinking and feeling nature in man. Our thoughts are prayers, and we are always praying. It is therefore very important that we entertain the right thoughts. When we are connected to God in prayer, we gain insight in understanding the laws of life, and we experience the kingdom of God within us.

Our consciousness will attract that which we desire, and failing to acknowledge our Christ nature will result in willfulness, a belief in separation that brings on hardships of all kinds. If we fail to demonstrate, it is not God who withholds our good, but rather our own willfulness and belief in negation.

God is principle, and according to the law of cause and effect, we reap that which we sow; our thoughts and deeds hold us accountable to the law, and we therefore punish ourselves according to the law. However, because God is always good, we do not have to stay in negation. With a repentant attitude, the law of grace acts on our behalf and our debts are cancelled, allowing us the opportunity to begin again and again and again. We always have the opportunity to change our circumstances by simply changing our thinking.

There is only one presence and one power in the world—God, the good and omnipotent—and everything He made was good. Any experience other than good is mind-created and not made of God. If we concentrate on pain for instance, the pain will increase, because what we actually do is give power to the pain. We cannot concentrate on God and the pain at the same time and expect release. God stands alone. There is no God and anything else. To concentrate on anything other than God is to give our power away to something inconsequential, and we consequently lose our blessing.

Whatever we focus our attention on will become a reality in our lives. Some time ago, I went on a much-needed vacation to visit my siblings. As shopping has always been my favorite pastime, I looked forward to spending a lot of my time visiting the malls. Unfortunately, I exercised some bad judgment, getting trapped into buying many things, most of which I did not really need. Deep within me I felt a sense of guilt, and although I tried desperately to curtail the habit, I continued to indulge myself day after day with what I consider to be impulsive and senseless shopping.

My vacation finally came to an end, and with so many things acquired during my shopping spree, I literally had to cram my two pieces of checked luggage, as well as my carry on, onto the airplane, and further ship another piece of luggage by the postal service to accommodate my overindulgence. In retrospect, my senseless compulsion made me very remorseful and unhappy. I was sad that I was not able to exercise better judgment with my shopping.

Arriving home in St. Croix after a long vacation was a joy, but I was extremely disappointed when one piece of my checked luggage did not arrive with me on the flight. I filled out the necessary paperwork to retrieve my luggage and left the airport hopeful that it would arrive by the end of that day. Unfortunately, my suitcase never did arrive that day, or any other day. As one can imagine, I felt very agitated, as most of my prized possessions were in that particular suitcase. Weeks of searching for the missing suitcase proved futile, and I finally surrendered, putting in my claim for my missing luggage.

It did not all end there. Having finally come to terms with the reality of the situation, I anxiously awaited my other piece of luggage shipped by the United States Postal Service. When I finally received a notice that it had arrived, I was happy and relieved. Unfortunately and unbelievingly, it was déjà vu all over again. This time the luggage did arrive, but not in one piece; most of the contents were missing! At this point I began to rationalize, wondering why these unforeseen incidents had happened one after the other. There had to be a divine reason, I thought.

Trying desperately to find clarity and consolation, I began to reflect on my entire vacation when it suddenly occurred to me that I had unconsciously decreed the disappearance of my luggage with my frequent feelings of guilt concerning my compulsive shopping. Not only did I set up a negative thought pattern, but I had also attracted it into my experience.

The lesson I learned after that experience is that the Universe, which is always on our side, brings into expression whatever we focus our attention on. Consequently, my initial thoughts of extreme guilt about my excessive shopping had actually played itself out with the missing items.

To experience positive results from prayer, we should therefore deny negation and affirm the good that we desire. If we pray for a specific outcome to a situation, and in fear we entertain doubts, it is almost certain that the feeling of fear will attract that which we do not desire. Job experienced this truth when he declared "The thing which I greatly feared is come upon me and that which I am afraid of is come unto me" (Job 3:25).

The most effective prayer is a prayer from the heart, with thoughts and feelings communicating the same language. "And ye shall seek me, and find me when ye shall search for me with all your heart" (Jeremiah 29:13). Overall, praying to God involves both talking and listening.

Another important element of prayer is to *believe*. God wants us to have our desires fulfilled, and His will is always good will. We should remove doubts and limitations from our minds, and cease from taking the negative attitude that it might not be His will for us to have the good that we desire. In fact, we should be fully convicted that no person, situation, or power can interfere with God's deliverance. God is the only presence and power in our lives and in the world, and His goodness is from everlasting to everlasting.

Frank B. Whitney says in his book *Mightier Than Circumstances*,

> "When in praying you get the realization that what you desire is already yours, you may be sure the answer to your prayer will soon appear in manifestation. You may be sure you have entered the high consciousness in which prayer and answer, are one."

Different Types of Prayer

1. Contemplative Prayer

> "Come ye yourselves apart into a desert place and rest awhile: for there were many coming and going, and they had no leisure so much as to eat."
>
> (Mark 6:31)

> "The root of prayer is interior silence."
>
> Thomas Keating

Contemplative prayer helps us to quiet the mind and connect with the mind of God. With this kind of prayer, we release and let go of all encumbrances, and in the stillness we invoke the presence and power of God into our lives. In this awareness, we realize that there is no higher attainable goal here on earth than an inner communication and realization of the power of God within. When there is a mental connection with the divine presence, the outward manifestation is health, prosperity, and peace.

While prayer is talking to God, meditation is simply listening to God. Regular periods of meditation induce interior silence and initiate self-knowledge. God is absolute cause, absolute power; the giver of all good things and the underlying force behind everything in this world. In essence, God is the answer we seek to every desire, every situation, and every need in life. Whenever we have the consciousness of the Christ presence, everything falls into place. God is all that we are. "Son, thou art ever with me and all that I have is thine" (Luke 15:31).

There is always place of quietness instantly available to us, "the secret place of the most high," the holy place where God dwells (Psalm 91:1). To enter into this quiet place we still our minds, relax our bodies, and retire to this place of stillness. Here, we commune with the spirit of God within us and find rest for our souls.

No matter where we are or what is going on around us, at any moment we can retire to this "secret place of the Most High." God's healing, guiding, and prospering presence fills our souls, establishing harmony within us and within everything that concerns us. Through the realization of this indwelling presence, harmony is radiated from us unto others, ultimately fostering understanding and cooperation. Calmness, peace, and poise prevail, and our lives flow with the goodness of God.

God is absolute good, and having the consciousness of God is all that we need to live life fully. The presence and power of God never leaves us; it never forsakes us; there is no sending or giving of anything except the giving of itself. With God there is ultimately freedom from worry, fear, lack, and limitation.

When human rights, human might and opinions, human will or desires, human power, and all like concerns are relinquished, the world surrenders to us. "Be still and know that I am God" (Psalm 46:10). Charles Fillmore, author and cofounder of Unity says in *Dynamics for Living*,

> "God is Spirit. We are the offspring of this Spirit. God is Mind: man is the thinker. God is Life: man is the living. God is substance: man is form and shape. God is Power: man is powerful. God is Wisdom: man is wise. God is Love: man is loving: God is Truth: man is truthful."

In the book of Mark chapter 5:24-35, a sick woman who had an issue of blood for over twelve years did all she could humanly do to heal herself, but to no avail. She no doubt had prayed conversational prayers, enduring prayers, impersonal prayers, uplifting prayers, and yet her condition remained the same. In dire need she contemplated her dilemma, and she was convinced that there must be a way.

She thought of Jesus and instantly a wave of hope came over her. She believed with all her heart that Jesus could heal her. He had performed many miracles healing the sick, restoring sight to the blind, causing the lame to walk, and He even fed the hungry with what appeared to be limited substance. She was sure that he could heal her condition as well. She heard news that Jesus was visiting Galilee, so she devised a plan to see Him.

There was one problem however. Because she was bleeding, she was considered unclean and people therefore kept their distance from her. With that many people thronging after Jesus, anyway, she doubted if she could ever get near Him. Slowly, a calm assurance came over her, and a force within her—a belief, a hope, a kind of faith so strong—engulfed her. In that moment she realized that she did not have to speak to Him, nor did she even have to touch him physically! All she needed was to tune into his aura and she would experience his presence in every part of her being.

She began to formulate a plan to touch the hem of his garment as he passed by. His Spirit was so strong and powerful that she was convinced that she would be healed. She saw Jesus coming in the distance, but the throngs of people were so great! It would be a challenge to accomplish her goal, but she would give it her best shot. She had to be healed!

Jesus finally approached the huge crowd, and the woman began to activate her carefully devised plan. She inconspicuously stooped down along the side of the road and awaited her chance to touch the Messiah's garment. No words were necessary, only her deep abiding faith.

The woman was so spiritually connected to Jesus that Jesus instantly felt her touch His garment. "Someone touched me," He said. Being surprised at his instant acknowledgment of her, the woman owned up to her act and openly requested her healing. "Daughter," Jesus said, "Go your way, your faith hath made you whole."

This woman employed a contemplative form of prayer to the utmost degree, a prayer of the heart in which she initiated a deep sense of trust and surrender. She withdrew from all mental activity, closed the door to negation, handed all her concerns over to God, and focused on the presence of God within her. Once in the silence, she surrendered, and having reached the ultimate place of awareness, she became whole.

To touch the hem of Jesus' garment was a display of deep, abiding faith. When we absolutely resign ourselves to God's will and tabernacle with His presence, an outward manifestation of whatever is necessary for us becomes evident in that moment.

This transcendental Spirit is here and it is now; it is within and outside of our very being. We become enfolded in its presence whenever we claim its authenticity. When this is achieved, a feeling of euphoria flows throughout our entire being, and we become one with it; we feel it and we know it. In this state of awareness, all things become possible.

In God's presence there is fullness of joy, and in His right hand there are pleasures forevermore. It is in the silence that we meet and commune with God. Sometimes no words can really convey the depth of our feelings when there are intense feelings of joy.

A story is told about Thomas Carlyle and Ralph Waldo Emerson, who both shared an ecstatic experience in the silence some time ago when the two met for the first time on a chilly winter evening. It is said that both Thomas Carlyle and Ralph Waldo Emerson had enjoyed a long relationship for years via correspondence, but the two had never really met each other. Eventually, the time came when Emerson, who had made a special trip to Europe, decided to make a special trip to Scotland so that he could meet his special friend, the renowned essayist and historian, face to face.

Upon arriving in Scotland, Emerson was greeted warmly by Carlyle. He offered him a pipe, lit one for himself, and the two men sat together in virtual silence until it was time to retire for the night. At this point the two men warmly shook hands, and praised each other for the wonderful and fruitful evening they had shared together.

Even though no words were exchanged between the two men, spiritually both were connected at a very deep level to the unseen yet rather tangible presence within them both. From that vantage point of awareness, they became one with each other, one with everything around them, and one with the divine presence within them. There was no need for any verbal exchange as the spirit within is universal and speaks louder than mere words.

Spending quiet time in the stillness each day will free us from worry and tension. We will be energized and renewed, and we will find strength to face any challenge with courage and confidence. We will experience love, joy, wisdom, strength, and peace and understanding. "But they that wait upon the Lord shall renew their strength; they shall mount up with wings as eagles; they shall run, and not be weary; and they shall walk, and not faint" (Isaiah 40:31).

2. Intercessory Prayers

> "Confess your faults one to another, and pray for one another that ye maybe healed."
>
> James 5:16

Intercessory prayers are prayers for others, which Jesus modeled in John 17.

> "And now, O Father, glorify thou me with Thine own self with the glory which I had with Thee before the world was. I have manifested Thy name unto the men which Thou gavest me out of the world; Thine they were, and Thou gavest them me; and they have kept Thy word. I pray for them: I pray not for the world, but for them which Thou gavest me; for they are Thine" (John 17:5-6, 9).

Praying for others initiates a sense of compassion and ultimately heightens self-awareness. This is a very powerful form of prayer that has dual effects. Both the healed and the healer receive some sort of healing. To offer intercessory prayer requires a deep sense of surrender, as the focus becomes the Divine presence within and not the condition that requires healing.

Some time ago I attended an afternoon class at our church. It was a long day, and I was tired and exhausted after a hectic day at work. At the end of the class, I found myself having a very excruciating headache. All I wanted was to get home to my bed. That desire did not immediately materialize, however, as help was needed at our prayer ministry, and despite my headache, I volunteered.

My assignment was to hand-write letters of encouragement and hope to people with various needs. These letters were dictated at a very fast pace, and in order to keep up, I had to focus intently on writing. After a while, I became so engrossed in writing healing letters that I completely forgot about my own headache. It was obvious that by shifting the focus from myself unto others in need, I had initiated my own healing.

3. Conversational Prayers

There are times when we are burdened and overwhelmed with concerns for ourselves or others and no words are necessary to convey our worry, but God understands our humanity so well that even before we talk to Him, He answers.

Nevertheless, there are times that we heighten our relationship with God and find release, when we speak to Him as a friend to a friend. It is always comforting to unload all our burdens unto God, who is always ready to give of Himself. Not only does He hear all our concerns, but they are also safe with Him. God never fails to comfort us in our needs. When in Gethsemane, Jesus poured out His heart to God and He found comfort and strength in facing Pilate. When we pray in sincerity with our lips and commune with God from our hearts, we learn patience and trust that reinforces our belief in God's omnipresence, omnipotence, and omniscience.

4. Uplifting Prayers

Uplifting prayers are prayers of thanksgiving. Before we ask, God has already answered, so our prayers should be in the affirmative, not begging or pleading, but giving thanks to God who gives to all men liberally. The Father of the prodigal son reminded the older son that he ought to be grateful, as he already had everything. "Son thou art ever with me, and all that I have is thine" (John 15:31.) All that the Father hath is ours, and a thankful attitude opens the way for greater blessings.

Thanksgiving is a very necessary part of prayer. Jesus demonstrated the effects of thanksgiving in the raising of Lazarus, when first He looked up to heaven and prayed, thanking God in advance for His desired demonstration. He then called Lazarus forth from the tomb, and Lazarus, who was dead, came forth alive.

During the feeding of the of the five thousand people, Jesus again looked up to heaven and gave thanks for what appeared to be limited substance, and he was able to feed five thousand people with only five loaves and two fish. Jesus tells us that we too can do these things, but we have to follow in His footsteps, staying connected to God in prayer and giving thanks always.

Sometimes we do not know what we should pray for, but God knows our needs always, even before we do ourselves, and He will take care of them. When doubts linger in my mind, my thoughts confused, and my words muffled and incoherent, I pray anyway. When challenges seem unbearable and God seems distant—and even though I seem to falter—I still pray anyway. I instinctively know that the spirit of God broods over my desolation and responds with understanding and love. Before I know it, the dark clouds roll away and God's presence within me becomes a reality once again.

> "But if we hope for that we see not, then do we with patience wait for it. Likewise the spirit also helpeth with our infirmities: for we know not what we should pray for as we ought: but the spirit itself maketh intercession for us with groaning which cannot be uttered" (Romans 8:25-26).

Prayer and Surrender

During times of uncertainty, I have come to realize one thing: *You cannot entertain thoughts of God and problems at the same time.* As God and materiality cannot coexist, an attitude of surrender is required in order to demonstrate Good.

The first thing to do when faced with adversity is to acknowledge the problem. Next, we deny or cross out flawed thinking by focusing on the presence and power of God within us. We then endeavor to fill that space with a positive thought reinforced with a positive act in believing. This may take the form of a simple affirmation of God's promise, or we may just simply let go and wait expectantly in the silence for God to reveal Himself to us.

Every challenge in life sets the tone for the manifestation of something good. I once found myself in a very stressful situation that was very difficult for me to let go of. No amount of praying helped, and I realized that I was holding onto the situation mentally, not daring to let it go. I prayed for God's intervention, but to no avail.

My escape seemed hopeless, and the experience left me delirious. One moment I thought I was free, and the next moment my escape seemed distant. *How could God even allow this?* I thought. As I struggled with the problem, I realized that my escape lied not in God fixing anything, but in my ability to step out in faith and claim my freedom of mind and spirit. No one could do it for me. All I needed to do was surrender to my old ways of thinking and being, and resurrect myself by drinking from the fountain of truth within me.

This didn't happen overnight, however, as letting go of the old and stretching forth into new territories sometimes seems more intimidating than inviting. And so I clung to what appeared to be my comfort zone, continuing in the struggle, trying over and over again to resurrect myself. The more I used my mind to find release, however, the more I seemed entangled in my web of frustration and uncertainty, wrapped up in misery and desolation.

With an intense struggle to free my mind, I persevered in the struggle, knowing that the journey would continue until I discovered the truth about myself and experienced my oneness with Spirit. When nothing seemed to be changing, I finally remembered the words of the psalmist, "Be still and know that I am God." (Psalm 46:10.) Finally, the realization came that of myself I could do nothing, but with God I could do anything. Actually, I realized that the condition would never change until I released it all into the hands of God.

Sometimes, in an effort to find release, letting go seems most difficult, and conflict arises between thoughts and feelings. Although Job was highly spiritual, holding onto his faith quite successfully, his challenges proved that there was room for perfection. He was a godly man, but limited in his humanity and unable to grasp the depth of his spirituality within. Job struggled to find his purpose when he said

> "Behold, I go forward, but He is not there; and backward, but I cannot perceive him: On the left hand, where He doeth work, but I cannot behold Him: He hideth himself on the right hand that I cannot see Him. But He knoweth the way that I take: when He hath tried me I shall come forth as gold." (Job 23:8-10).

The gift in all the pain and frustration is the ability to begin again and again. God meets us wherever we are, and no matter how many times we fail, God is always with us, awaiting our submission.

I now view all challenges as stepping-stones that allow me the opportunity to acknowledge and examine my fears, process and transform my feelings, and channel my energy in the right direction. Without the understanding that God is always with us, our prayers are futile. "He performeth that which is appointed for me to do" (Job 23:14).

Our responsibility is to *let go* and practice patience and non-resistance. Praying "Thy will be done" helps us to let go and opens our capacity to receive God's unconditional love and bounty.

Prayerfulness

No matter how long we engage in the study of Truth, there is always an opportunity to learn more and rise higher in consciousness. We cannot possibly outgrow our divine potential. It is therefore necessary to stay focused through our trials, persevere, and pay attention to what shows up during the process.

Our aim during prayer should not be for selfish reasons, but rather to attain spiritual fulfillment. "Seek ye first the kingdom of God and His righteousness ad all these things shall be added unto you." Having the experience of God in our lives is the ultimate demonstration. When this is achieved, there is freedom from worry and fear. There is no need to strive or toil for anything; God is everything, therefore, when we seek Him first all things will be added unto us.

While it is important to engage in daily prayer and meditation, assuming an attitude of prayerfulness is even more beneficial. There is an interesting difference between prayer and prayerfulness according to Dr. Larry Dossey MD in his book *Healing Words.*

> "Intercessory prayer has a tendency to ask for definite outcomes, to structure the future, to tell God what to do, such as taking the cancer away. Prayerfulness on the other hand "is accepting without being passive and grateful without giving up."

While I was in ministerial school, most of my instructors told me that my gift of faith shone through in everything that I did. My peers also told me that I had a "prayer consciousness." Quite frankly, I was not consciously aware of the attributing factor attached to this compliment.

At the end of my ministerial training, seeking employment out of my country was the furthest thing from my mind, so when without active search l was offered a job as the minister of a church in the U. S Virgin Islands, everyone was taken by surprise. One of my classmates remarked, "Marjorie, I have never seen anyone demonstrate as quickly as you do without even lifting finger." It was then that it suddenly dawned on me that despite my unassuming attitude, I was living and demonstrating a life of prayer, and a light was shining through.

When we make prayers the most important activity of our lives, we can experience outstanding miracles. Ultimately, we have to be truly conscious, believing with conviction that God is able to do all things in and through us. Consequently, we give ourselves permission to heal, and we know that our prayers are answered, not with an outward demonstration of our perceived good, but when there is a feeling of peace in our hearts and in our minds.

A faithful and consistent prayer life fully equips us for unexpected trials and temptations. Jesus demonstrated this in the wilderness when He was tempted several times by the devil. Had He not been prayerfully prepared, He might have given in to the wiles of the devil, but Jesus lived His life in total awareness of His Father and negativity could not control or disarm Him.

Prayer is about accepting what is happening in the moment and taking responsibility for our actions, surrendering to God's will and purpose for our lives. When we stay connected to God through daily times of prayer and meditation, He will reveal Himself to us according to our needs and according to His will and purpose for us. There is nothing too good for God to give us. He is our father and our mother. He loves us unconditionally, and He hears us always, no matter what we are going through.

How to Pray

Prayer is for the purpose of changing us, not God. Pleading and begging God will not coerce God into pleasing us. We pray therefore not to change God, but to change our limited ways of seeing things. God is principle, unchanging and eternal. God is and forever will be. "All things were made by Him and without Him, was nothing made that was made" (John 1:3). We pray not to impress God, but to impress upon our subconscious minds the truth that already is. "Whatsoever God doeth, it shall be forever: nothing can be put to it nor anything taken from it" (Ecclesiastes 3:14). Our responsibility is to seek God as the answer, instead of the things that we seek.

Our beliefs and attitudes are shaped to a large extent by our upbringings, and the way we perceive God is indicative of how we experience Him. God is not a punishing God. We are punished according to our beliefs. If we believe that God is a stern God who punishes us when we are bad and rewards us when we are good, through our minds we will constantly live in fear. Conversely, if we believe that God is all good and loves us unconditionally, we will experience Him as a loving and forgiving Father who is willing to give us the opportunity to redeem our lives and experience the best of everything.

Prayer can be a very complex subject, and there are many different ways in which one can pray. There is no wrong way or right way to pray; it is the intention behind our prayers that matters most. Prayer involves the mind and includes anything that we do consciously like meditating, listening to music, gardening, doing the dishes, walking, or even dancing. In fact, we live a life of prayer daily, as we are always praying. Prayer can be spoken out loud, silently spoken, or it can be a total attitude of surrender to God, who is all-knowing, all—powerful, and all present.

The method of prayer is not so much important as the reason for praying. Many words are not necessary in prayer, but the more time we dedicate to prayer, the more effective will be our prayers. The important thing is to be present to the now moment. God speaks to us from the stillness of our hearts, and our hearts are still only when thoughts and feelings are united.

Every prayer brings rewards, but we must follow instructions and move our attention inward instead of outward. During the Sermon on the Mount in Matthew 6:6, Jesus taught his disciples how to pray by first giving them an instruction. “When thou prayest, enter into thy closet, and when thou hast shut thy door, pray to Thy father which is in secret; and thy Father which seeth in secret shall reward thee openly.” To enter the closet is to retire within and close the door to all outer distractions. When we focus on the presence of God within, whatever we need to know will be revealed to us.

Flowery words are not necessary in praying to God. Most of all, our prayers should be sincere and from our hearts.

> “But when thou pray, use not vain repetitions as the heathens do; for they think that they shall be heard for their much speaking. Be not therefore like unto them; for your Father knoweth what things ye have need of, before you ask Him” (Matthew 6:7-8).

There is a story about a Hindu teacher who used the analogy of a wounded dog to illustrate the meaning of prayer.

> There was once a dog who was attacked by a pack of wild dogs. He fought his way free, limped home bleeding, and presented himself to his owner. The owner carried the dog indoors where he treated his cuts and bruises. He cared for the dog every day, giving him food and water and a soft bed. Soon the dog recovered.

The point of the story is that the dog did not ask for a thing. He just presented himself to his master, who subsequently took care of his needs. "That is how you pray," the Hindu teacher said. "For if you ask for a shirt you will get a shirt, and if you ask for trousers, you will get trousers, but if you simply present yourself, blessings will be yours." God is with us always to comfort, protect, guide, and direct us toward our good. He understands our fears, our doubts, and our weaknesses. We should therefore learn to be still and trust in His divine plan for our lives.

Most of all, our prayers should not be for selfish reasons. They should be for the good of all concerned. The Dalai Lama once said, "I have found that the greatest degree of inner tranquility comes from the development of love and compassion. The more we care for the happiness of others, the greater is our own sense of well-being."

How to Demonstrate through Prayer

1. Live in the Present Moment

> "Yesterday is history.
> Tomorrow is mystery.
> Today is a gift.
> That's why it's called the present."
>
> Eleanor Roosevelt

The past is behind, and the future is yet to be. Therefore, this present moment is the only reality. We can never experience the future in the present because we are always in the present. Although the past helps to shape the present and the present helps to shape the future, we are always in the present, so in reality all that we can do, we can only do in the present moment.

The Bible says in 2 Corinthians 6:2, "Now is the acceptable time. Behold now is the day of salvation." Not yesterday, not tomorrow, but right now. In this moment lies wonderful possibilities, but we have to be present to realize them, and to be present is to become still. When we acknowledge the present moment, we become aware of our thoughts, actions, and feelings. We become aware of our surroundings and the needs of others. The more aware we become, the more our experiences will be real and the more our light will be revealed.

2. Pray Without Ceasing

To pray without ceasing is to live in the kingdom of God and establish oneness with God. This practice reinforces our belief that what we pray for is already done unto us. God knows our needs and our desires even before we ask Him, so the discipline of praying without ceasing establishes oneness with God and with all things. God can do for us what He can do through us, and If we put Him to the test, He will open the windows of heaven and pour out blessings that we won't even have enough room to receive. God is the only reality in our lives, and in Him there is no darkness.

Jesus constantly demonstrated to us the benefits of praying without ceasing. As the Son of God, He had the power to do great things while He was on earth. Nevertheless, Jesus lived in constant awareness of His Father, frequently going apart to make contact with God. Because of His connectedness to His Father, Jesus never failed to demonstrate from healing to supply.

3. Seek First the Kingdom

To seek the kingdom first, is, to focus our attention on God within us in all our needs, and not on our needs themselves. God is the only reality. Things will be added unto us, but they are not lasting and they do not make us happy.

The kingdom of God is a pure state of being, a realm where we access divine information. It is not a physical place where we go after we die. It is here and now. It is attainable to all who seek it, and it becomes evident when we function in tune with the divine mind of God. But in order to find it, we have to diligently seek it, not for selfish or material gains, but to have sufficiency in all things. Jesus tells us in Matthew 6, "Seek ye first the kingdom of God and His righteousness and all these things will be added unto you." "All things" include peace of mind, harmony in relationships, financial gains, perfect health, and also material things.

Jesus tells us in Matthew 6:24, "No man can serve two masters: for either he will hate one and serve the other, or else he will hold on to one and despise the other. You cannot serve God and Mammon." When we put God first, we will experience lasting joy and spiritual fulfillment. God is everything that we desire. He is all-knowing, all-present, and all-powerful. When we seek Him first, we experience "the fruits of the spirit: love, joy, peace, long suffering, gentleness, goodness, faith, meekness and temperance" (Galatians 5:22-23). There is nothing in the world that prayer will not conquer, no situation that prayer cannot change. Let us stay connected to the source of all our good, God the good, the omnipotent.

9

From Fear to Freedom

Living a life of prayer no doubt frees us from crippling emotions, such as fear, which at times robs us of our joy, leaving us spiritually and emotionally exhausted, unable to enjoy life. But fear for some of us is a vague constant that plagues us indiscriminately, in the most inopportune times, leaving us emotionally exhausted and lacking.

Sometimes fear hits us so greatly that we want to fight or run away. When faced with obvious danger, fear can be a perfectly natural emotion; it can be used as a tool for survival. When fear lurks around indiscriminately in our emotional life, however, it tends to hold us in bondage and prevent us from making necessary improvements in our lives.

Letting Go of Fear

The best way to conquer fear is to step right into it with faith, knowing that "underneath are the everlasting arms." God wants us to be brave like David was when he faced with the giant Goliath.

In biblical times the Hebrews faced a formidable foe, Goliath of Gath. Goliath was tall and heavily built. Goliath challenged that if his Hebrew opponent conquered him, then the Philistines would become servants of the Hebrews, but if he conquered his Hebrew opponent, the Hebrews would surrender to the Philistines.

No one from the Hebrew side wanted to challenge the formidable Goliath. They were afraid of his appearance. He looked big, and most people were intimidated by his stature, but a small boy named David accepted the challenge. He had no fear. He remembered how the Lord had saved him once before, and thought that this time would be no different.

So David stepped out in faith. He had no armor to protect him. All he had was a sling, some stones, his faith in God, and his courage. Goliath sneered as David faced him, thinking that this small boy could not possibly defeat him.

How wrong Goliath was! What he didn't know was that besides physical strength, David also had what he didn't have—spiritual strength, the greatest strength of all. "Not by might, not by power, but by my spirit says the Lord" (Zechariah 4:6). So David faced Goliath, and out came the stone from his sling, hitting Goliath right in the forehead and killing him with ease.

When we step out with faith in God like David did, He will ease our fears and help us to overcome our challenges. "And he led them on safely, so that they feared not; but the sea overwhelmed their enemies" (Psalm 78:53). Viewed from a metaphysically perspective, enemies represent doubts and fear, and the sea, our mental potential. Consequently, whenever we step out in faith, anchored in the presence of God within us all fears, doubts, and anxieties are subsequently dissolved. Once we face the world and our fears, we will discover inner strengths, talents, and skills we never realized we had for coping with challenging situations.

Appearances can be deceiving, but the Truth is real, and although a challenge may appear insurmountable, God can turn around any difficult situation into a blessing. We must first acknowledge Him as the ultimate problem solver and surrender to His presence.

The best way to combat fear is to make friends with it by acknowledging its non-power over us. It has been reported that the building of the Golden Gate Bridge in San Francisco, which is the highest and longest single-span bridge in the world, created a lot of fear for some of the builders. The height of the bridge, which looked down into the dark waters of the bay, was enough to scare even the most experienced builder.

The bridge cost thirty-five million dollars to build, and there was a superstition that for every million dollars spent on the bridge a human life would be sacrificed. Five lives had already been lost due to this superstition regardless of the safety measures that were put in place. One day it was decided to put a safety net under the bridge. This net was woven with steel strands just like a fishing-net. It was put under the bridge and stretched from one end to the other. If anyone fell, the net would automatically catch them and they would be pulled back to safety.

The height of the bridge remained the same, the slippery conditions the same, the water just as black and far below, but the amazing thing is that there were no more accidents; from that time onward no one has fallen off the bridge into the net. This is because the presence of the safety net removed the fear factor.

Fear Has No Power

In our quest to overcome fear, we need to take a closer look at ourselves and realize that fear in itself has no power except the power we give to it through our thoughts, and that we can change our thoughts in moments. Fear is a lack of belief in oneself, but faith in oneself will banish all fear. God is the only power, all good, everywhere present, within and without, and we were made in His image and likeness, so there is absolutely nothing to fear "For God hath not given us the spirit of fear; but of power, and of love and of a sound mind" (2 Timothy 1:7). This divine potential is inherent, which somehow manifests whenever we are pushed to the edge; suddenly before we know it we move right into it setting ourselves free.

There is a story about a mother eagle that once flew to the top of a great mountain. There amidst the rocks and crags she decided to build a nest. Down into the valley below she swooped and picked up twigs from the thorn trees that grew in great abundance. Trip after trip she made until at last the nest of thorn branches was complete. She swooped down again to find soft moss from the floor of the valley with which to line the nest. She sat upon the nest until a single egg hatched and her baby was born. He was comfortable and warm in the mossy nest.

Daily his mother made trip after trip, bringing food from the earth. The baby eagle grew rapidly. Soon black and white feathers adorned his mighty body, and at last he was almost grown. The young eagle was so happy. He was warm and safe, and there was plenty of food to eat. He loved to peer over the edge of the nest and watch the magnificent scenery below.

One day the mother eagle did a strange thing. Bit by bit she began to pluck bits of moss from the nest, and thorns began to break through and stab the young eagle. "Why are you doing this?" cried the young eagle. "If you loved me, you would not do such a thing!" But the mother eagle did not reply. She just continued to take away the moss.

At last the pain from the thorns became so intense that the young eagle leaped from the nest. The wind caught under his wings and he soared high and strong into the sky. Thus it was only through discomfort and pain that the young eagle was able to experience true freedom, becoming the creature of triumph.

When we embrace fear in the light of God, we will transform it, ultimately discovering what powerful creatures we are in

Christ! "Greater is he that is within you than he that is in the world" (1 John 4:4).

Our difficulties are often mind-created, and we view them according to our limited perception of the truth. If we live in fear, we will encounter fear. If we live with a sense of victory, we will not only experience victory, but we will also view our challenges as stepping stones, conquering them and experiencing victory in Christ.

Moving Beyond Fear

Fear often shows up in our lives no matter who we are. The important thing is how we handle it. As the Israelites prepared to enter Canaan, the Lord advised Moses to send men to survey the land. They were to see whether the people were strong or weak, and whether the land was rich or poor.

The men finally returned and reported that the land was indeed full of milk and honey. There was a problem, however. The people were strong and the cities were walled and very large, and so they thought it best to stay away from those people.

Caleb, who went with the men, had a different report. Yes, the land was fertile and the people appeared strong, but God had made a promise to them and He would keep it. He believed that they should go right into Canaan and take possession of the land, as God would be there to protect them.

The people still doubted, and they rejected that idea. They looked liked grasshoppers compared to the people of Canaan who looked like giants. They did not want to be devoured by them.

Poet and author William Shakespeare once said, "There is nothing good or bad, but thinking that makes it so." If we see our challenges as giants, they will become giants. If we look beyond the appearances, however, we will see God in them all then we will not be intimidated by fear—"For God hath not give us the spirit of fear; but of power, and of love, and of a sound mind. (2nd Timothy1:7).

The journey of the Israelites into Canaan reflects the different aspects of our consciousness which we display as we face challenges in life. We all have the qualities of Moses embedded within us, which represents the law; the consciousness of the children of Israel, who represent sense consciousness; the quality of Caleb, representing fearlessness, and the consciousness of Joshua, representing victory through overcoming. It is entirely up to us, through the power and presence of God to find balance and harmony in every aspect of our lives.

Our release of fear and subsequent degree of victory is therefore incumbent on our ability to face fear with love; knowing that in itself fear has absolutely no power over us. We can do anything with the help of God.

10

Acknowledging the Divine Self

> "A man should learn to detect and watch that gleam of light which flashes across his mind from within"
> Ralph Waldo Emerson

The goal of all mankind is to experience oneness with the divine Self within and to live life from that perspective. To have this experience is to be conscious of our thoughts and the way we live. "Let this mind be in you, which was also in Christ Jesus" (Philippians 2:5). The daily practice of prayer and meditation allows us access to the mind of Christ, from which flows a fountain of Divine ideas.

The book of Genesis states that God created man in His own image and likeness; blessed everything He created, and gave humankind dominion over everything.

> "And God said, 'Let us make man in our image, after our likeness: and let them have dominion over the fish of the sea, and over the fowl of the air, and over the cattle, and over all the earth, and over every creeping thing that creepeth upon the earth.' And God blessed them and God said unto them, 'Be fruitful, multiply and replenish the earth and subdue it and have dominion over the fish of the sea, and over the fowl of the air, and over every living thing that moveth upon the earth" (Gen. 1:26, 28).

To multiply and replenish the earth is to grow in the Christ consciousness, taking responsibility and doing the will of God. We can make a difference to any situation in our lives by changing our thinking and believing in the power of God within us. "To whom God would make known what is the riches of the glory of this mystery among the Gentiles; which is Christ in you, the hope of glory" (Colossians 1:27).

We have the power within us to heal the sick, raise the dead, cast out demons, calm the storms, and overcome death, but we must believe. "Verily, verily I say unto you, He that believeth on me, the works that I do shall he do also; and greater works than these shall he do; because I go unto my Father" (John 14:12).

Throughout the Bible we are reminded of our divine potential:

- "But if the spirit of him that raised up Jesus from the dead dwell in you, he that raised up Christ from the dead shall also quicken your mortal bodies by his spirit that dwelleth in you."
  Romans 8:11

- "All authority is given unto me in heaven and in earth. Go ye therefore and teach all nations baptizing them in the name of the Father, and of the Son, and of the Holy Ghost."
  Matthew 28:18-19

- "And the seventy returned again with joy, saying "Lord, even the devils are subject unto us through Thy name."
  Luke 10:17

- "Behold I give unto you power to tread on serpents and scorpions and over all the power of the enemy; and nothing shall by any means hurt you."
  Luke 10:19

As co-creators with God, humankind is therefore endowed with authority and dominion over thought, with potential for success and full provision for all needs. Unfortunately, humankind departed from spiritual consciousness, as demonstrated in the story, "The Tower of Babel," in the book of Genesis, resulting in mixed states of consciousness.

We sometimes doubt our divine potential like Moses did, or sometimes we are intimidated by a task at hand, that may seem too great for us to handle. However, God's presence within us makes us capable of achieving anything we desire but in order to receive Good, we have to be ready and receptive. Our good doesn't necessarily come packaged in fancy wrapping paper but with God's presence and power within us we have the inner capability to use what we have to our gain.

Moses was transfixed at the sight of the burning bush and the ultimate realization of the presence and power of God within him, but subconsciously he was ready to go on his God appointed mission to free the Israelites from bondage in Egypt.

The first thing that we need to do is to believe that God would never leave us or forsake us, and wherever He leads, He provides. Because Moses had doubts, God eased his mind by redefining his divine potential, instructing him to remove the shoes from his feet, as the place wherein he stood was holy ground. Feet, according to Charles Fillmore in *The Revealing Word*, represent understanding, so in order for Moses to receive spiritual understanding, he had to remove limitation and negation from his mind (remove his shoes from his feet).

God is absolute good, everywhere equally present, within us and without; so wherever we are, God is. No matter what we are going through, God is working in and though us to bring forth good. God further used a rod to demonstrate His power in Moses. First, He instructed Moses to throw the rod on the ground. Moses obeyed and the rod turned into a snake. God then told him to pick the rod up, and when Moses did, it turned back into a rod.

Next, God told Moses to put his hand into his bosom and then take it out. When Moses did, his hand became white with leprosy. God further told Moses to put his hand back into his bosom and take it out once again. When he did, the leprosy was gone.

These demonstrations proved that the power of God is always within and without, available at any time to conquer any circumstance, to accomplish good.

How to Express Your Divine Potential

1. Exercise humility

A proud person often misses out on God's guidance because he or she is not prepared to pray about it. Jesus was born in the humblest of circumstances, and yet he was rich in spirit. He could demonstrate from healing to supply at the drop of a hat. Although he was the Son of God, he never failed to demonstrate humility in all walks of life, always giving God the glory and acknowledging God as the giver of all good things. In Philippians 2:5-8, the Apostle Paul also reminds us to be humble.

> "Let this mind be in you which was also in Christ Jesus, who being in the form of God, thought it not robbery to be equal with God. But made Himself of no reputation, and took upon him the form of a servant, and was made in the likeness of men: And being found in fashion as a man, he humbled himself, and became obedient unto death, even the death of the cross."

In order to enter the kingdom of God, we need to acknowledge our powerlessness and give God the glory in all things. We of ourselves can do nothing, but with God we can do anything. "All things were made by Him, and without Him was nothing made that was made" (John 1:3).

2. Put God first

We cannot serve God and at the same time put our trust in outer things or people. "Thou shalt not bow down thyself to them, nor serve them: for I the Lord thy God am a jealous God" (Exodus 20:5). God is the only power, and the only presence in our lives and in the world. He is the vine and we are the branches. He is the source from which all our good comes. When we acknowledge Him first, all things are added unto us.

3. Pray without ceasing

To pray without ceasing is to trust God with carefree abandon, knowing that we are one with Divine presence and His will for us is absolute good . . . God is the source of everything. He is creator and sustainer of all life and without him we can do nothing.

When we pray without ceasing we focus our attention on the presence and power of God within us, as the answer to all our needs. From this awareness He will reveal to us all that needs to be revealed, and heal all that needs to be healed. "And ye shall seek me and find me when ye shall search for me with all your heart" (Jeremiah 29:13).

4. Ask in faith

All that the Father hath is ours, and it is His good pleasure to give us the kingdom. "If any of you lacks wisdom, let him ask of God that giveth to all men liberally, and upbraideth not; and it shall be given him generously to all without finding fault, and it will be given him. But let him ask in faith, nothing wavering. For he that wavereth is like a wave of the sea driven with the wind and tossed" (James 1:5-6).

God has already supplied all our needs, even before we ask (Isaiah 65:24); therefore, we do not have to plead or beseech. We should ask in faith, claiming our divine inheritance and giving thanks that we have already received that which we ask for.

As for the brother of the prodigal son, who was obviously in doubt about his inheritance, the Father reminded him that he already had everything, so there was no need to envy his brother. "Son, thou at ever with me and all that I have is thine" (Luke 15:31).

5. Believe that with God all things are possible

It is easy to believe what we have seen, but to believe what we have not seen is a test of our faith. "Faith is the substance of things hoped for, the evidence of things not seen" (Hebrew 11:1).

The fact is we cannot achieve anything in life without first believing.

"All things whatsoever that you ask in prayer, believing, ye shall receive" (Matthew 21: 22).

In the gospel of John, when Jesus appeared to some of His disciples after His resurrection, Thomas, who had been absent, found it hard to believe that Jesus had risen. He wanted to see Jesus with his own eyes and touch the place where the nails had pierced as evidence that Jesus had truly risen.

Jesus knew that Thomas had doubts, so He appeared unto him and showed him his pierced hands and side. Thomas then believed and he said, "My Lord and my Master." Jesus told Thomas afterwards, "Because thou has seen me, thou hast believed: blessed are they that have not seen, and yet have believed" (John 20:29).

At times many of us doubt like Thomas did, as it is not always easy to believe something that we have not seen, but even though we have not seen Jesus physically like some of those disciples who did, we can nevertheless exercise our faith and experience Him in our hearts.

Many great things in life are often unaccomplished due to unbelief. In Matthew chapter 17, after Peter, James, and John came from the Mount of Transfiguration with Jesus, a man asked Jesus to heal his lunatic son who was possessed by the Devil. After healing the boy, the disciples who were left behind were puzzled. Why were they unable to heal the boy on their own? They asked Jesus, and Jesus told them

> "Because of your unbelief: for verily I say unto you, if you have faith as a grain of mustard seed, you shall say unto this mountain, Remove hence to yonder place, and it shall remove, and nothing shall be impossible to you. This can only be accomplished by prayer and fasting" (Matthew 17:20).

Praying and fasting is to deny error thinking and affirm the truth. "If my people which are called by my name shall humble themselves, and pray, and seek my face, and turn from their wicked ways; then will I hear from heaven, and will forgive their sin, and will heal their land. (2nd Chronicles 7:14).

The depth of our belief is the first requirement to demonstrate our desired good. This is emphasized throughout the Bible. Jesus often asked those who went to Him for healing if they believed, after which He would then tell them, "According to your faith it is done unto you."

Of ourselves we cannot accomplish a single thing. Jesus said, "I am the way, the truth, and the life. No man cometh to the

Father but by me." Having the consciousness of Jesus is therefore the way through which all can achieve fullness of life. "And if I be lifted up from the earth, will draw all men unto me" (John 12:32).

To attain the consciousness of the Christ spirit within requires self-discipline, determination, and a firm belief in one's divinity. Although others may help us with our navigation, no one can do the actual work for us—not even Jesus, our way shower. Nevertheless, Jesus understands our humanity, and He is always willing to assist us in our weaknesses. The father of the epileptic boy in Mark chapter 9 who asked Jesus to heal his lunatic son confessed that his faith was weak. "Lord I believe, help thou my unbelief," he said. Jesus then took the boy by the hand and healed him.

6. Allow Love to rule in your heart

Love is the key factor in demonstrating the divine Self. It is the inner light that enables you to see good in all persons. When one is in tune with God's love, one sees good everywhere, even in trying and even unforeseen circumstances. Love heals all physical and emotional discords, setting us free from turmoil and discomforts, establishing peace and harmony in our lives, prospering and harmonizing our relationships

> "And we have known and believed the love that God hath to us. God is love; and he that dwelleth in love dwelleth in God, and God in him. Herein is our love made perfect, that we may have boldness in the Day of Judgment: because as he is, so are we in this world" (1 John 4:16-17).

7. Acknowledge your body as God's temple

"Ye are the temple of the living God: as God hath said, "I will dwell in them, and talk in them, and I will be their God, and they shall be my people" (2 Cor. 6:16).

The overcoming of worldly consciousness is essential in demonstrating and maintaining a happy and healthy life. We enhance our spirituality and bring our divinity to the forefront by honoring our body and its functions with regular exercise, adequate rest, nourishing foods, and regular periods of prayer and meditation.

As we devote more time to our spiritual practices, we will maintain a healthy and productive life. We will become more calm, and patient in times of crisis and our lives will become rich, more meaningful, and more successful. Ultimately, our blessings will unfold in expected, unexpected and wonderful ways, and everything will flow in divine order.

11

Knowing God's Will

> "And we know that all things work together for good to them that love God, to them who are called according to His purpose."
>
> Romans 8:28

> "In everything give thanks: for this is the will of God in Christ concerning you."
>
> 1 Thessalonians 5:18

God's will is the same for all mankind; perfect and good. God is also principle and we cannot therefore cajole God into pleasing us. To experience His will however we need to acknowledge Him in all our ways, whereby absolute Good or God's will, is established in our lives.

We should therefore trust God with all our concerns. He knows our needs even before we do and He never makes a mistake. He is always on our side. When we live in compliance with the word of God we have nothing to fear. "Because all things work together for good to them that love God, to them who are called according to his purpose". (Romans 8:28).

Despite all trials and tribulations, the will of God for us is always to demonstrate Good. Despite conditions that prove contrary to His promise, we need to stand firm, trust God, and further prove our allegiance by giving thanks that His will which is perfect and good be done. "In everything give thanks: for this is the will of God in Christ Jesus concerning you. (1 Thessalonians 5:18). The more time we devote to the divine presence, the more God's will is revealed to us. By simply trusting and acknowledging God's will, we can accomplish mighty things in our lives.

In John chapter 2, Jesus showed us how the seemingly impossible could be made possible by simply doing the will of God, as He turned water into wine at a wedding feast in Canaan. Of great significance was the fact that before this great miracle took place, Mary, the mother of Jesus, gave an instruction to the servants: "Whatsoever he saith unto you, do it" (John 2:5).

After obeying Mary's instructions the servants did what Jesus instructed them to do, and wine was manufactured from water in an instant. From this demonstration the lesson is clear: by doing the will of God, which is in essence doing what Jesus says, the impossible will become possible. Metaphysically speaking, "servants" represent our thoughts, so preceding any demonstration we ought to focus our thoughts on the Word of God.

Prior to the miracle of turning water into wine it is interesting to note that Jesus chose His disciples with an invitation "Follow me." (John 1:43). It can be concluded therefore that the seemingly 'impossible' can be overcome simply by listening to divine instructions and following in the footsteps of Jesus.

To follow Jesus is to seek God first, acknowledging Him in all our ways, and to show love to everyone, even those who have done us wrong. It means to be kind, humble, compassionate, forgiving, and to think of others and not just of ourselves.

Sometimes we may feel empowered to tackle great tasks, but there are also other times when in our humanity we feel hopelessly intimidated by doubts and fear, resulting in undue anxiety and uncertainty. During these challenging times, there is always a choice to turn within to the Christ presence at any given moment, and there we will find all the strength, power, and peace we need to fulfill our every desire.

Willfulness induces disobedience, and disobedience is one of the biggest hurdles to our spiritual lives. There is nothing to gain from such a self-inspired mentality, only limitation and bondage to materiality. We should always pray for God's will in our lives regardless of the outcome. God's will is good will, and when things go wrong we should not fear, because He is able to do all things in and through us. "He performeth the thing that is appointed for me" (Job 23:10, 14).

Jesus trusted that God's will, for Him, would have been perfect and good, even during his ordeal at Gethsemane. He proved his obedience by doing the will of God, and God was with Him always. In his pain and agony, Jesus prayed, "Father, if thou be willing, remove this cup from me, nevertheless not my will, but Thy will be done." Amazingly in that moment of surrender, an angel appeared unto Him from heaven and strengthened him. (Luke 22:42-43).

In the book of Genesis, Abraham also acknowledged God's will, when he agreed to offer Isaac, his beloved son, as a sacrifice. Abraham had no fear. He had deep abiding faith even in the most adverse situation, knowing that God would always provide. Because of Abraham's faith, God intervened at the appointed time and provided a ram for Abraham to slaughter instead of his son Isaac. As a result of his obedience to the will of God, Abraham was subsequently rewarded with abundant blessings.

God's will is not to be found in events or circumstances. His will is found within our own heart. God's will is never for humankind to suffer in any way. His love for us transcends all adversity, all unwelcome events or circumstances.

Any desire from the heart can be seen as God's will for us. The authenticity of the desire is often substantiated when everything flows in divine order and for things to flow in divine order there has to be total trust and surrender of self. This was the case for me a year or two after finding my spiritual home at Unity of Jamaica. Having enjoyed a successful business for a number of years, the time had come when the zeal and enthusiasm I once experienced abruptly came to an end, leaving me completely in the void.

My business subsequently lost its fervor and sales went down drastically, lessening my reserves and threatening my sanity. Frankly, I went right down to rock bottom, and it soon became evident that I had no choice but to close my business. This unraveling of events must have been divinely orchestrated as it seemed that I had no choice but to listen and go with the flow.

After months of soul searching and seeking spiritual counseling, it became obvious that I was going through a transition, being called to a higher purpose. I began to accept the series of subsequent events as the heralding of a new direction. It was evident that a paradigm shift was about to take place.

As I continued with my spiritual practices, one day I was summoned to the Sunday school at my church to improvise for an absent teacher. I was humbled and honored for the vote of confidence, but quite shy and uncertain of my divine capabilities. I loved the challenge, but I had doubts.

I contemplated my decision, and I was guided by the Holy Spirit to take on the challenge. Deep down I knew it was a divine appointment, so eventually I surrendered, accepted my assignment in faith, and handed the experience over to God, affirming "divine order."

To my surprise, interacting with the teens proved to be a very rewarding and enjoyable experience. It was effortless and wonderful, as they were open, receptive, and willing to express themselves freely.

This turned into a permanent assignment without much warning. Initially, I felt overwhelmed and hesitant about sacrificing Sunday morning worship experiences, fearing that my spiritual growth would be affected. My inner voice reassured me, however, that this was a divine appointment, and I had more to gain than lose. Finally, resolving that there had to be a bigger picture, I consequently answered the call to serve with an inner knowing that Divine guidance would lead me and divine wisdom would inspire me, making my way easy and successful.

Eventually, the experience turned out to be an adventure in faith, one of the most fulfilling and joyful experiences of my life. As I took the plunge in faith and surrendered, I felt guided and directed by the Holy Spirit. I served willingly and enthusiastically, and the children were eager to learn and grow. There were challenges, of course, that helped me to develop my spiritual muscles as my patience and my listening and caring skills greatly improved. I was truly motivated to continue serving for as long as it was required of me.

The wealth of knowledge and inner satisfaction I gained from serving was unequalled. Not only did I develop self-confidence, but I was also encouraged to expand my awareness both intellectually and spiritually and to stretch my imagination creatively in order to interact with a group of teens who obviously needed to be challenged and inspired. Since then there has been no looking back, and I continue to give generously of my time, talent, and treasure.

This was not only a time of giving, it was also a time of receiving, and as I taught, I learned. I was truly amazed at the depth and profundity of the children's wisdom. They expressed themselves judiciously and without limit. It felt wonderful to be with them and to experience this remarkable exchange!

This was a blessing, and it has had an indelible effect on my life.

After a year or two I was asked to assume the role of director for the Sunday school. This was even a bigger stretch for me, having had no prior experience in this field, but this time the decision was easier because I had served as sponsor for the past year.

Before accepting the offer, I took it into prayer and meditation, listening earnestly for divine guidance. One day while I was in church, I received my confirmation when a little girl not more than four years old held onto my leg and lovingly exclaimed, "Auntie Marjorie!" This made me aware of the bond I had established, and I realized that the Sunday school had become a part of me. From that moment on, I made the decision to assume the responsibility of being a spiritual mother to over sixty children ranging from ages two to sixteen.

Being lovingly called "Auntie Marjorie" by this little angel finally propelled me to accept my new position as director of the Sunday school, and I made a decision to give it my best shot, knowing that with God as my silent partner, adviser, and instructor, I could not fail. I subsequently ventured out in faith once more, preparing myself to serve gladly.

Not having been in a leadership position in this arena before, I still doubted my capabilities. Nevertheless, I stepped out in faith. Soon after, however, I was challenged by one or two volunteers who openly displayed their dissatisfaction of my agenda during a meeting. I almost retorted in consternation, but I somehow managed to hold my peace and maintain my composure. Although I managed to remain silent, inwardly I wanted to run away and hide. The spirit of God seemed to have intervened, however, when a voice from within me compelled me to smile and turn the other cheek. "Be still and know that I am God."

It seemed that I had no choice in the matter, as I found myself totally defenseless, responding with love and showing no outer sign of indignation or fear. The meeting ended with a wonderful feeling of victory, and I thanked God for coming to my rescue.

On my way home, however, I felt saddened and uncertain. The tears came and I let them flow profusely and uncontrolled. Instinctively, I was warned to be strong and of good courage, as there would be many more challenges ahead. Knowing that God was my defense and my deliverer, I dried my tears and remembered God's promise to the prophet Isaiah

> "I will go before thee, and make the crooked places straight: I will break in pieces the gates of brass, and cut in sunder the bars of iron: And I will give thee the treasures of darkness, and hidden riches of secret places, that thou mayest know that I, the Lord, which call thee by thy name, am the God of Israel" (Isaiah 45:2-3).

With that beautiful promise I later affirmed with power and conviction, "I can do all things through Christ which strengtheneth me" (Philippians 4:13).

There are no mistakes in life, and everything works for a good purpose. We often become the target of persecution because of our own inner thoughts. We attract circumstances, conditions, and people into our lives for a reason—in order to learn and grow from them. In order to improve my faculties of strength, confidence, patience, willpower, and understanding, it appeared that I had been challenged by these personalities, when in fact they were only helping me to unravel my insecurities. The experience worked as my stepping stone, allowing me to face my shadows and transform my weaknesses into strength.

The Sunday school continued to function remarkably well, and shortly afterwards the two volunteers completed their assignment. They later resigned and went on their individual journeys. I thank them for their contribution to the Sunday school, blessed them, and wished the best for them.

The remaining volunteers continued to be supportive, always willing and eager to assist in whatever ways they could, and the Sunday school continued to thrive and flourish. Within a short time, there was enough volunteered help that no one felt any undue pressure.

The Spirit of God was in charge, directing and preparing us for loving service, and we gave of ourselves unconditionally. We buzzed with new ideas that initiated growth and development for our center, and we worked together in an atmosphere of peace, love, and harmony. There was cohesiveness among us all, and our team functioned as one. Everyone had an input, and every voice was authentic. There were no hidden agendas, there was no animosity, and we all served willingly and gladly, teaching, learning, playing, and growing together.

Our activities at the Sunday school were many and varied, and the children learned to prioritize their time wisely. One of our objectives was to foster spiritual awareness by encouraging a display of love and compassion to those less fortunate. We visited homes for mentally challenged and homeless children, and the experience was an eye opener for most of our group. Ultimately, we all learned to appreciate and to be thankful for what we had.

Another activity of great success at the Sunday school was the youths leading Sunday worship services at the church on Youth Sundays. This was the highlight for them, and they looked forward to this time when their creativity was greatly exposed. It was a wonderful experience to see the caterpillar turn into a butterfly in many children who were viewed as unassuming. They shone in all their glory to the honor of the

Christ within, as they often rose to the occasion and displayed talents and abilities they never thought they had.

The volunteers were a willing, constant, and ever-present resource for them, and although self-reliance and freedom of expression were encouraged, we also instilled good morals with honest and open communication. Soon afterwards, the Sunday school was the talk of the town and our success was eminent.

As I opened up myself to be used by God, step by step the butterfly in me began to emerge, and after a period of soul searching, I received confirmation of being in my rightful place. I volunteered most of my time to the development of the Sunday school, and my spiritual life took precedence over everything else in my life. The joy I received from serving and the success I achieved from working with eight other volunteers at the Sunday school served as confirmation that there was a bigger picture in store for me. This was only the beginning.

The closing of my business, as well as the series of events ensuing after, were all a part of the divine plan, unfolding the path to my ministerial career. I was very passionate about becoming a minister of religion, but not confident enough to disclose my innermost desire to anyone for fear of being invalidated, and although doubts constantly surfaced in my mind, I kept my desire close to my heart and allowed it to unfold in God's divine will.

Now, many years later, I have come to realize that it is always God's will to give us the desires of our heart. All it takes is a belief in one's self, and a sheer determination to succeed. With the help of God, I managed to take the stand of the little shepherd boy David and confront the giant of fear, the Goliath within me, with love, faith, and courage, transforming feelings of negativity into a blessing, proving that God's will is good will, and finally making my dream become a reality.

12

A Reality Check

> "Seek ye first the kingdom of God and his righteousness; and all these things will be added unto you."
>
> Matthew 6:33

No matter how successful we are in demonstrating God's will, there is always an opportunity to advance in our spirituality. God's ways are not our ways, nor are His thoughts our thoughts, so life itself is a mystery. There is no given. We have no control over what happens from day to day.

Although we dedicate ourselves to thinking only the best and doing only the best, sometimes our best is not good enough and we seem to wind up at the foot of the ladder, trying all over again and again. Because of this, we have to be fully prepared at all times to combat unforeseen circumstances.

There are times in life when we fail miserably, but we can recover from failed dreams—and succeed—if we seek divine guidance and act on it. The feeling of God's beauty and happiness within us gives us hope, courage, and strength to deny drabness, monotony, and darkness. When trouble and misfortune seem to crush us to the ground, God places a light in every window for those who seek Him. "My Father is still working and I am also working" (John 5:17).

Without God's help we are bound to fail right from the start. We may not know why unforeseen things happen at times, but our responsibility is to trust the divine process, knowing that God is our Father and our Mother, and He understands our trials, our fears, and our weaknesses, and He can change all things around into a blessing. Jesus reminds us in John 14:10, "It is not I, but it is the Father within us that does the work." The presence of God within us will give us the power to overcome all negation and limitation. On the whole, we prove over and over again that all things work together for good.

Sometimes our challenges help us to exercise our spiritual muscles. God's love will uphold us in the most trying circumstances, even when we feel too weak and discouraged to help ourselves. Although fear may clutch our hearts and we may think that all is lost, God is right there at our side urging us to return home.

A little boy once found the cocoon of a beautiful butterfly. The butterfly seemed to be struggling to get out, because of the silk of the cocoon. Wanting to help, the boy tore open the silken covering. Instead of flying away, the poor butterfly waved its wings a few times and dropped to the ground. Years later, the boy learned that the cocoon offered just enough resistance to the butterfly so that during the struggling to get out, its wings would be strengthened. It was only when the butterfly had developed enough strength in its wings to break the silken chains that it would have enough strength to fly.

Sometimes our trials may be giving us enough strength to break the cocoon of our earthly life. The challenges we face sometimes help us to develop enough strength to fly with the wings of Spirit. We need only to try to live one minute at a time, facing one difficulty at a time the best way we know how, and we will be astonished at how lighter they become. Knowing that we are children of God, we can face each difficulty with quiet confidence.

I learned this lesson soon after graduating from high school, when my life took on a new dimension. I became increasingly distracted, and my spiritual life took a backseat, as I lived a very fast and disorganized life. My parents tried to intervene, but I chose not to listen, and I finally moved out of on my own.

In June 1976 I met and married a wonderful man who became the main focus of my life. People thought we were two peas in a pod. He pampered me and gave me almost anything I wanted. We were viewed by many people as the ideal couple, and we were the envy of most of my friends. He was not only fun-loving, but also sociable and charming. Most people who knew him loved him, including my family. He was the life of the party and he loved to entertain.

After two years of marriage we decided to start our family, but months and months of trying proved futile, leaving me extremely pressured, anxious, and uncertain. I prayed, asking God to intervene, but to no avail. God seemed distant. Depression began to set in, and I cried profusely each month thinking with guilt that I was letting my husband down and ruining our marriage.

My husband's lack of compassion made matters worse. His insensitivity to my emotions was unbearable, and we communicated less and less. Each month when I failed to conceive I would sink in despair, and he would just look at me and simply walk out of the house without any word of consolation or compassion, leaving me alone in my misery.

I felt guilty, lonely, and abandoned. As a result, our relationship began to deteriorate and he began to stay away from home. We grew further and further apart, and I became frightened. I tried to reason with him, even suggesting counseling, but he would not concede. Where did I go wrong? I searched myself, but there were no answers.

As my own lack of understanding and impatience took a toll on my health, I suggested a short separation, hoping that with time he would eventually see reason and try to reconcile our differences. To my surprise he agreed. He gladly moved out of the apartment, and I was devastated! I cried for almost a month thinking I could not live without him.

Not wanting to witness his departure from our home, I took a trip to Miami, Florida, with the intention of distracting my thoughts with shopping. On the flight I met a friend who was to be my guardian angel not only on that trip, but also for a long, long time after. During our flight I shared the current happenings in my life, and he listened with compassion and understanding.

On arrival in Miami, he drove me to my hotel, promising me that he would pay me a visit later that evening. Alone in the hotel room, I felt helpless and despondent. A deep depression took hold of me, and I wanted to hide myself from the world. I realized that I had made a grave mistake in taking the trip, as I was in no shape whatsoever to be alone in a foreign country with a pending separation from someone I loved.

My friend arrived that evening finding me in a state of great depression, bathed in tears. I was happy to see him, as I felt lost and alone, frightened and forsaken. He must have sensed my pain, as he instinctively took my hand in his, looked me in the eye, and said in a very gentle and caring way, "Marjorie, this is not the end of the world. You are an attractive girl, you have a lot going for you, and you have a lot to offer. Don't let anyone steal your joy."

He further reminded me that there were tremendous opportunities awaiting me, and soon I would experience a brighter tomorrow. "This too shall pass," he told me. I tried hard to believe this truth, but the reality of the moment was that my husband had walked out on me and I was frightened.

After awhile my friend's counseling seemed to have taken root, as I suddenly fell into a deep and comfortable sleep, something I had not done for quite some time. The next morning I woke up to find him on his way out. As there were two single beds in the room, he had slept on the other one and watched over me like a guardian angel, as he thought that I was in no condition to spend the night alone. He later left and promised me that he would return soon that day.

After he left that morning, I decided to go back home to Jamaica to face the music. I was surprised to see him return to the hotel just before I left for the airport. I told him of my plans to go back home, and without a spoken word he took me to the airport and sent me off with his blessings. I expressed my appreciation for his help and support, and thanked God for sending him to me.

I boarded the plane with a sense of disillusionment, but oddly enough my breathing seemed less erratic than it had been for awhile. Not knowing what to expect, I dreaded my arrival in Jamaica, but strangely enough, as the plane took off from the airport in Miami, I literally felt my burdens lift and dissolve right into space. It was quite uncanny, but I actually felt peaceful and free, and I experienced a sense of relief that I could not explain.

This separation from my husband was a subsequent wake-up call and the beginning of my freedom. As painful as it was, gradually I learned to release the emotional discomfort and pain I had inadvertently imposed on myself. Soon I began to develop a new perspective on life; I reasoned that it was a part of the process. Sometimes we have to lose in order to win. I was convinced that there was a bigger picture involved, and I looked forward to another chapter of my life. Starting over again is never easy, but it seemed like I had no choice but to go with the flow.

13

Finding Joy in Sorrow

Life happens. It is not easy to be happy and cheerful all the time. Jesus said in John 16:33, "In the world you might have tribulation: but be of good cheer; I have overcome the world."

Jesus was a man of sorrows, acquainted with grief, and yet Jesus demonstrated a joy that was far beyond human understanding. In the gospel of John, Jesus teaches us how to deal with sorrow and sadness, and to find new meaning to life. Before He faced his death on the cross, He said to His disciples in John 15:11, "These things I say unto you that my joy might remain in you and that your joy might be full."

Sadness might stem from an unfortunate situation, a disappointment, a failure, a lost opportunity for love, or the death of someone we love. We may experience severe pain, but what is done is done; we cannot change it, but we can learn from it. The more severe the pain, the greater is the joy in overcoming it. "Blessed are they that mourn: for they shall be comforted" (Matthew 4:5).

To conquer depression, we have to find the cause, confront it, and act to remedy the situation. The Bible teaches us how to rejoice in times of sorrow. Rejoicing reinvigorates our spirits and allows us to conquer our challenges. It helps us to find new sources of joy despite our sorrow. The apostle Paul also tells us in Romans 5:3-4, "We glory in tribulations also: knowing that tribulation worketh patience, and patience experience, and experience hope."

A preacher once said, "When trials come, God is weaning us off our dependency on worldly things." Feeling low once in a while is quite all right; we do not have to hide or be ashamed of our feelings. When we persevere in our trials and trust God for a divine solution, soon there will be a day of resurrection, the ultimate experience of a newfound freedom that is unequaled.

Why We Lose Our Joy

1. People

It is amazing how people get in the way of our happiness, but we have to live with people, so we need to learn *how* to live with them. What we need to realize is that people come into our lives for a reason, most often as our teachers, and the ones who push our buttons the most are our greatest teachers. Consequently, as we have to live with each other, we ought to realize our oneness instead of our differences.

2. Circumstances

We have no control over unforeseen circumstances in life, so rather than making ourselves miserable over them, we need to accept them and go with the flow. Challenges happen sometimes—not to threaten or harm us, but to show the wonder of the working power of God in our lives. It is said, "Behind every dark cloud is a silver lining." Life happens, and times of joy and pleasure can easily pass by, leaving nothing but a wonderful memory. Dark clouds and stormy weather can suddenly interrupt bright sunshine, but it is almost certain that the storm will disappear or move on, and the sky will once again be as radiant and bright as before. Sometimes things happen to expose the treasure that lies underneath. If we get discouraged or frightened during times of challenges, we only miss the lesson to be learned and ultimately lose the blessing.

3. Things

Jesus tells us that a man's life consists not in the abundance of the things that he possesses. Things never make us happy. The more we have, the more we want. Having too many things make us just as unhappy as not having many things does. Things are not lasting; they decay, and thieves will break in and steal them. When we focus on God and not on outer things, we will find lasting joy and an abundance of every good thing.

4. Worry

Worry not only brings us unhappiness, but ill-health as well. Worry is actually wrong thinking and wrong feeling. Most of the time the things that we worry about never happen anyway, so why worry? Realistically, if we pay too much attention to what people say or think about us, we would be unhappy most of the time. So why worry about things that are insignificant? "What is that to thee? Follow thou me" (John 21:22).

We often feel a sense of guilt with sorrow, thinking that we are responsible for our dilemma, but what is done is done, and rather than focusing on the past, we need to learn from it and make room for a new and better way. In order for joy to expand and grow in us, we need to get the old sorrow out of the way and make room for joy.

How to Achieve Happiness

Happiness can be a cultivated habit. It comes to us when we actively reach for what we love and want. It certainly will not come to us when we sit and brood passively over what we find difficult to attain, nor does it come to us, when we brood over misery. The kingdom of heaven is within us and we have the potential to live our lives in happiness and joy by actively pursuing after it.

A woman who once suffered great sorrow and sadness went to an old wise man and asked him for a charm that would ward off all feelings of sorrow and sadness. The man looked at her with pity in his eyes and told her, "I will give you such a charm on one condition; you will bring me a handful of earth from a house into which sorrow has never entered."

So the woman went forth to every house she asked, "Has sorrow ever entered this house?" At every house the people nodded their heads; she never came across any house where sorrow had not entered.

As she went across the country and discovered that sorrow had indeed entered every house, her heartache and grief seemed to change. As she witnessed sorrow everywhere, her heart softened and she stopped being overwhelmed with her own sadness. She became compassionate toward others, and her tears of self-pity turned into tears of pity for others. She had not forgotten her own sorrows, but she became lost in the sorrow of others instead.

In Matthew 13:44-46, Jesus told two parables about the kingdom of heaven, each with a different connotation. In the first parable Jesus describes the kingdom of heaven like a treasure hidden in a field, which a man found and covered up; then in his joy he went and sold all that he had to buy that field. In the second one, Jesus likened the kingdom of heaven unto a merchant in search of fine pearls who, on finding one pearl of great value, went and sold all that he had to buy it.

In the first parable, the treasure was undiscovered; thus it appeared hidden. Our happiness is dependent on the discovery of the kingdom of God within us, but we often fail to find it simply because we often look for it in the wrong places. When we find it, however, nothing else compares with it, and we subsequently release all outer distractions in order to claim it.

In the second parable, Jesus tells us that we should not become too complacent, as spiritual work is continuous. The more we engage in our spiritual work, the more good unfolds. When the realization of the Christ presence within is achieved, everything else is inconsequential, as the Christ presence within is the answer to every desire and every challenge.

Most of us can identify with both parables. In one instance, happiness is right within our very reach, and yet we are still searching for it. Consequently, instead of taking time to uncover our treasure and being vigilant in claiming our happiness, we become complacent in complaining about how miserable and unhappy we are.

When we put God first in our lives, we grow from strength to strength, and the more we grow, the happier we become in Christ. It is interesting to note that Jesus said that the kingdom is like a merchant in search of treasure, not just the treasure itself. In other words, if we search for it, we will find it.

> "'When you search for me you will find me if you seek me with all your heart. I will let you find me,' says the Lord, 'and I will restore your fortunes and gather you from all the nations and all the places where I have driven you,' says the Lord, 'and I will bring you back to the place from which I sent you into exile'" (Jeremiah 29:13-14).

Sometimes we know that the treasure is in our own backyard, but because of willfulness we fail to claim it, as did the rich young ruler in Mark 10:17-28. Because he was unwilling to let go of his earthly treasures of materiality, self-centeredness, vanity, and pride, he was unable to receive treasures in heaven.

Although Jesus was sorry for the rich young ruler, He could not help him, because he was unwilling to participate in his own healing. In *Anatomy of the Spirit*, Carolyn Myss says

> "Healing is above all a solo task. No one can heal on behalf of another person. We can assist others, but no one can for instance, forgive someone on behalf of someone else. Nor can any of us cause someone to release the painful memories or experiences that he needs to release in order to heal."

Unfortunately, nearly everyone makes the same mistakes in searching for happiness, believing that outer circumstances will make us happy. If we experience unhappiness, we blame it on the fact that we do not have something that we want. We fantasize about winning the lottery or finding the right companion. We feel that the right job or car would make us happy. Jesus assures us that the treasure is there for us, if only we will take a few risks; if we only let go and let God.

The sorrow I experienced during the breakup of my marriage was pronounced. As my whole world had previously revolved around my husband, I could hardly imagine a world without him, and the happiness I once experienced seemed to be replaced with a perennial sense of doom and gloom.

After almost three months of grieving the separation and what seemed like the end of my marriage, I gradually began to recuperate, slowly letting go of past memories thanks to my two dear friends—Carol, who actually spoon-fed me to keep me from starvation, and Pamela, who never went anywhere without literally dragging me along with her.

With time, the wounds began to heal, and I gained strength day by day. The final breakthrough came the moment I realized that I had a choice to either remain in my misery or rise above my misery, which I could do by focusing on the presence of God within me as my strength, my power, my peace, my understanding, my wisdom, and my abundant supply. I accepted the latter, and knew with an overwhelming relief that a subsequent death of the old was simply the heralding of a new beginning.

A new day was dawning, and I looked ahead with confidence and a firm conviction that even greater blessings were ahead. “Weeping may endure for a night, but joy cometh in the morning” (Psalm 30:5).

PART II

14

The Power of the Spoken Word

> "For the word of God is quick, and powerful, and sharper than any two edged sword, piercing even to the dividing asunder of soul and spirit, and of the joints and marrow, and is a discerner of the thoughts and intents of the heart."
>
> Hebrews 4:12

Words are used to communicate our feelings and our intentions. Behind every word is an idea, and ideas take root and grow into expressions. Words can be spoken out loud or they can be spoken silently. Sometimes we say words that are uplifting, inspiring, and loving, and sometimes we say words that are despicable, uninspiring, or unkind. Author Alice Steadman says in *Who's The Matter With Me?* "Every loving suggestion plants a seed that comes up at the right time and flourishes. Every angry command flings a seed that may get results immediately but it is sick and tries to die as soon as possible."

The Word of God as Creative Principle

All ideas have origin in the Divine mind. They are our inheritance from God. Whenever we lay hold of them through prayer and meditation, they become vehicles of expressions within us. The more I grow in my awareness of the truth, the more I realize how important it is to use my words wisely and constructively, as words have the power to perform our every intention.

The living Word of God is spiritual principle. It is omnipresent like the air we breathe. It is available to all to use at will. "Word," as used in the Bible, is a translation from the Greek *logos,* which means reasonable speech or reasonable thought.

Divine mind is the source of all divine manifestations. "In the beginning was the Word and the Word was with God, and the word was God" (John 1:1). In order to manifest harmony in Divine mind, all ideas must be in tune with Divine mind. Words spoken from the consciousness of Spirit have the power to heal and transform our world. "And the word was made flesh and dwelt among us, (and we beheld his glory the glory as of the only begotten of the father,) full of grace and truth" (John 1:14).

As co-creators with God, we have the power to use our minds to transform our lives and achieve good. Words by themselves have no power, but it is the thoughts or the intention behind the words that carry power. Thought involves the combined energies of thinking and feeling that ultimately find expression in words, and words subsequently have power to take form in our lives. "So shall my words be that goeth forth from my mouth, it shall not return unto me void, but it shall accomplish that which I please, and it shall prosper in the thing whereto I sent it" (Isaiah 55:11).

The Power of Thought

We were made equipped with dominion over thoughts and feelings, and we are therefore responsible for our creations. If we experience sickness in mind, body, or affairs, it has nothing to do with God. It simply means that we are not creating with God as principle.

Because we are made in God's image and likeness, mankind is endowed with power and authority to create good by separating the darkness from the light. God then gave us dominion over all things.

> "And God said, Let us make man in our image, after our likeness: And let them have dominion over the fish of the sea, and over the fowl of the air, and over the cattle, and over all the earth, and over every creeping thing that creepeth upon the earth" (Gen. 1:26).

By the power of the spoken word, or by thinking and speaking words that are uplifting and life changing, we can therefore call forth the light to any negative situation that confronts us.

Thinking is just as powerful as speaking, and the words that we use repeatedly create our experiences. "As a man thinketh in his heart, so is he" (Proverbs 23:7). By our thoughts we can transform our inner as well as our outer world, as thoughts can culminate in our bodies and in our environment. The quality of our lives is therefore a reflection of the thoughts we have previously entertained. Consequently, the thoughts that we hold in this moment will create tomorrow, and the next day, and the next.

Sometimes we use our words carelessly, not realizing the adverse effect they can have on our lives. Jesus said in Matthew 28:18, "All authority has been given to me in heaven and on earth." It is therefore important that we pay attention to our thoughts and measure the words we use very carefully, making sure that they convey the right intentions.

Martin Luther King, Jr. stands out as one of the most outstanding persons who not only believed in his dream, but also achieved many goals by the power of his thought. He has on many occasions proved the power of thought, overcoming limitation and mental abuse. Martin Luther King, Jr. has proved that whatever the mind conceives and believes it can achieve.

There is a divine process for living a successful life that is outlined in the first two chapters of Genesis. By the spoken word, God called forth the light. "And God said, 'Let there be light:' and there was light." God demonstrated that the darkness had no power by separating it from the light, and God further pronounced the light good. "And God saw the light and it was good. And God divided the light from the darkness" (Gen.1: 4).

Most of us cannot help having destructive thoughts from time to time, but Jesus showed us how we may drive them away. They will invade our consciousness, but we must not entertain them. Though adverse thoughts arise, they must not take control. We do have the power of choice, so we have the power to drive them away by the spoken Word of God.

Some time ago, someone I know who planned to get married asked a mutual friend of ours, who was a seamstress, to design and make her wedding dress. After enquiring about the cost, she was repeatedly told not to worry, as the cost would be reasonable and affordable. With this understanding she agreed to have her dress made. For the sake of convenience, it was agreed that she would get dressed for the wedding at the home of the seamstress.

The wedding day arrived, and this person was happy and elated. Not having been told the cost beforehand, she took it for granted that she could pay after the wedding, as she was no stranger to the seamstress and their homes were in close proximity.

Her happiness was quickly dimmed, however, when the seamstress' daughter told her that she couldn't have the dress without first paying for it. This poor lady experienced sheer panic and total disbelief at this request, as she had not traveled with any form of payment.

By then it was already late, and almost everyone had already left for the church. She tried desperately to apply reason, promising faithfully to honor her obligation right after the wedding, but the seamstress flatly refused.

With tears streaming down her face she said a silent prayer, hoping that someone would be at home to rescue her. Her prayers were miraculously answered and her sister, who had not yet left for the wedding, rescued her.

As soon as the payment was received, everyone's attitude suddenly changed and everything was quickly transformed. She was dressed in an instant, made up in the most beautiful way, and sent off—finally—to her wedding.

She finally made it to her wedding and although she was quite late she managed to maintain her composure, not giving the slightest clue as to her earlier discomfiture, and the wedding service took place beautifully without anyone's knowledge of her prior ordeal.

At the end of the wedding, family and friends who were most pleased with the outcome of the wedding gathered together to reminisce. Everyone was in shock when the bride related her unfortunate experience. In their anger and disgust for the seamstress, many people spoke unkind words about her. One person exclaimed, "She is going to die an awful death."

Exactly one week following the wedding, the daughter of the seamstress and her two children boarded a train to attend another wedding in the country. The train crashed, and one woman jumped to her death. It was the daughter of the seamstress who had demanded payment from my friend in exchange for her wedding dress on her wedding day!

It was a very sad story, and even though we may not know why or how this tragic accident happened, all those who had passed negative remarks about the seamstress were full of remorse. "So shall my words be that goeth out of my mouth: It shall not return unto me void, but it shall accomplish that which I please, and it shall prosper in the thing where to I sent it". (Isaiah 55:11).

The Word is the presence of God within humankind. It is not necessarily a spoken word. The word is any definitely formulated thought. Charles Fillmore states that all thoughts are formative but all thoughts are not creative. For thoughts to be creative they have to function in tune with Divine Mind. In this state of consciousness we call forth what we will and it is done unto us. Author Emmet Fox says in Take your Thinking in Hand, "Every carefully formulated thought is an order that you send into the future, unless you overtake it with a denial".

A mutual friend once worked at a job where she felt totally unappreciated by her employer. She did an excellent job but was never shown any form of appreciation. She often complained to her friends and relatives how cold and exact this employee had been and everyone agreed with her that her employer was taking advantage of her.

My friend was ready to retire from her job but because of her financial dilemma she kept putting off her retirement yet at the same time she kept complaining about the injustice shown to her by her employer. Each day she went to work against her will.

One day she tripped and fell over an object injuring her right arm. Unable to drive or use her right arm for work she was laid up for a couple of weeks. During her recuperation she learnt to relax and enjoy her friends and family and conceded that she would finally retire.

Not long afterward, her employer called her with a new proposal. Deep within her she did not want to accept, but the reality of the situation was that she needed funds to take care of her responsibilities. My friend thought there was no way out so she accepted the new proposal with a 'heavy heart'. One week after she did, the unbelievable happened; she once again fell, this time injuring her right foot!

We get out of life whatever we put into it, and because her heart and her mind were not in sync my friend unconsciously sustained injury to both her right hand and her right foot. She unconsciously willed this situation unto herself, which enforced her retirement.

The power of the spoken word was demonstrated during the Babylonian captivity in the book of Ezekiel, when Ezekiel received a vision in which God showed him a valley of dried bones. God told Ezekiel to speak to the bones, instructing them to listen to God's Word. God said He would cause breath to enter into the bones so that they would live again. When Ezekiel prophesied to the bones, they assembled into skeletons and muscles, and skin covered them.

God further instructed Ezekiel to prophesy to the wind or spirit, and the four winds breathed life into the reassembled bodies and the dead bones became alive. "So I prophesied as I was commanded: and as I prophesied there was a noise, and behold a shaking, and the bones came together, bone to his bone" (Ezekiel 37:7).

The spoken word that Ezekiel used was the Word of God charged with the Holy Spirit. It is therefore the spoken Word of God that brings all things into manifestation. The breath of God is the essence of all life. This breath is within each individual as power, strength, and authority. "The Lord God formed man of the dust of the ground, and breathed into his nostrils the breath of life; and man became a living soul" (Gen. 2:7).

Again Jesus demonstrated the power of the spoken Word when He brought Lazarus back to life in John chapter 3. After instructing the people who were present to remove the stone from the tomb of Lazarus, Jesus acknowledged the power and presence of God in the situation by first praying, "Father I thank you for hearing me always and for hearing me now." Then with a loud voice He cried, "Lazarus come forth!" and Lazarus came forth, bound in his grave clothes. Jesus further advised them, "Lose him and let him go." And Lazarus came forth alive.

Before Jesus made His ascension He reminded His disciples of the power they would possess if they believed in Him.

> "And these signs shall follow them that believe; in my name shall they cast out devils; they shall speak with new tongues; they shall take up serpents, and if they drink any deadly thing, it shall not hurt them; they shall lay their hands on the sick and they shall recover" (Mark 16:17-18).

The mind is the connecting link with God, and there are unlimited possibilities opened to us when we commune with God through prayer and meditation. When we acknowledge God's all-creating power within us, we can move mountains of challenges that face us daily. Like Ezekiel, God is instructing us to speak life-affirming words. We can charge them with love, life, wisdom, substance, power, strength, and all other ideas that express divine attributes, healing our families, our friends, our loved ones and our world.

15

Creating Spiritual Abundance

In his book *The Mysteries of Genesis*, Charles Fillmore, author and cofounder of Unity, metaphysically outlines seven spiritual steps used in relation to the creation story. These faculties, which he identifies as the calling forth of seven faculties of being, are identified as light, faith, imagination, will, understanding, wisdom, and rest.

Light

The meaning of light, according to Webster, is something that makes vision possible. In the first book of Genesis, God made spiritual vision possible by calling forth the Light. "And God said, Let there be Light; and there was Light" (Genesis 1:3).

Light as used in the Bible can also be interpreted as:

1. Illuminated intelligence; a symbol of wisdom represented by "the I Am." e.g. "I am the light of the world." God is the source of everything created, and humankind is an extension of that light (In Him was light, and the light was the light of all men" John 1:4). God is ever present in our lives as light or illumination, and the light of God is available to all humankind, which through prayer and meditation manifests as divine ideas.

Charles Fillmore relates from the Mysteries of Genesis—

> "The first step in creation is the awakening of man to spiritual consciousness, the dawning of light in his mind, his perception of Truth through the quickening of his spirit. Light represents intelligence, and darkness represents undeveloped capacity."

2. The quality of lightness, which is the opposite of darkness or heaviness.

No matter how much darkness surrounds us or no matter where we are in consciousness the Light of God shines forth from within us, and there is always the choice to experience the Light of God.

> "In the beginning God created the heavens and the earth. And the earth was waste and void; and darkness was upon the face of the deep: and the spirit of God moved upon the face of the waters. And God said, 'Let there be light' and there was light." (Gen 1:1-3).

The darkness and the light are opposite ends of the same stick. They both exist together. In the Silence of the Heart, author Paul Ferrini says, "When you get to absolute pitch blackness, there illumination is found. Blackest black becomes radiant. Sadness turns to unaccountable joy. Despair turns to hope without measure".

The Light of God Dispels All Darkness

God or "Light" is the only Power and Presence in our lives and in the world and "Light" cannot coexist with darkness.

> "And God saw the Light, that it was good: and God divided the light from the darkness. And God called the light Day, and the darkness He called Night.

> And the evening and the morning was the first day" (Genesis 1:4-5).

God is the only power and the only presence in our lives. There is absolutely no other power, and therefore nothing can harm us or stand in our way except our own negative thoughts. When we acknowledge God in all things, we automatically call forth the light erasing darkness or negativity. "I am come a light into the world, that whosoever believeth on me should not abide in darkness" (John 12:46).

As long as we live in the physical world, there will be challenges to overcome, and darkness will appear in our lives from time to time, but we cannot overcome them by running away from them. We should not be afraid; we do have the power through God to overcome it. "To everything there is a season, and a time for every purpose under heaven." (Ecclesiastic 3:1).

The darkness is not to be feared. It serves the purpose of helping us appreciate the light and reminding us of our divinity. "All things work together for good" (Romans 8:28). Unless we acknowledge the darkness, we cannot appreciate the light, and acknowledging the darkness does not mean being overcome by it, but being aware of its non-power over us. Authors Jack Kornfield and Christina Feldman write in their *book Soul Food*, "We must be willing not to turn away from or shun the shadows in our lives, but to turn toward them. This is the first and most significant step, for in turning we begin to cast away our fears, despair and self doubt. It is not darkness that is our opponent but our rejection and denial of it."

In order to move out of a restricted state of consciousness, we first need to acknowledge the situation and then exercise our God-given potential, trusting God and moving beyond the situation. After Lazarus' death, Jesus was overcome with compassion, as He acknowledged the humanity around Him, and He wept. (John 11:35) Jesus knew however that the light of God makes a difference to any situation, and He demonstrated this by calling upon the power of God, and after thanking God in advance for the desired manifestation, He called Lazarus back to life. When Mary expressed her dismay over the death of Lazarus, He reminded her, "Didn't I tell you if you believe you would see the glory of God?"

Experiencing the Light through the Darkness

Humankind, being made in God's image and likeness, is connected to God through individual consciousness. We manifest the "Christ Mind," or "Light of God," when we surrender to the higher Self, or the Christ within us. "If any man should come after me let him deny himself, take up his cross and follow me" (Matthew 16:24). To deny self and follow Christ is to deny that part of us that keeps us in bondage, or to deny our attachment to things that do not serve us by declaring "Let there be Light."

In the Bible, John the Baptist is regarded as the forerunner of Jesus. "I am not the Christ but that I am sent before Him" (John 3: 28). Metaphysically, John the Baptist represents the illuminated intellect. The illuminated consciousness, however, cannot stand alone by itself, so although John the Baptist was aware of his divinity to some degree, in order to arrive at that perfected place of being he had to let go of his lesser self by acknowledging Jesus as his higher Self.

The higher Self or the Light of God is within all humankind and is always seeking expression in and through us. The way to experience the light of God and manifest good in our lives is to let go of the ego and acknowledge the Spirit of the Christ within us. Jesus tells us "I am the way, the truth and the life: no man cometh to the Father but by me" (John 14:6). John knew that he could accomplish nothing on his own, but with God he knew that he could do anything. He was enlightened enough to know that he had to subdue himself so that the Christ within him could take expression. "He must increase, but I must decrease" (John 3:30). During spiritual unfolding, the lesser part of us has to be relinquished so that the greater part of us, the light of God, can be realized.

When divine ideas are received, they go through the process of spiritualization before they become manifest. This was demonstrated in the book of Genesis. Esau, the first-born of Isaac, who was a hunter and a lover of things of the appetite, represents the flesh, while Jacob, the second child, a lover of the home environment and the quiet spiritual things of life, represents the mind or the intellect. According to Charles Fillmore, the natural man comes first in the process of evolution, and then the spiritual man or intellectual man illuminated by Spirit takes control, and then gets the blessing. Consequently, Jacob deceived Esau and received the blessing from Isaac.

Likewise, Cain and Abel displayed the effects of surrendering to the higher Self. Cain, the firstborn, was a tiller of the soil. Abel, the second child, was a shepherd. In *The Metaphysical Bible Dictionary* by Charles Fillmore, Abel represents the physical nature, while Cain represents the mental, which is more closely related to the spiritual consciousness. Although Cain was the firstborn, his offering was rejected while Abel's were accepted. Cain was angry, so he killed his brother Abel. God cursed Cain as a result, but despite Cain's felony, God put a mark on Cain that no one could harm him. In this scenario, Charles Fillmore metaphysically explains that no matter how deeply the body has transgressed, it still bears the stamp of God and should never be killed.

We should always remember that no matter where we find ourselves, the light of God is always available to dispel all darkness when we declare "Let there be light."

Faith

> "Faith is the substance of things hoped for, the evidence of things not seen."
>
> Hebrew 11:1

Without faith nothing can be accomplished. The power of faith can remake our entire lives. Faith opens closed doors and reveals hidden secrets. Faith arouses healing and restorative forces within us.

> "Let there be a firmament in the midst of the waters and let it divide the waters from the waters. And God made the firmament and divided the waters, which were under the firmament from the waters, which were above the firmament: And it was so. And God called the firmament heaven. And there was evening and there was morning, a second day."
>
> Gen 1:6-8

In the book *The Mysteries of Genesis* Charles Fillmore says "The second step in creation is the development of faith or the 'firmament.' Waters represent unexpressed possibilities in mind. There must be a firm starting point or foundation established."

Faith is Inherent

The faculty of faith is inherent, but first we have to believe. "And all things whatsoever ye shall ask in prayer, believing ye shall receive" (Matthew 21:22). We cannot build our lives effectively unless we build with the consciousness of the Christ within. In Matthew 16:13, when Jesus asked his disciples "Who do you say that I am?" Simon Barjona replied, "You are the Christ the son of the living God" (Matthew 16:16). Jesus was impressed with Simon's response because he displayed the quality of faith. Jesus then renamed him "Peter," which means "rock."

> "Thou art Peter, and upon this rock I build my Church; and the gates of hell shall not prevail against it. And I will give unto thee the keys of the kingdom of heaven: and whatsoever thou shall bind on earth shall be bound in heaven: and whatsoever thou shalt lose on earth shall be loosened in heaven" (Matthew 16 18-19).

The rock that Jesus spoke about symbolizes a firm foundation. This rock of Faith is the firm foundation on which we build our dreams, our hopes, and our desires.

To have faith in something is to have a firm conviction that it is true, even when there is no visible evidence of it being so. A small amount of faith can remove mountains of challenges.

Faith Requires Action

Secondly, we have to put it to work. In the book of James, Paul tells us that in order for faith to be effective we need to put it to work, as faith without action has no merit. "Even so faith if it has not works is dead, being alone" (James 2:17). As co-creators with God, we have a responsibility to do our part. When we step out in faith, it is certain that God will help us accomplish our goals like he did the lame man at the pool of Bethesda in John chapter 5. Although the lame man at the pool of Bethesda had some faith in going to the pool, he doubted his divine potential, and consequently he waited thirty-eight years for his faith to be activated. Going to the pool was the first step, but that was insufficient. He needed to act.

Finally, something within the man stirred, and he encountered Jesus. He suddenly came to himself, realizing his strengths and his divine potential. He was now willing to put his faith to the test, and with the help of his Christ spirit within him, he arose from the place of mental limitation to a place of pure potentiality. So he took up his bed, his problems, and he walked. It suddenly dawned on him that he had unconsciously kept himself in bondage, and he alone could free himself.

Peter later demonstrated his faith when he tried to walk on the water to meet Jesus. Unfortunately, because he looked away from Jesus, he began to sink. But the saving grace of the Christ presence recognized his effort and rescued him from sinking. Metaphysically, water in this sense represents emotions. Peter, in his attempt to find the Christ within, tried to control his emotions by walking on them.

We must cultivate the habit of using our faculty of faith in productive ways. With faith the impossible is made possible; but the true basis of our faith is "action": we must believe that whatever we desire can be accomplished, keep on trying, doing whatever we can humanly do to make to happen, and claiming it as our divine birthright.

Abraham demonstrated the working of faith in the book of Genesis by obeying God's instruction to offer his son Isaac as a sacrifice when most of us would regard this assignment as an inhumanely difficult task. When God is foremost in our thoughts as the source, creator, and giver of all good things, however, there is no need to fear, as no harm can touch you or your loved ones.

> "Because thou hast made the Lord, which is my refuge, even the most high, thy habitation; there shall no evil befall thee, neither shall any plague come nigh thy dwelling. For he shall give his angels charge over thee, to keep thee in all thy ways" (Psalm 91:9-11).

Because Abraham trusted God with carefree abandon, he later proved that God was able to do mighty works far beyond his capacity to even fathom. Just as Abraham was about to put Isaac to the slaughter, God intervened in the nick of time, providing a ram for Abraham to slaughter instead of Isaac. "The foolishness of God is wiser than men and the weakness of God is stronger than men" (Cor.1:25). Abraham's obedience and trust in God worked in his circumstances to produce absolute good, and he was subsequently blessed abundantly with riches and posterity. Abraham has demonstrated that in putting God first in everything we will reap bountifully. God's love is the source of all good things, and He will give us the desires of our hearts. "Seek ye first the kingdom of God and His righteousness and all things will be added unto you" (Matthew 6:33).

Ask, Believing

The correct way to exercise faith is to ask in belief. (Mark 11:24) "You ask, and receive not, because you ask amiss" (James 4:3.) To ask amiss is to doubt, or to ask for selfish reasons. In her book *Dare to Believe*, author May Rowland writes, "When faith becomes a flame in man's mind, he sees by the light of this flame and there are no impossible situations. He knows that there is a way through every difficulty."

Lack of faith is the biggest obstacle that prevents us from achieving our good. When Jesus went to the mount of transfiguration with Peter, James, and John, the remaining disciples were unable to heal the sick in the absence of Jesus. Jesus told them that this was a result of their unbelief. Metaphysically, according to Charles Fillmore in *The Metaphysical Bible Dictionary*, Peter represents faith, John represents love, and James represents wisdom. In order for healing to take place, the Christ within has to be realized through acts of faith, love, and wisdom. Jesus told the disciples that healing could only be accomplished through the consciousness of the Christ spirit within that can only be achieved through prayer and fasting. To pray and fast is to center oneself in the presence of God always by erasing negative thoughts and outer distractions.

A certain lady was told by her doctor that she had an incurable disease, and she was given only a few months to live. Refusing to accept this sentence, she decided to visit her spiritual healer who counseled her and encouraged her to pray, affirming, "Lord, I believe that you can and you will heal me." The woman continued with this ritual for about two weeks, after which she noticed that she was receiving a deep spiritual healing. Whenever her faith got weak, she joined the father of the epileptic boy in the Bible and affirmed, "Lord, I believe, help Thou my unbelief." She continued praying in faith each and every day, and within three months she was completely healed of her disease.

We do not receive answers to our prayers simply because of unbelief, as for most people seeing is believing. "While we look not at the things which are seen, but at the things which are not seen: for the things which are seen are temporal; but the things which are not seen are eternal" (2 Cor. 4:18).

The power of *belief* is demonstrated throughout the entire Bible. In Matthew 9:27 when the blind men went to Jesus for healing, Jesus first asked them, "Do you believe that I can do this?" They said unto him, "Yes Lord." He then touched their eyes and said, "According to your faith be it unto you." And their eyes were opened.

The words "according to your faith" used by Jesus are of great significance. It means that the degree of the demonstration is entirely dependent upon the individual's faith. Evidently, had the blind men not believed that Jesus could heal them, their eyes would not have been opened. "Faith is the substance of things hoped for, the evidence of things not seen" (Hebrews 1:11).

Sometimes when challenges seem insurmountable, exercising faith can be very difficult for some of us, but when we acknowledge our powerlessness and ask the Father to strengthen us in our weaknesses, He will always come to our rescue. When the father of the epileptic boy in Mark chapter 9 asked Jesus to heal his son who had been ill from childhood, Jesus told him, "If thou canst believe, all things are possible to him that believeth." The father of the boy in humility confessed, "Lord I believe. Help thou my unbelief." Jesus was moved by the man's humility and acknowledgment of his powerlessness, and He took the boy by the hand and healed him.

The more we affirm the omnipresence, omnipotence, and omniscience of God's truth, the more positive the results we will get from our prayers. The potential of faith is not limited only to a special few. We all have been blessed with the faculty of faith and have the same capacity to exercise our faith in believing.

Unfortunately, we sometimes allow willfulness and outer distractions to get in our way and we fail to accomplish good. "In whom the god of this world hath blinded the minds of them which believe not, lest the light of the glorious gospel of Christ, who is the image of God should shine unto them" (2 Cor. 4:4). But all is not lost. There is always hope through the indwelling Christ spirit.

> "We having the same spirit of faith, according as it is written, I believed, and therefore have I spoken; we also believe, and therefore speak; knowing that he who raised up the Lord Jesus shall raise up us also by Jesus" (2 Cor. 4:13-14).

How to Exercise Faith

We rekindle our faith with daily periods of prayer and meditation. The more faith we exercise, the more our faith increases. Most of us have the desire to walk on our emotions of doubts, fear, and willfulness, but in our humanity we sometimes take our spiritual eyes away from the truth, and it appears as if we are sinking. When we acknowledge our powerlessness, however, we are always saved through grace, when like the father of the prodigal son Jesus comes to meet us right where we are in our humanity.

Biblical stories help to remind us both of our humanity as well as of our divinity, and through them we are encouraged to exercise our faith. We make mistakes on the path, but when we acknowledge them we can always learn from them and start anew. The Christ Spirit is within us regardless of our circumstances, and so is our faculty of faith, represented by Peter who tried to walk on the water to meet Jesus.

According to *The Metaphysical Bible Dictionary*, 'firmament' means faith in mind power, or a firm unwavering place in consciousness, and 'water' means unexpressed possibilities in mind. In order to exercise faith we need to cleanse our minds from negation with the use of denials and establish good with affirmations. During difficult times we should acknowledge the Christ Spirit within us and our faculty of faith (Peter), which wavers at times, will be lifted up.

In her book, *Lessons in Truth,* author Emily Cady says there are two kinds of faith; there is blind faith, and there is understanding faith. Blind faith, she says, is "an instinctive trust in a power higher than us, while an understanding faith is based on immutable principle." We may think that we do not have enough faith, but all we need to do is use what faith we do have. A small amount of faith can work wonders. In other words, the seemingly impossible will become possible according to our faith.

There is a story about a young man by the name of James Stegalls who went through trying times while he was in Vietnam. He always carried a small Gideon New Testament in his shirt pocket, but he couldn't bring himself to read it. His buddies were all destroyed and terror was a reality for him. James thought that God was nowhere in sight. His twentieth birthday came and went, and James felt despondent. He thought he couldn't go on.

On February 26, 1968 he prayed for it all to end and deep in his heart he thought he would die before dusk. As sure as fate, his base came under attack that day and he heard a rocket coming straight toward him. He began counting the seconds he had left to live. Three, and then two . . . and suddenly a friend pushed him into a grease pit. He waited for the rocket to explode, but there was only a surreal silence. The fuse had malfunctioned.

James knelt in that pit for five hours. Finally, his shaking hands reached into his pocket and took out his Bible. Starting with Matthew, he read the first eighteen chapters. Then he came to Matthew 18:19-20, and after reading it he instinctively knew that everything would be all right.

Long after James returned home, he went to visit his wife's grandmother, Mrs. Harris. She told him of a night years before when she was awakened in terror. Knowing James was in Vietnam, she thought that he was in trouble. She began to pray, asking God to spare his life.

Just before dawn she read Matthew 18:19-20. "If two of you agree down here on earth concerning anything you ask, my father in heaven will do it for you. For where two or three gather together because they are mine, I am there among them."

She immediately called her Sunday school teacher, who got out of bed and went to Mrs. Harris' home where together they claimed the Lord's promise as they prayed for James until they felt reassured by God's peace.

After she told James the story, Mrs. Harris opened her Bible to show him where she had marked the passage. In the margin were the words *James, February 26, 1968.*

This poem reminds us how to develop our faculty of faith and achieve abundant good:

"Set aside a time every day, a definite time,
And pray whether you believe it or not . . .
If you will persistently affirm truth, even
Though you do not believe it at first,
You will find that your prayers have power.
Faith is like a mustard seed and it will grow.
Pray, pray, and keep praying; affirm and yet
Affirm once more. Your persistent prayers
Will succeed."

Charles Fillmore

Faith Works Wonders!

When I went to ministerial school at Unity Village, Missouri, my faith was severely put to the test. I had been out of high school for over thirty years, and as I had never been to college, I did not know what to expect, and I was intimidated by classroom instructions. I knew that God within me was my refuge and my strength, so I constantly affirmed, "I can do all things through Christ who strengthens me" (Philippians 4:13).

With this comforting promise and reminder, I decided to step out in faith. A new chapter of my life had begun, and I moved forward on my journey to Unity Village, Missouri with a strong conviction that my call to ministry was authentic, and I would therefore be successful in all my endeavors.

As much as I tried to convince myself of this reality, there were nevertheless moments of uncertainty. Although I had traveled countless times back and forth to visit the United States, I was mildly intimidated with the idea of being a student and living in foreign country with extreme weather conditions for two years! Not only was I terrified of the winter, but I also had to adapt to different living conditions and reshape my boundaries, which seemed most disconcerting. Nevertheless I said yes to the call of Spirit, and I decided to trust the process knowing that the Spirit of God would not lead me where It wouldn't provide for me.

On my arrival at Unity Village I felt enormously captivated and bedazzled with the wonderful surroundings, but at the same time I felt lonely, bewildered, and uncertain. I tried to calm my frazzled nerves with a prayer for strength, faith, and serenity, and as I settled down to face the reality of the moment I could actually feel the energy of those students who had preceded me on their journey. I acknowledged my blessings, confessing that living in such a beautiful and spiritually endowed environment was truly an honor. I was momentarily engulfed in a surge of hope and encouragement, and I held firm to my faith, remembering the grand prize at the end of my journey—to be ordained a minister!

Still suffering from a sense of disorientation, however, I felt sadly disenchanted, as my accommodation left much to be desired. Not having lived in a campus environment before, I didn't know what to expect, but the sparse furnishings were hardly what I had envisioned.

With an impulsive change of thinking, a feeling of guilt and remorse suddenly swept over me when I thought of the many, many people all over the world who would have done anything to trade places with me in that moment. I then acknowledged that my blessing was indeed a reality, and with this reminder I decided to shed my melancholy and thank God for this wonderful opportunity to be a part of this environment, for my humble but adequate accommodation, and also for the many anticipated blessings yet to be manifested.

Getting around Lee's Summit without my own transportation, however, posed a challenge, as Unity Village was nowhere near the vicinity of the shopping areas and I was not financially equipped to charter taxicabs. To make myself comfortable I needed to shop around, and with no transportation, my movements were virtually curtailed. I sat on the unmade single bed and cried. *Did I make the right move in coming here?* I wondered.

I dried my teary eyes, said a prayer, made my bed, and decided to make the best of what I had. Then a miracle happened. An angel appeared. Things began to unfold in a positive manner the moment I met Leiris, my roommate. Not only did she know her way around Kansas City, but she had a car as well. Although Leiris was Hispanic, she spoke adequate English and she was warm and caring. We connected instantly, and soon we became like two peas in a pod, shopping constantly, sometimes late at nights. Soon our living quarters were significantly transformed. Leiris became my friend and my confidante, and together we prepared ourselves for our class orientation.

The environment of Unity Village was most loving and supportive, and everyone seemed willing and eager to help in one way or another. One only had to make a request and sooner or later someone would come to the rescue. Little by little everything miraculously began to fall into place, and blessings of every nature unfolded, one after the other. I felt heaven established right there on earth with angels hovering all around me. I felt safe and secure, and most of all I felt very blessed.

Paulette, from the senior class also shared living quarters with us. She was highly spiritually motivated, and she helped to keep us centered and focused. She acted as mother, spiritual advisor, and counselor for both Leiris and myself and played a big part in calming our fears by preparing us with the realities of living on campus.

The other international candidates were also of great support, especially Claire and Vernon, ministerial candidates also from Jamaica. It was very comforting to be able to communicate and bond with two people from my own culture. Altogether, we were one big happy family.

Recapitulating my past experiences, I reveled in the vote of confidence I received at my farewell function from my minister and the congregation at the church in Jamaica, and I was ecstatic. My minister cited my potential as a minister, and judging from my farewell message, she concluded that I was already a minister in the making. Family, relatives, and friends all attested to my readiness, conceding that they could only see distinction in my future. My self-confidence soared high, and I was convinced and assured that I would handle myself perfectly in any situation.

My high self-esteem was short-lived however as reality soon began to take shape and I realized that I had a long way to go to measure up to these expectations. Many worthwhile lessons awaited me in later months, and I gradually learned that in order for growth to take place, I had to go back to the womb of darkness and start all over again.

In a multi-cultural environment, challenges do arise, not to intimidate or threaten, but to expose innermost fears and insecurities and subsequently heal them. The once solid ground on which I stood began to shake violently, and with a feeling of dismay, I found myself uneasy and at a low ebb. One by one the challenges surfaced, leaving me frightened, unsure, and discouraged.

As I got ready for our class orientation, I acknowledged that an old chapter of my life had closed and another one was about to begin. It was evident during the orientation exercises that many students were similarly self-confident as I was, perhaps on account of past accomplishments, commendations, and accolades from their home churches, thinking with glee that they were in the category of the "fully prepared and ready." As we shared our individual qualifications, adventures, experiences, and our call to serve in a ministerial setting, each person reiterated with joy the magnificent journey that consequently landed them in the ministerial program. Their experiences were all fascinating, individually carved, and pertinently validated. Disconcertingly, I acknowledged that my circumstances were in no way isolated.

I listened in awe to the bevy of potential ministers all adorned in their respective glory, and I found my trembling feet slowly giving way to the weight of my body, and the ground on which I stood felt shaky. Not only did I learn that virtually everyone was just as fully prepared as I thought I was, but I realized also with a sense of inferiority that I was the only one in the group of twenty-nine students without a college degree. My Jamaican high school diploma, a General Certificate of Education, experiences at my home church in Jamaica as platform assistant and superintendent of the Sunday school, my experience as a garment manufacturer, and my deep abiding faith in God were all I had as my credentials. That certainly did not seem equivalent to the master's and doctorate degrees that were floating around. There was no mistaking that I definitely stood in the minority, and that was enough to intimidate me.

Almost paralyzed with fear, I had to seek refuge from my Christ Self within. Interacting with twenty-nine students highly educated and experienced, was something to reckon with. *Would I be ever measure up?* I wondered, doubts filling my mind. Things were changing so rapidly around me that that even my prayers were difficult to utter.

Classes finally began and the experiences continued, with everyone anxious to uncover their destiny. When it was time for me to speak, I could only mumble a few incoherent words and my once confident spirit felt completely shattered. I did not trust my voice to utter a word, thinking that it would only betray my feelings. Thank God this was a Christian adult learning environment, and I did not have to expose my fears. As the days and weeks progressed, I had the feeling of being on a roller coaster, some days being challenged by the experience, some days enjoying it, and some days just wanting to run away from it all.

As I struggled with my fears, I recapitulated an unhappy experience during high school when a teacher openly displayed her dislike for me because the boys in my class found me attractive. I felt constantly intimidated and unjustifiably abused, as she deliberately picked on me with the sole purpose of embarrassing me. One day I decided to retaliate by not answering a question, and she verbally abused me with a long lecture about my purpose for being in school. I never did forget the pain and misery I suffered as a result, and I reckoned that somewhere deep within my subconscious mind lay a feeling of insecurity that was now surfacing. With my new sense of awareness I was determined to release that feeling of negation and regain my composure and my identity.

We all continued to share our individual stories in the classroom, and those of us with haughty spirits soon came to ourselves. All who answered the call to become ministers consented to go on a journey where the light would be revealed, exposing our innermost selves, and taking us from self-centeredness to "Christ-Centeredness." Ultimately, it became evident that everyone, both the educated as well as the uneducated, was blessed with a divine potential, which is realized according to the degree of receptivity and self-reliance.

This was a painful journey for some of us, as hidden agendas of past hurts, disappointments, and pain surfaced. During classroom instructions, however, we were encouraged to face our shadows and transform them with the power of love. This made a lot of sense; in order to minister, we had to first heal ourselves.

Each day was a new experience for me, and to survive this environment I had to go back to the drawing board, focus on my initial intention, and accept responsibility for whatever showed up. I kept remembering the words of Paul in Philippians 1:6: "He which hath begun a good work in you will perform it until the day of Jesus Christ," and with each new day came the opportunity of seeing the bigger picture.

Denials and affirmations coupled with a nonresistant attitude became my defense and my anchor, helping to renew my sense of commitment, increasing buoyancy, encouraging self-confidence, and instilling within me the courage to follow the wisdom of my heart. I subsequently opened myself to the cohesiveness and support of the universe, and little by little it became easier to adjust to circumstances and conditions around me.

But old stuff continued to emerge, and the roller coaster ride continued as unfounded fears of failing daunted me, and my faith seemed threatened. Feeling desolate and unsure, I was prompted into quitting many, many times, but my inner guide reminded me that I had gone too far to ever turn back and that winners never quit, nor do quitters ever win. I soon realized that the cure for the pain was in the pain itself, and that the pain had no control over me, so I made a conscious choice to live in the moment by facing my pain and trusting the process.

Determined to find release, I realized that my salvation laid not in something miraculous happening to me from the outside, but only in my own ability to face my shadows and transform them, incorporating the power of knowledge, wisdom, and authority entrusted to me from the beginning into my routine and acting from that place of love.

My first class assignment and challenge was to write a seven-page essay on values for my metaphysics class. I went home, stared at the computer, and cried. Not only did I not know how to use the computer, but I also had no idea how to write an essay, especially on values, having not being in school for over thirty years.

Nevertheless, I found courage to read the required text and tried hard to concentrate. My frazzled nerves were a force to reckon with, however, as I felt overwhelmed with constant feelings of inadequacy. After what seemed like hours, I prayed the prayer of faith, a Unity affirmation of truth, and eventually I got some courage to begin my assignment.

God is my help in every need;
God does my every hunger feed;
God walks beside me guides my way
Through every moment of the day.

I now am wise, I now am true,
Patient, kind, and loving too
All things I am, can do, and be
Through Christ, the Truth that is in me.

God is my health, I can't be sick
God is my strength, unfailing, quick;
God is my all; I know no fear,
Since God and love and Truth are here.
Hannah More Kohaus

After a moment of praying this profound prayer, my unfounded fear was released, and I suddenly found myself beginning to type. The ideas came one after the other; little by little; and before I knew it, my paper was complete. Still thinking that I had not measured up to my full potential, however, I turned it in with reservation.

I anxiously awaited the result, fearing that I didn't make the grade, but thank God I did, as indicated by my instructor's comments. Deep in my heart, however, I knew the paper could have been better, but nevertheless I felt good knowing that I had done my best. I didn't allow insufficiency to hold me back; instead I gave myself credit for making the first step forward, reminding myself that "the journey of a thousand miles begins with one single step." I was happy that I had made my very first step forward. The next was bound to follow.

There were other challenges during my ministerial training besides academics. There were twenty-nine students in my class, most of whom were very qualified and experienced. Being the only one in the class without a degree was intimidating to say the least, so prayer became my only defense. To measure up with the rest of the class required determination, persistence, perseverance, and a great deal of hard work. Most of all, it required a tremendous amount of faith.

Perhaps my biggest challenge was to speak in front of my classmates, as I thought that they were more equipped and qualified than I was. I often dreaded those Monday mornings when I would be required to give a twenty-minute talk and then be critiqued after by my classmates and my instructor. Even though I was confident that my messages were profound, each time that I stood in front of them, I would be overcome with such fear that my voice often betrayed me.

I would reflect on my church home in Jamaica and recapitulate with pride the many times I spoke with relentless passion and conviction, often satisfying the appetites of many people. As I remembered the self-confidence I displayed then, I wondered why I suddenly felt inadequate and what had made the difference. My level of education was obviously a cancer in my mind, affecting my equilibrium, deceiving me of my divine potential. I was determined to prove to everyone that this had absolutely no power over me, as God was my true and abundant source of every good thing, and that I could do all things through Christ who strengthened me (Philippians 4: 13).

Our communication instructor must have understood my fear, as he was most understanding and encouraging, always making me feel that I was better than I thought I was. I remember telling him once that he was going to be proud of me one day, and he told me that he was already proud of me.

Soon after, I began to find my voice. One day after hearing me speak my instructor Tom said to me, "Marjorie, I see you addressing thousands." There were times when my classmates would look at me in total astonishment and disbelief, wondering if they were listening to the same unassuming person who could hardly say her name.

Persistence, hard work, and faith in our dreams are the prerequisites for success. According to our faith, the blind will see, the lame will walk, disharmony will be transformed into harmony, lack into abundance, despair and unhappiness into joy and happiness, and sickness into health. My unwarranted self-consciousness continued to prey on my subconscious mind, overriding my emotions and threatening my very being.

In a state of fear and self-doubt, I thought sadly that I had unavoidably reflected my insecurities, and secretly I envisioned criticisms and invalidation from my classmates. But my defiant attitude interrupted the raging storm within me, and with conviction and determination I embarked on a mission to revert this feeling. I shouted in defense "It is not I, but the Christ within me that does the work!" I acknowledged and affirmed that I was as smart as everyone else in the class, and I had every right to be there. Everyone would eventually see me as I am—a child of God filled with wisdom, knowledge, power, authority, and understanding!

This took a lot of faith and courage, however, as my self-persecution continued. Being very hard on myself, I would look forward to the end of class when I would seek refuge from the confines of my abode. I would close the door behind me, wrap myself in self-pity and hide myself—from myself. I dared not betray my feelings of inadequacy and expose my innermost feeling of incompleteness to anyone.

The waging war continued, and the unwelcome face of insufficiency continued to show itself. One moment I felt on top of the world, and the next moment I felt downcast and completely inadequate. With time, however, I became increasingly aware that I was fighting my own war and I acknowledged that all my discomfiture was mind-created and totally unfounded. I had absolutely no reason to engage in this mental conflict, as I was actually treated with utmost respect and kindness by my all my classmates.

In the midst of all my mental agony I kept remembering the words of St. Paul in the book of Philippians 1:6: "He, which hath begun a good work in you will perform it until the day of Jesus Christ." With a great resolve I pressed on, looking ahead with sheer determination to achieve my desired goal. In order to survive, I knew I had to live in the presence of God at all times.

So my practice of prayer and meditation became more intense, and I slowly I began to be gentle with myself. I subsequently began to effect a change in consciousness when I acknowledged my powerlessness incorporated with an intense desire to take responsibility and overcome my self-imposed limitations. With a sheer determination to succeed, I realized that fear had no power over me, and with the spoken Word of God and deep abiding faith I would be transformed by the renewing of my mind. Each day I kept affirming my divine potential and continued to give thanks for the many lessons worth the while. The time for the singing of the birds had come.

Faith is not something cultivated; it is something embedded deep within.

The Buddha once said:

> "Do not believe in anything simply because you have heard it
> Do not believe in anything simply because it is spoken and rumored by many.
> Do not believe in anything simply because it is found written in your religious books.
> Do not believe in anything merely on the authority of your teachers and elders.

> Do not believe in traditions because they have been handed down for many generations.
> But after observation and analysis, when you find that anything agrees with reason and is conducive to the good and benefit of one and all, then accept it and live up to it."

Sometimes we see our challenges as insurmountable when they are only molehills, but all it takes is a belief in ourselves followed by one single step in the direction of our good, and like the mustard seed that has tremendous potential for growth, one small step will continue into a thousand, multiplying into wonderful and unlimited possibilities. Whenever we are ready to receive, God is willing to meet us right where we are. He can do for us what He can do through us.

The "Imagination"

The imagination plays a big part in creating our world. It helps us to project ourselves "And God said, let the waters under the heaven be gathered together unto one place, and let the dry land appear; and it was so. And God called the dry land Earth; and the gathering together of the waters called He the Seas: and God saw that it was good. And God said, Let the earth bring forth grass, the herb yielding seed, and the fruit tree yielding fruit after his kind, whose seed is in itself, upon the earth: and it was so. And the earth brought forth grass, and herb yielding seed after his kind, and the tree yielding fruit, whose seed was in itself, after his kind: and God saw that it was good. And there was evening and there was morning, a third day". (Genesis 1:9-13).

Charles Fillmore states "The third step in creation is the beginning of the formative activity of the mind called imagination. This gathers the waters together unto one place so that the dry land appears. Then the imagination begins a great multiplication of forms and shapes in the mind. We create our world with our thoughts and with our words, but behind every word and every thought is the imagination."

Within us is the kingdom of God, a realm of divine ideas, and we gain access to divine ideas through regular periods of prayer and meditation. Before ideas take form, we picture them in our minds, using our imagination. If there is no mental picture, there can be no form, as the imagination shapes and forms substance. Charles Fillmore says in *The Twelve Powers of Man*, "The imagination is the formative power of thought, the molding power of the mind. It is that which gives shape and color and tone to thinking. Every word we say and every thought we have has back of it an image and these images mould our lives. "

Dreams, Visions, and the Imagination

Some people have a very vivid imagination that manifests as dreams and visions. We all have the gift of the imagination, but it can only be developed with a deep sense of self and who we were created to be. Whenever we become open and receptive and work with divine principle, the light of God shines forth in and through us, and our guidance becomes clear and certain.

We are powerful beings blessed with the innate potential to accomplish good, and the right use of the faculty of imagination prepares us for impending dangers and prepares the way of success for our loved ones and ourselves. This was the case with Joseph, the beloved son of Jacob, in the Old Testament.

Jacob was an avid dreamer and interpreter of dreams. Because of this special gift, Joseph felt elated, as his father loved him more than all his other siblings. Joseph allowed the images he received from his divine source to work for him, and as a result of his gift of dreaming he became a source of blessing to himself, his family, and ultimately the entire nation.

In one of his dreams, Joseph dreamed that the sun, the moon, and the eleven stars bowed down to worship him. When he told his father about the dream, his father rebuked him, thinking perhaps that Joseph was self-serving and wanted others to worship him.

Because Joseph was able to use his great gift of imagination in such a wise and profound way, his brothers resented him and plotted to kill him. When the opportunity arrived, they threw Joseph into a pit, stripped him of his coat, and sold him to merchants who took him to Egypt.

Not knowing what to tell Jacob, they killed an animal, dipped Joseph's coat in its blood, and told Jacob that a wild animal had attacked Joseph. Jacob was very saddened with this news, thinking that his son had died a very tragic death.

Despite all that Joseph went through, God was with him all the way. He prospered in every way after his arrival in Egypt, and soon became known as an interpreter of dreams.

Pharaoh was impressed with Joseph's ability to interpret his dreams, so he made him his chief officer in charge of operations. One night Pharaoh had a very disturbing dream that Joseph was asked to interpret. Joseph predicted that a famine was imminent, and it was therefore necessary to store food in preparation for the famine.

Pharaoh trusted Joseph's intuition, and so preparations were made in order to combat the effects of the famine. The famine did come to Egypt, and as a result of Joseph's ingenuity, many people's lives were spared. There was enough grain in store for everyone, and people from other lands came to Egypt to buy grains for their families.

Joseph often thought of his family back in Canaan. He held nothing against his brothers who tried to murder him. His father had since then accepted that Joseph had died, and his brothers had no idea what had become of Joseph.

The famine got very severe, and as Egypt was the only place with food, Jacob sent ten of his sons to Egypt to buy food. He did not feel comfortable in sending his youngest son, Benjamin, fearing that he might suffer the same fate as Joseph did.

They arrived in Egypt and Joseph knew at once who they were, but they had no idea that Joseph was still alive much less living in Egypt and experiencing such prosperity. Joseph was secretly overcome with emotion, but he didn't reveal himself to them. He gave them ample food to take back with them and returned their money hidden in their bags. To verify that Benjamin was still alive, Joseph asked them to return to Egypt with their youngest brother Benjamin to prove that they were not spies.

On their journey back home they discovered that their money was returned in addition to having much more food than they had presumably purchased. They were all confused. When they arrived back in Canaan they reported the incidents to Jacob, who wondered in awe. *How could this be?* he thought. He was reluctant to send Benjamin back with them, as he did not want to lose Benjamin like he had lost Joseph. His other sons reassured him, however, that they would take care of Benjamin, so Jacob finally consented to send Benjamin along with them to Egypt.

On their arrival in back in Egypt, with tears in his eyes, Joseph eventually revealed himself to his brothers! They were stunned. He assured them that he held nothing against them. "What you meant for evil, God meant it for good," he told them. Joseph treated them royally and sent them back to Canaan with the good news: "Joseph is alive and well" which Jacob was truly happy to hear.

The imagination plays a big part in our evolutionary process; when we are in tune with God through our minds, all things work together for good. Because of Joseph's ability to focus on the presence of God, he was able to use his imagination in a creative way, not only sparing his own family but also sparing a whole nation from hunger.

Charles Fillmore, author and cofounder of Unity and an avid dreamer himself, also used his gift of the imagination to show a profound working of divine order. Having reached a crossroad in his life, he had decisions to make that would affect his future as well as the health of his wife, and he was shown how to proceed with his life in a very significant dream. James Dillet Freeman relates this incident in the book *The Story of Unity:*

Charles was a very talented businessman with many different interests, but he was also a very spiritual man. Charles Fillmore displayed his power of the imagination during his different adventures that brought him to Kansas City, Missouri. One of his interests was mining, and he was intent on returning to Colorado where he had previously been with a business in mining. Many things attributed to this desire. Among them was his interest in mining as well as weather conditions that he thought would have been more conducive to his wife Myrtle's health. Despite all, Charles found himself remaining in Kansas City.

It is said that Charles later reported

> "I had a strange dream. An unseen voice said, 'Follow me.' I was led up and down the hilly streets of Kansas City and my attention called to localities I was familiar with. The presence stopped and said: 'You will remember having a dream some years ago in which you were shown this city and you were told you had a work to do here. Now you are being reminded of this dream and also informed that the

> invisible power that has located you will continue to be with you and aid you in the appointed work.'"

When he awoke, Charles said he remembered that he had the dream some time ago, but had simply forgotten about it.

Despite the fragility of Myrtle's health, Charles Fillmore obeyed the promptings of the spirit within him, and like Joseph later proved that "all things do work together for good to those who love God to those who are called according to His purpose" (Romans 8:28). Not only was Unity born from this divine decision, but Myrtle's health also improved greatly, and although she was given only a few years to live, she was completely healed of tuberculosis and went on to live for another forty years.

The Power of the Imagination

Thoughts held in the mind create after their kinds; therefore we should guard our thoughts and cleanse our minds daily. In order to cleanse our minds of negative thoughts and beliefs, we need to focus our attention on God and deny thoughts of negation. When we harmonize our thoughts and feelings, our desired manifestation will then become clear.

Whenever we receive a divine idea through prayer and meditation, we first have to believe that it is possible. Next, in order for our imagination to bear fruits we need to picture it in our minds and whatever the mind conceives and believes it will achieve.

Finding my new church home at Unity of Jamaica was like finding the pearl of great price. The Bible became my compass for living, my companion, my rock, my shield, and my hiding place. The metaphysical interpretations inspired me greatly, and for the first time in my life I began to understand that every story, every teaching, and every incident and character related to my life represented some aspect of me.

I could now read the stories of the Bible not as ancient history unrelated to the present time, but I could now read with the understanding that the Bible is very much alive, and very much a part of my existence.

Light was revealed through prayer and contemplation, and I was able to draw from the rich resources of truth embedded within the scriptures. My life was thus enriched with new meaning and purpose, and I found the answers for many challenging situations and circumstances.

The more inspiration I received, the more grounded in principle I became, and it became obvious that my life was taking on a new meaning. I wasn't sure how it would all manifest, but I knew for certain that something within me was beckoning and prompting me into some sort of change.

One day while I sat in church, I found myself daydreaming. I saw myself as a minister at the podium giving a message. As I sat there I distinctively pictured my mannerisms, my posture, my voice projections, and even my eye contact with the congregation, and it all felt very surreal. These images continued for quite some time. Not only did they persist, but they actually felt good.

I felt more and more invigorated with the truth as I opened myself to receive, and despite my presumably unassuming nature, people began to see me in a different light. The minister then, the late Enid Bailey, must have recognized a light from within me and my willingness to serve, as she later asked me one day to assist her on the platform, leading the meditation and doing the welcome and announcements. I must confess that at first I was a bit taken by surprise and totally overwhelmed, but something deep inside was elated and spurred me on to accept. Many people were in awe at my initiation. I was comfortable and composed, and as I allowed myself to be used by God, I seemed to have connected with the congregation in a very positive way. This experience was unforgettable and encouraging, and so each time I sat in church I continued to visualize my—self at the podium as a minister.

Soon, however, I began to doubt myself. *Were the images I received real, or was it just my ego out of control?* I wondered. In my humility, I subsequently surrendered and resorted to my one and only authentic resource—prayer—and asked God for clarity. If this was a divine calling, I requested an opportunity to deliver a Sunday message at the church. I further bargained that the response I received from the congregation after the message would validate my request. I left my request at the altar, surrendered to the will of God, and kept my desire close to my heart, not daring to divulge it to anyone.

Shortly afterward, as the director of the Sunday school, I was requested to accompany a few of our children to a youth conference at Unity Village, Lees Summit, Missouri the headquarters of the Unity Organization.

On arrival at this blessed place, I instantly felt a sense of belonging. It was quite an exhilarating experience, as I connected with many souls all on the same path, and I experienced more inner peace, love, and joy than I ever dreamed possible. The energy was very high, and everyone seemed invigorated with spirit. It was surely a time of giving and receiving, and the atmosphere was filled with what seemed like magic. There were many activities to connect us with each other and with the presence of God, and after attending a workshop entitled "Coming Home," my life's purpose began to unfold.

I knew then that my trip was divinely orchestrated, and I was sent to Unity Village to confirm my mission. I didn't have the slightest clue how it would unfold, but it was not for me to know at that point in time. I consequently let the matter drop, and continued to enjoy my trip affirming divine order.

It was sheer fun as I did everything I could mentally to familiarize myself with the routine of the Village. I began to visualize myself as a student living on campus, studying in the library, browsing in the bookstore, eating at the restaurant, and walking along the grounds of Unity Village. I admired the ministerial students as they walked around on campus and saw myself in them. I even had myself photographed at the podium of the Myrtle Fillmore chapel, assuming a speaking position!

Unity publishes a popular little book called "Daily Word" each month, and there is a message written for each day on different subjects. Sometimes the word for the day and the corresponding message speak directly to one's particular needs or circumstance. As was customary, many people who went to Unity Village for the first time went to the archives to research the daily word reading for the day they were born.

My reading for the day I was born was "Employment." The corresponding message was very awe inspiring and seemed quite relevant to my circumstances as they were at that time! It stated that employment is much more than a job, and anyone seeking to fill this need is brought to his own place of employment. The reading reminds us that everyone is needed. Ultimately, one will be guided to his place of employment by looking within and discovering particular skills and abilities one may have. Finally, the most fulfilling work comes from serving others. One should therefore look for a need to fill, develop a responsive and confident attitude, and one will be brought to his place of employment.

This daily word reading was quite a remarkable revelation, as I was between jobs during that time with the idea of ministry uppermost in my mind. Most of all, the scripture quotation was even more synchronistic. "A man's gift maketh room for him" (Proverbs 18:16). I couldn't help but believe that this was a clear signal for me to pursue my ministerial career.

I went back to Jamaica literally energized, feeling on top of the world, and looked forward to sharing my experiences and my new-found joy with family and with the church. As I landed in Jamaica, I enthusiastically called our then spiritual leader Maxine Martin, now an ordained minister, eager to share my joy and relate my experiences while I was at Unity Village. What I didn't know was that I was about to experience the biggest surprise of my life and prove the wonderful and mighty power of God.

After sharing my experiences with Maxine, I was in awe, speechless, and moved with tears of joy when she asked me to give the message at the church the following Sunday! This was all surreal; God had answered my prayer, and I was going to give a message after all! Now I would see if my call to ministry was real or not. My delivery and the response from the congregation would now be the deciding factor. Was my desire to pursue my dream as a minister authentic, or was it just a wild imagination? Time would tell!

That entire week was spent in mental, physical, and spiritual preparation for my assignment and I decided to use "Coming Home" as my theme, based on the story of the prodigal son, which was the theme, used at the youth conference I had attended. I fasted and prayed relentlessly for light and divine order, and soon divine ideas came pouring in and through me, one after the other.

When I was satisfied with my material I handed it over to God and decided to surrender to God's will and purpose for my life. I had done my part and now God would do the rest. I didn't want to appear egotistical, but somehow in a very humble way I could smell the flavor of success, and something deep within me knew what the outcome would have been. Nevertheless, I was completely unattached to the outcome.

On that Sunday the church was almost full. I felt a sense of purpose deep within me, and I was elated to the umpteenth degree, soaring high as the clouds, but at the same time feeling a deep sense of gratitude and humility. It felt amazingly familiar and comfortable. It felt as if I had been there in that capacity before.

I stood at the podium in total surrender and handed the experience over to God. As I began to speak, I observed different expressions on many faces. I looked at each one with confidence, pride, and with love. God was with me, so I could not fail; and even if I failed, it seriously would not have mattered. I was at that place of total surrender, unattached to the outcome, knowing that God's purpose would be fulfilled one way or another, and it would all be for good.

At the end of the talk there was a huge applause, and everyone stood in ovation. I felt delirious with this obvious and overwhelming vote of confidence, and temporarily experienced what could be described as an out of the body sensation. *Was this real?* I wondered, *or was I in a dream?*

I was brought back to reality when Maxine approached the lectern to continue with the morning's program, and then the reality of it all began to sink in. I did it! I was thrilled, humbled, and happy that my prayer had been answered. When I regained my composure, I closed my eyes and silently said, "Thank you, God."

With the assurance that God had spoken in the affirmative, I was convinced that I was on the right path to pursue my ministerial career, and I was overcome with humility and a sense of gratitude. I continued to pray for guidance and direction on my chosen path, continued to visualize myself at the podium as a minister, and within a couple of years I was on my way to Unity Village to realize my dream. My visualization activities had truly become a reality. Thank God!

How to Develop the Faculty of Imagination

1. Sit in silent meditation each day and declare, 'Let there be light.' Listen to the divine guidance within you.
2. Picture the image that you desire every day, in every detail. Allow your mind to wander. Let your imagination stretch you to the fullest degree.
3. Keep a journal and write down every idea you receive through divine inspiration.
4. Formulate a realistic 'how to' plan, and take one step at a time.
5. Believe that whatever you conceive you can achieve.
6. Do not share your dreams with anyone except God.
7. Give God thanks every single day for the perfect results unfolding.

Will and Understanding

The fourth step in creation according to Charles Fillmore's The Mysteries of Genesis is the right use of the faculties of the will and the understanding. "The will is the executive faculty of the mind, the determining factor in man. What man wills or decrees comes to pass in his experience. Spiritual Understanding is the quickening of the spirit within. It is the ability of the mind to apprehend ad realize the laws of thought and the relations of ides one to another."

Spiritual understanding is the quickening of the spirit within, which is achieved through desire, and the will helps to formulate the desire. We all have access to spiritual understanding, but in order to gain it we have to be centered and focused in the light of God with the practice of daily prayer and meditation with the study of God's Word. Through prayer and meditation when we declare, "Let there be light," we receive divine ideas from within us. "And God said, Let there be lights in the firmament of the heaven to divide the day from the night; and let them be for signs, and for seasons, and for days, and years: and let them be for lights in the firmament of heaven to give light upon the earth: and it was so. (Genesis 1:14) We then utilize our faculty of faith, believing that with God all things are possible (Matthew 19:26). As the light of truth dawns on us, we picture the form we desire using the imagination (Jeremiah 23:17). Next, using the will and spiritual understanding we act decisively, doing what is necessary to bring forth the manifestation (Proverbs 3:5-6).

The greater light as stated in Genesis represents understanding, and the lesser light represents the will. "And God made two great lights; the greater light to rule the day, and the lesser light to rule the night: he made the stars also" Genesis 1:16) The will and the understanding work together; the understanding guiding the will and the will inspiring the understanding into action. "And God set them in the firmament of heaven to give light upon the earth, and to rule over the day and over the night and to divide the light from the darkness: and God saw that it was good. And there was evening and there was morning, a fourth day" (Genesis 1:17-18)

Guided will and understanding should be our aim. God's will does not mean punishment, suffering, or retribution. We must realize that good and only good is our salvation. God cannot give us any less than we can give ourselves, only good and better.

In her book Lessons in Truth, Emily Cady states, "Understanding or realization of the presence of God within us is as Peter said, 'the gift of God' (John 4:10). It comes to any and all who learn how to seek it "aright."

Learning to Trust God's Will

At times willfulness, impatience, and disobedience to the laws of God can result in a lack of spiritual understanding, and confusion and disorder reign in our lives. We may then confuse God's will with self-will, but God's will is always good will. When we declare 'Thy will be done,' we surrender self-will for God's will, and good and only good will subsequently materialize.

We often ask for proof from God, because we do not trust our inner instincts. But when we earnestly seek the light, we shall find that the presence of God is always there to guide and direct us. After the crucifixion of Jesus, the disciple Thomas wanted with all his heart to believe that Jesus had risen, but in his humanity he was doubtful, so he needed physical evidence. Jesus knew that Thomas doubted, so He revealed himself physically to Thomas, showing him evidence of the nails that pierced His hands and His side. Only then did Thomas believe, exclaiming, "My Lord and my King!"

Sometimes when adversity surrounds us because of doubts, fear, and a lack of self-confidence, we often deny our divine capabilities, but God's guidance is always sure in times of decision-making and trouble. For this to become a reality, however, we have to seek God continually, trust Him, and believe in the divine aspect of self as Gideon did in Judges 6-8.

Gideon, a judge who was of humble means thought that he was inadequate. There were adverse conditions facing the Israelites and Gideon felt helpless. When the angel of the Lord appeared unto him and told him that God was with him, he doubted the angel. How could God be with him when there were such adverse conditions facing the Israelites? He wondered.

But in reality, God does not cause hardships; God is absolute good, always with us, even in times of trials. By the law of cause, however, we reap what we sow, but God gives us the opportunity always to change our thinking and begin anew. The hardships that the people experienced were the results of their own disobedience.

Like Thomas who wanted to believe that Jesus had risen but needed physical evidence, Gideon, who also doubted what the angel had said, asked for a sign that God was with him. Gideon received the sign that he requested of God, but Gideon still limited in his understanding and wanted more signs from God.

But God believes in all His children, and even though we act in fear and often miss the mark, He sees us as perfect in His image and after His likeness. Despite Gideon's self-doubt, God knew that he was capable, so God chose him to represent the Israelites in battle. Still unsure of himself, Gideon once again asked God for a sign that He was with him. Again this sign was granted, and Gideon finally answered the call to serve.

But Gideon still had more doubts. Once again Gideon was haunted with disbelief. Before going to battle with the enemy, Gideon wanted to be sure that God would be with him to protect him and give him victory, so he asked yet for another sign. Again the sign was granted.

Finally, after an inner struggle to harmonize his will and his understanding, Gideon surrendered to God's Will and became victorious. Gideon was persistent in asking for signs from God, because he had not quite surrendered.

It is good to be persistent in asking for what we believe is rightfully ours, as persistence helps us to become still and wait on God, ultimately cultivating a good relationship with Him. Whenever we become still we develop an inner ear for listening, and the world surrenders to us. From that place of surrender we then ask whatever we will and it will be done unto us.

Like Gideon, during life's challenges we sometimes have an inner knowing that God is always with us, but when sense consciousness gets in the way, we seek proof from God that we are on the right track.

When I received the call to serve as a minister some time ago, I thought that I was not worthy, so I doubted that this call was authentic. Not trusting my inner guidance, I asked God for proof, "If this voice I am hearing is authentic let me know by giving me an opportunity to give a message at the church, and I will know from the people's response if I am on the right track."

Despite the doubts that surfaced, my intuition guided me, and my request for the signal to proceed served its purpose; I subsequently developed a deeper relationship with God while I waited, and although doubts surfaced, I was still convinced that my calling was authentic.

In February 2000 when I was accepted into the ministerial program, I was told that I would later receive a follow up letter of confirmation. I waited and waited and waited. Nothing arrived, and so the whole process of trying to exercise patience started all over again.

At the end of March when I did not receive the letter of confirmation, I decided to call the school. They reassured me that the letter was sent, and encouraged me to exercise patience. Patience, I must confess, was not one of my virtues, and my vulnerability was exposed resulting in a chronic stomach pains.

My prayers seemed futile as I waited, and although I knew better, I found myself being captive to my thoughts. "Maybe God is too busy with other details, or perhaps this is some sort of punishment," I even thought. I quickly became aware of my mental aversion, admitting that my circumstances were presenting the lessons I needed in exercising patience. I subsequently decided to take responsibility for my limited thoughts, promptly denying negation and affirming the truth that God never fails.

In exhaustion I finally found the strength to hand it over to God when something very uncanny happened. My minister suggested that I go to the post office to see if they were holding the package there. I didn't see the likelihood in this, but decided that it wouldn't hurt to try.

Miraculously, the documents were held at the post office because of an incomplete address. They were just about to return the package to the school unclaimed, but thank God, I got there in the nick of time. That was lesson number two in impatience and willpower. Lesson number three was in the making.

I was supposed to be in school at the end of June in preparation for orientation, so as soon as I got the letter of confirmation I headed toward the United States Embassy to apply for a school visa. This was another hurdle to pass; there were no guarantees that I would receive the school visa. Although the school granted me a scholarship, in reality my finances were quite inadequate. Once more I took comfort in affirming that this was what God wanted for me, so nothing could stand in my way. But doubts and negation lingered, and there were many questions. *What if I am denied that school visa? What if this is not God's divine plan for me?* The uncertainty of the outcome was more than I could endure. "God," I prayed, "I believe in Your divine plan of good for my life. Good and only good can come to me from this situation. I now hand over all my cares, all my desires, and I rest in peace. Thy will be done".

Yet in another breath I also prayed, "God, you know that it is my greatest desire to go. Please make a way for it to happen." One minute I prayed "Thy will be done," and the next moment I prayed, "Let my will be done." The uncertainty of the situation weighed heavily on me, but deep within me I knew the truth: I would never experience relief of God until I surrendered to the will of God.

I joined the line at the American embassy in Jamaica for my interview, and after waiting for hours to get to the information line, my heart sank when my arrival was deemed premature and I was redirected. It was obvious that my lesson in exercising spiritual understanding was still in progress.

All being said and done, I knew that exercising patience and waiting for another month, not knowing what the outcome would be, was going to be extremely difficult. The rollercoaster ride continued; trusting one moment, and doubtful and anxious the next moment. As a result, the pain in my stomach intensified and severe inertia began to set in.

Finally the day came for my interview with the American Embassy, and my exhausted spirit seemed to have given way to a final act of surrender, as for some reason my anxiety seem to have diminished at the appointed time. The grace of God must have intervened, as I felt a peaceful calm deep within my soul, and my anxiety was somewhat under control.

I tried to release myself from being too attached to the outcome, although I had an uncanny feeling that everything would be all right. With a confident feeling that the grace of God had converted my weakness into strength, I pressed on with a renewed faith and courage, truly, truly trusting God for the right and perfect outcome.

I continued to feel a calm sense of awareness as the interview approached, and I affirmed with convicted faith, "God knows my need even before I ask, and it is His will to give me the desires of my heart." I looked straight ahead with confidence, right into the eyes of the interviewer, and the Christ within me beheld the Christ within him, and we became one in Christ. The interview was short, easy, and successful, and as I allowed God to speak through me I felt strong and empowered by the Holy Spirit. My answers were precise, truthful, and right on target and I expressed myself with confidence. I was not the least bit perturbed as I fully focused my attention on the presence of God within, and I felt secure in knowing that "it was not I, but the Christ within that does the work." I knew without reservation that God was my all-sufficiency, and nothing could ever stand in the way of my good.

The gentleman who interviewed me seemed to have sensed my sincerity and validity after hearing my truth, and seemed to have had no other alternative than to grant me my long-awaited school visa that God had already preordained. I was told to pick up my visa later on that day, and my joy was full to overflowing.

As I made my exit from the room of the interview that day, I was humbled and elated. My steps were sure and steady, my mind calm and serene, my body light, and my joy complete. My prayers of thanksgiving were superfluous and came from an overflowing heart. "My God shall supply all my needs according to His riches in glory" (Philippians 4:19). What a mighty God we serve!

I was given a three-year school visa to enter ministerial school, and I was ecstatic. My blessings were a constant reality! Looking back, I am able to conclude that the ups and downs in life are a natural part of the process, and we will continue to experience them as long as we are physically alive. There will always be good days and bad days, but ultimately survival depends largely on finding a solid place to anchor oneself.

Gradually, I became increasingly convinced that God had chosen me not only because I could rise to the occasion, but also because I applied myself to the truth and had consented to be used by the process. My initial fear was subsequently transformed into faith, courage, and confidence and I knew that with God as my partner, I could not possibly go wrong. "I can do all things through Christ who strengthens me" (Philippians 4:13).

Releasing Personal Will

As the uncertainty of my future journey and the responsibilities of ministry weighed heavily on my mind, I thought of John the Baptist and his willingness to surrender to the will of God.

When John the Baptist was thirty years old, he left his home and went throughout the land of Judea, preaching to the people, "Repent, for the kingdom of heaven is at hand" (Matthew 3:2). His message was very powerful, and people came from all walks of life to hear him. His fame grew, and there was none like him for over four hundred years. John was very much in tune with God, so certain things were revealed to him.

As curiosity stirred in the people of Jerusalem, the Jews sent priests and Levites to enquire about John the Baptist. They wanted to know whether he was Elijah or some other prophet. John assured them that he was neither. "I am the voice of one crying in the wilderness, make straight the way of the Lord," was his reply (Matthew 3:3).

The people were still curious, so they continued to ask, "If you are not the Christ, Elijah, or a prophet, why do you baptize people?" John reassured them, "I baptize with water, but there is one coming whose shoes I am not worthy to unloose. He will baptize you with the Holy Spirit" (Luke 3:16).

Jesus was thirty years old when he left Nazareth and went to the Jordan River where John preached and baptized people. When John saw Jesus in the crowd, he cried out, "Behold the lamb of God, which taketh away the sins of the world. This is the one that is greater than I," (John 1:29-30).

But the arrival of Jesus was not to show His power. Jesus had come to be baptized by John. John was curious when Jesus requested to be baptized by him. "But John forbad him saying, I have need to be baptized of thee, and comest thou to me? (Matthew 3:14). Jesus replied that it was the will of God. So

John baptized Jesus right there in the river Jordan. Following that the heavens were opened, and the Spirit of God in the form of a dove came and rested on Jesus. Then and a voice from heaven said, "This is my beloved son, in whom I am well pleased," (Luke 3:22).

John made it clear to some of his disciples, as well as the Jews who questioned him, that he was not the Christ, but was sent only as a forerunner of the Christ. He further expressed his profound joy in the fact that Jesus had come to take His rightful place. "He must increase but I must decrease," (John 3:30).

And so it is with the personal will. This story of John the Baptist reminds me of my powerlessness; I was reminded that in order for me to be true to who I am, I had to let go of my lesser self so that my Christ-self could be realized. Sometimes this is easier said than done, as during challenges we invariably doubt our divine potential, making mistakes and losing our way. When we learn to turn it over to God, however, like St. Paul, we will be able to affirm, "I live, yet not I, but Christ lives in me" (Gal 2:20).

In order to be successful, we need to spend more time focusing on the Christ presence within so that the faculties of will and understanding can be harmonized. Personal will has to be released so that the understanding of the Christ presence can take its rightful place in us. Surrendering personal will for the will of God takes a lot of strength. It does not happen overnight, as there are many rivers to cross, many deaths, and subsequent rebirths.

Before my initial departure to ministerial school, I went through my personal belongings trying very hard to separate the essentials from the non-essentials. This was difficult for me, as I had grown very much attached to many treasured possessions. I prayed for strength to let go, but periodically my faith wavered, and my packing was frequently interrupted with periods of intermittent sobbing. Feeling lost and confused, I called my prayer partner. “Millie,” I said, “I don’t think that I can make it. It is too difficult.” Millie hesitated for a while before responding, and after a period of profound silence, she sweetly said, “Marjorie, how can something that’s right be wrong?” I contemplated Millie’s profound statement of truth that somehow brought me some amount of solace and peace, and within a short while I was able to continue with my release, which surprisingly became much easier.

The ending of a very important chapter of my life was imminent, and with the heralding of a new beginning I still felt engulfed with uncertainty. Each time I felt in control, some other emotion would surface, signaling urgent attention. These unscheduled emotional feelings warned me that my healing and transition would be a long process.

And so I prayed “Lord give me the strength to change the things that I can change, courage to accept the things that I cannot change, and wisdom to know the difference.” I know that everything happens at the most perfect time, in divine order, so I learned to be still and trust the process. “Be still and know that I am God,” (Psalm 46:10). I finally reached the acceptable level of surrender, or at least so I thought, and with a renewed sense of purpose I looked forward to starting my ministerial journey.

God is good all the time. He will meet us right where we are. He believes in us even when we do not believe in ourselves. When we walk with God nothing can hurt us, harm us, or stand in the way of our good. Like Moses who was doubtful of His divine capabilities to save the Israelites from the harsh rule of Pharaoh, the power of God within us can change any adverse conditions in our lives resulting in victory.

God will make a way for us even when there seems to be no way. He will never leave us or forsake us. He will work to the end to see us through our trials.

Together, the "will" and the "understanding" both play a very important part in creation, and nothing can be accomplished until perfect balance is achieved in both mind and heart. Had I not been so self-willed, my journey might have been accomplished with much less anxiety. Nevertheless, the many worthwhile lessons I learned during the process have undoubtedly become wonderful stepping stones for greater good to unfold. "All things work for good to those who love God, and to them who are called according to His purpose" (Roman 8:28).

The true prize is ultimately discovered when we surrender to the presence and power of God within us, when we acknowledge Him in all our ways. I now acknowledge the power of God in my life more and more each day, and conclude that there are absolutely no mistakes or coincidences, only lessons to be learned and God to be revealed; everything is perfectly timed and in perfect balance.

I am now convinced of the fruitfulness of challenges, knowing that the Christ experience does not always thrive in the midst of material comfort. Someone once wrote, "Character cannot be developed in ease and quiet. Only through the experience of trial and suffering can the soul be strengthened, vision cleared, ambition inspired, and success achieved." Thus I consider all my challenges a blessing.

> Happy is the man that findeth wisdom,
> And the man that getteth spiritual understanding.
> For the merchandize of it is better than the
> merchandize of silver,
> And the grain thereof than fine gold.
> She is more precious than rubies;
> Not to be compared unto her.
> Length of days is in her right hand;
> And in her left hand riches and honor.
> Her ways are pleasantness, and all her paths are
> peace.

The Lord by wisdom hath founded the earth;
By understanding hath he established the heavens.
By his knowledge the depths are broken up, and the
clouds drop down the dew.

Proverbs 3:13-20

"Judgment"

"Do not judge by appearances, but judge with right judgment."

John 7:24

"Ye judge after the flesh; I judge no man. And if I judge my judgment is true, for I am not alone, but I and the Father that sent me."

John 8: 15-16

"Judge not, that ye be not judged, for with what judgment ye judge, ye shall be judged."

Matthew 7:1-2

Judgment is the ability to judge wisely and to discern the truth behind appearances. This can be used in two ways, from sense or from spiritual perception.

Charles Fillmore states "In the fifth day's creation ideas of discrimination and judgment are developed".

"Let the waters swarm with swarms of living creatures, and let the birds fly above the earth in the open firmament of heaven". (Gen. 1:20).

"The fishes and fowls represent ideas of life working in mind, but they must be properly related to the unformed (seas) and the formed (earth)) words of mind. When an individual is well balanced in mind and body, there is an equalizing force flowing in the consciousness and harmony is the evidence."

We cannot help making judgments as we face responsibilities and as we live and interact with others from day to day and making decisions can sometimes be a difficult exercise unless one is guided by the Holy Spirit. Judgments which are made from a sense perception often have dire consequences. We make wrong choices and costly mistakes based on insecurities within us, which inevitably find their way into action. Authors Jack Kornfield and Christina Feldman say in *Soul Food*, "Our judgments are the visible expression of our disconnection and separation from others, and from our own hearts. They are a breeding ground of pain, alienation, and division."

If our actions are done to the glory of God we can be certain that we are on the right track. Jesus cautioned us to beware of false judgment in John 7:24, "Judge not according to appearances, but judge righteous judgment." Jesus was often misjudged because he went against the expectations of many people, doing what they considered to be wrong from their own perspective. He healed and fed many people on the Sabbath, and He often kept company with prostitutes, thieves and beggars. They often thought that He was blasphemous even when He extended Himself toward the good of others.

Jesus was however acting from the place of righteousness within Him, and whatever He did, contrary to their opinions he did to the glory of the Father. In the book of John chapter 4, during His encounter with the woman at the well, Jesus demonstrated the right use of the faculty of judgment. Although He was a Jew and she was a Samaritan she felt at ease with Him, and although she had many issues, she felt safe to discuss them with him. He didn't seem cold or calculating, nor did she feel intimidated by him. She didn't have to tell him about her issues, because as strange as it seemed, he already knew everything about her.

Most of all, He did not judge or condemn her; he merely exposed her to the bigger picture and showed her how to rise above her limitations and experience complete wholeness. Just the mere encounter with this stranger gave her a sense of freedom.

As a result, she acknowledged her weaknesses and embraced the incumbent opportunity for transformation. As the light of truth dawned on her, the little ills and the demands that society placed on her were no longer of consequence. This stranger, Jesus, offered her living water, which he told her would quench her thirst forever. She would no longer have to journey to the well in the midday heat in fear of being chastised, nor would she have to subject herself to the cold hostility, criticism, and prejudice society dished out to her. Not only could she now face all her fears and limitations squarely and without self-condemnation, but she also could now face her past with courage, wipe the slate clean, and start all over again. How she longed for this day of reckoning!

The Samaritan woman's meeting with Jesus at the well was perfectly timed. At that time of day she hardly expected to meet anyone at all, most of all a Jew who not only could tell her all about her past, but who also gave her an opportunity to heal and begin afresh. This was obviously not a chance encounter. This was definitely a divine appointment. She had obviously reached the end of her rope and the point of surrender. She was ready to be transformed and willing to find a new and better life. Jesus chose to go through Samaria, because he wanted to demonstrate righteous judgment, as He knew what awaited Him there. Someone once said, "When the student is ready, the teacher appears."

Making Right Judgment

Making the right judgment is about taking risks. It is about stepping out in faith. Unless we step out in faith, we will not experience the Christ within us, which is the hope of glory. The woman of Samaria exercised good judgment when she went to the well despite all the negativity that faced her daily, and she was empowered, healed, and transformed by the presence of Jesus.

We ought not to take matters into our own hands by trying to execute judgment on our own, as we are all mirrors for each other and none of us is perfect. We all fall short, and therefore we should not to be too quick to judge our fellow man. Every judgment we make on others is a reflection of what we do not like about ourselves. Instead of judging others, we should concentrate on ourselves and leave the rest to God. "'Vengeance is mine: I will repay,' saith the Lord" (Romans 12:19).

The truth is—Jesus never condemns anyone. He welcomes everyone: publicans and sinners, Jews and Gentiles. Because He was connected to God, His judgment was always righteous. Despite our shortcomings, Jesus is able to look beyond the appearance to the truth that we are children of God, filled with the inner potential to be whole and perfect. God is in charge. He is the judge and the juror, He sees where we cannot see, and hears all that we cannot hear. Our responsibility is not to judge but to love our neighbors as God loves us, and He will take care of the rest.

In John chapter 8 when Jesus challenged the accusers of the woman caught in adultery to cast the first stone at her if they thought they were without sin, not one of them could; not because they were afraid, but because they suddenly realized that they too had transgressed the law, over and over and over again. They were therefore unable to cast a stone, as this would be purely hypocritical, so in total embarrassment they hung their heads, and one by one they quietly walked away.

Like Jesus, we too can exercise right judgment by living and doing the will of God, by looking beyond the appearances and letting go and letting God. Sometimes it is difficult to let go of the past, of things or people even though they do not serve us.

Jesus says in Romans 13:8 "Owe no man anything but to love one another, for he that loveth hath fulfilled the law." In *The Revealing Word,* Charles Fillmore says

Law, "is the faculty of mind that holds every thought and act strictly to the truth of Being, regardless of circumstances or environment. Man, by keeping the law of right thought, works in perfect harmony with divine law and thus paves his way into spiritual consciousness."

In loving one another rather than judging, we cultivate the right habit of thinking and being, regardless of the appearances and regardless of misgivings from others. We consequently reap the fruits of the spirit, which are, "love, joy, peace, long suffering, gentleness, goodness, faith, meekness, and temperance, against such there is no law" (Galatians 5:22).

According to Charles Fillmore's The Twelve Powers of Man, in the Bible the faculty of judgment is represented by the disciple James, and it is also quite significant that on certain occasions Jesus often took with Him Peter, James, and John. Charles Fillmore states that Peter metaphysically represents faith, James wisdom, and John love, respectively. Charles Fillmore states that these are the uppermost qualities we need to embody in order to make right judgment.

In The Twelve Powers of Man, Charles Fillmore also says

> "When we awaken to the reality of our being, the light begins to break upon us from within and we know the truth; this is the quickening of the James faculty. When this quickening occurs we find ourselves discriminating between the good and the evil. We no longer accept the race standards or the teachings of the worldly wise, but we judge righteous judgment."

Deep within our souls there is a fountain of living water. When we drink from this fountain of living water, we experience the Christ of our being, and our thirst will be quenched forever. Jesus the Christ is always within us, and He offers us the opportunity for redemption and to make righteous judgment.

As the two Unity churches in Jamaica had no vacancy for an additional minister, I had no idea what form my ministry would take after leaving school. Nevertheless, I looked forward to returning home. I envisioned myself pioneering, and I was enthused with the idea. As a result, I paid little attention to the writing of resumes. Close to the end of school, however, there was an unexpected turn of events; God had a totally different plan for me.

Early one morning, I received a telephone call from a friend in Florida asking if I would like to practice my ministry in the United States Virgin Islands. I instantly dismissed the idea, as being awarded a scholarship for my ministerial training warranted my return back to Jamaica or some other Caribbean island. Although St. Croix is actually in the Caribbean, it is a United States territory, and therefore it was quite unlikely that I would be permitted to go there. The prospect of going to the United States Virgin Islands intrigued me however, and as nothing beats a failure but a trial, I decided to explore the possibilities. After all, I had nothing to lose.

The approval from the Association of Unity Churches, in charge of the placement of ministers, was my biggest obstacle. To my surprise, however, the approval was instantaneous. Although St. Croix is a United States territory, it is in fact a Caribbean island, so all that I needed was a work permit.

I quickly brushed up my resume and faxed it promptly to the president of the board of directors at the Unity church in St. Croix. The board of directors and the congregation were very eager and enthused at the prospect of having their first minister, and everything was set and a telephone interview with the church board arranged. I prayed for divine guidance and prepared myself mentally. The interview went quite well, and judging from their responses, I thought I had passed the first hurdle. Now I had to wait to hear the verdict.

Most of us who sent out resumes awaited the results with anxiety. As we met with our prayer groups, we experimented with different methods of prayer, some praying direct prayers while others prayed indirect prayers. I had mixed feelings. I wanted to go home to be with my mother who was ailing in Jamaica, but at the same time I was open to the prospect of going to St. Croix, so my prayer was for God's will to be done. Being unattached to the result, I surrendered to the will of God knowing that His divine will for me was good, perfect, and just.

A few weeks went by, and I heard nothing from the church in St. Croix. Being unattached to the outcome, I told myself that it really didn't matter. Just after releasing it, I received a telephone call from the president of the board of directors in St. Croix who gladly told me that the church board unanimously agreed to have me come to St. Croix for a tryout talk. Still thinking about my mother, I had mixed feelings; neither was I joyful or sad, but I resolved that God was in charge, and I relied on Him for right judgment. God knows our needs even before we do, so I felt confident that God had already made this decision for me, and I decided to go with the flow.

Whenever we need direction and guidance in judging wisely or in making wise choices, we need to declare "Let there be light," as God showed us in the book of Genesis. And God said, "Let there be Light and there was Light" (Gen. 1: 3). God then separated the darkness from the light, which means He separated the essentials from the non-essentials.

When we therefore seek divine guidance in making right judgments through prayer and meditation, denying negation and affirming good, God will lead us safely to our desired destination.

I consequently prayed for the light to be revealed, and my willingness to surrender to the all-knowing mind of God later proved that "all things work together for good to those who love God and who are called according to his purpose" (Romans 8:28). God works in mysterious ways, His wonders to perform!

I made my plans to go to St. Croix the Friday before Mother's Day in May 2002, and I was required to do a workshop that Saturday afternoon, as well as a full-length message the next day. Giving a full-length message was not a problem, as my previous experience as a platform assistant back in Jamaica left me well equipped with the dos and don'ts of platform etiquette. Facilitating a workshop, however, was a little more challenging, as I did not have much experience in this arena. As a consequence, I decided to take a day off from school the day preceding my trip in preparation for my upcoming assignment in St. Croix.

On the day before my planned respite, I received a telephone call from Jamaica that adversely affected my trip to St. Croix. My mother who had been ill for some time had taken a turn for the worse! I was devastated! I pondered the reality of the situation, my dilemma, the implications and the consequences, and tried to arrive at a rational solution. Should I cancel my trip and go home to Jamaica, or should I continue with my original plans to go to St. Croix? I had mixed emotions. This was a tough decision, as the church board in St. Croix had already purchased my airline ticket and plans were already underway, but at the same time I wanted nothing more than to be with my mother who was obviously making a transition.

Sleep naturally eluded me that night, and rather than preparing myself mentally and spiritually the next day as I had planned, the next morning found me exhausted, in a state of confusion, and unable to concentrate or calm my frazzled nerves. My state of inertia persisted toward late morning, and in exhaustion I fell asleep.

I must have slept for about three hours that morning, and when I finally awoke, I felt much lighter and strangely peaceful despite my dilemma. As soon as I became fully conscious, I had a faint recollection of an encounter that took place in my subconscious mind.

I remembered very vividly a dream in which I was with my father, who was deceased, as well as with my niece and nephew, both of whom hold a very special place in my heart. My father, who appeared ill, was still, in contrast to my niece and my nephew, who were very playful and energetic. I began to complain that my sisters should not have sent my father to be with me in his state, knowing that I had to go on my assignment to St. Croix, but in response they all advised me to take them all with me to St. Croix.

The dream was uppermost in my mind, and as I pondered the dream I reckoned there had to be some spiritual significance, as my past state of sadness and uncertainty were duly replaced with a sense of calm and peace.

When my roommate returned from school that day, I shared my dream with her, hoping to receive some additional insight. In a flash she smiled and said to me, "I think the dream is telling you to go ahead with your plans to St. Croix, Marjorie. Despite what happens to your mother, life goes on."

That interpretation sounded quite relevant and acceptable, and after consulting with my siblings, they unanimously agreed that my mother would have wanted nothing more than for me to continue with my original plans in going to St. Croix. As a result I continued with my plans to fly out to St. Croix the next day, hoping desperately that my mother would at least hold on until after I left St. Croix.

As I began to pack for my trip, I tried hard to face reality. I kept thinking with a feeling of sadness that my mother might not be around for my ordination. I felt really saddened, knowing how much she had looked forward to this.

My roommate, who was aware of my emotions surrounding this issue, lovingly and wisely encouraged me to call my mother and release her. I thought the idea was preposterous, and being in a state of denial I flatly refused to do such a thing, as it was just too heartbreaking to acknowledge such finality with regards to my mother.

Mother had been ill for a while, and she gave us many false alerts on many different occasions, but this time somehow was different. Something warned me to prepare for the worst, as she gradually got weaker and weaker. As I meditated on the reality of the situation, I pondered my roommate's suggestion of calling my mother and releasing her, and slowly I came to terms with it. Eventually, after surrendering to the will of God and letting go, I consoled myself with an inner knowing that everything would be all right, and the next morning I boarded my flight to St. Croix to facilitate my workshop and do my "tryout talk" on Mother's Day.

I arrived on St. Croix on Friday, May 10, 2000, and was warmly welcomed by a member of the board of directors. I must admit that my first impression of the island was not an immediate love at first sight experience. As I drove into the interior of the Island, I felt a wave of disappointment. Not quite knowing why, I questioned myself about relocating, and again left it all to God's will. At this point I was completely unattached to the outcome, and I subsequently left it all to serendipity. I secretly comforted myself that if I didn't measure up to their expectations, the decision would be made for me, and I would be free to go back to Jamaica to be with my mother after my ordination.

And so once again I surrendered to God's will, declared divine order, and decided to let it flow, knowing that whatever happened would be for the best. Still, at the back of my mind was the thought of my ailing mother and my desire to be with her.

As I gave myself permission to relax, I began to feel a little more at ease with the surroundings, and with a sense of guilt, I asked God to forgive my thoughts of negation. I remembered my promise to God prior to my ministerial training, which was to go to any part of the world that needed me, and I felt my body relax. I quieted my racing thoughts, smiled, and proceeded to engage my greeter in conversation.

My accommodation made up for my previous misperception about St. Croix. The view below was captivating! This was a very beautiful island, I confessed. The hostess' hospitality added to the magic of the moment, and I had the feeling of being at home away from home. After settling in for the night, I closed my eyes and thought how brave I was in accepting this challenge to go to a foreign place with no friends or family. Before retiring for the night I prayed for comfort, serenity, and peace for my mother and for faith, guidance, and divine order for myself.

My first assignment was to facilitate a workshop on Saturday afternoon. As I relaxed within the confines of my resort accommodation that Saturday morning, I was prompted to call my mother, but decided to wait until Mother's Day. Instinctively, I decided to overrule that decision and called my mother's home, specifically to obtain a telephone contact for my aunt's family. As my aunt had passed away only the week before, I needed to pass on my condolences to the family, anyway.

This decision turned out to be one of the best decisions that I ever made, and definitely an act of serendipity. I thanked God for connecting with me in such a profound way that day, and I was happy that I had listened to the prompting of Spirit and followed through with divine guidance.

My sister sounded very grim when she answered the phone. My mother was not doing very well at all she told me, and she really doubted whether or not she would still be alive by the time I left St. Croix. I felt like an explosion went straight through me like a bullet, and with an instant tightening of my stomach I asked permission to speak with my mother. My sister warned me that she was wearing an oxygen mask and that she could only listen. Sadly, I reassured her that it was not necessary for my mother to speak; all I wanted was the opportunity to connect with her from my heart.

When it was time to speak to my mother, I was petrified. I didn't know what to say to my wonderful mother, who had loved, nurtured, supported, and cared for me with wise and loving counsel all through my entire life. At first words failed me when I thought that I might really be speaking to her for the last time.

Memories of my mother flashed back to me, and I remembered our last conversation while I was in ministerial school, when she comforted me during an illness. My mother always had the perfect remedy for any situation, and her encouraging words and love never failed comfort and institute healing.

This was the first time since my mother's illness that I was unable to have an interactive communication with her, and I sadly assumed that this was really the end of our physical contact with each other. How could I ever thank her for all that she had been to me with thousands of miles now separating us?

The telephone felt cold and impersonal, but I quickly got my wits together and gave God thanks for the divine inspiration to connect with her in that moment. This was certainly a divine intervention and proved to be a real blessing, as never again would I have been afforded this privilege of speaking to my wonderful mother on this earthly realm.

As I began to speak to her, words of adoration and praise came pouring out from my heart. My tears were uncontrollable, but it didn't seem to matter. Although she didn't say a single word to me, I could feel her presence right there within my very heart, a presence that was more powerful than words, and too strong to be severed even in death. Even though I felt her physically slipping away, at that moment I felt closer to her than I had ever been in my entire life.

I then remembered my roommate's suggestion to release her, and I finally found the courage to tell her that although I knew that she wanted to hang on to experience my ordination, I would understand if she couldn't hold on anymore and had to go before. This was hard for me to do, but I reassured her that we could never be separated in spirit, and that she would be in my heart always.

I had the sudden need to hug her, to look into her eyes and tell her how much I loved her. Nevertheless, I was grateful to connect with her over the telephone at a deep level of our spirituality. It was a very special moment, as I took refuge in the fact that I would always have her with me in my heart wherever I went.

It was a very sad moment for me when I hung up the telephone. I felt emotionally depleted, a deep sense of physical loss. In that moment, pain and sorrow were a constant reality. How I wished that I were there with her! Somehow, deep within me I knew that I would never speak to my mother or even see her physically alive ever again. I dried my tears, went to my bedroom, and quietly said a prayer of thanksgiving for her life and for soul's return to Spirit.

As I sat quietly in a chair in the bedroom, I closed my eyes and imagined myself taking flight and landing at her bedside. I envisioned myself resting in the cradle of her bosom, invigorated by her warm embrace. I imagined her sweetly smiling at me, softly whispering, "Peace, be still." I lingered for a moment, feeling comforted and at peace, and we became one in that moment. With peace, love, serenity, and faith filling my heart, I took a deep breath and slowly came back to the present moment, knowing with all my heart that the presence of God was watching over her, and that she was at peace.

I somehow found the strength later on that afternoon to facilitate the workshop for which I was scheduled, and to my surprise the workshop went remarkably well despite the fact that this was my first time facilitating a workshop in this setting, and despite the emotional crisis I was experiencing.

At the end of the workshop I felt the need to be alone, but I nevertheless accepted an invitation to dine with the members of the board of directors of the church. This is what ministry is all about, I thought. *It is about putting aside personal emotions and dealing with matters at hand.*

Dinner went well, and I welcomed the opportunity to bond with the members of the board in a more personal way. I was very thankful to them for their understanding and support, but at the back of my mind was the thought of my mother, possibly making her transition at that very moment, and I felt helpless and extremely saddened at the fact that I was thousands of miles away.

I arrived back at the hotel at about ten o'clock that night with an uncanny feeling that sad news awaited me. As I approached the bedroom door, I observed a note pinned onto the door. My heart skipped a beat, and I closed my eyes and prayed for strength. I held my breath as I read the note that said, "Call your sister Flora. It is important."

My intuition warned me to prepare myself for the worst-case scenario, and with trembling hands I timidly called my sister, fearing the worst. Being ripped apart herself with emotion, she sadly confirmed that my mother had really passed away, back to Spirit, earlier that afternoon. I sat in the chair in the bedroom and wept.

It seemed quite interesting that my mother died while I was on St. Croix, and I pondered the significance, as previously I was torn between the decision of accepting this assignment (if it was offered to me) or going back home to Jamaica to be with her. *Was this an omen?* I wondered. I knew that everything was in divine order, but I couldn't help wishing that she could have been around a little longer, or even that I could have had the privilege of seeing her physically alive before she died. In the end, I conceded that God knew best, and so I surrendered to His will. After all, when I last spoke to her I had indeed released her when I told her that I would understand if she chose to go before I had a chance to see her.

Despite the sadness I felt, I knew I had come to complete an assignment, so I prayed for courage and faith in order to complete it, and I became comforted with the words of St. Paul : "My grace is sufficient for thee for my strength is made perfect in weakness" (2 Cor. 12:9). I subsequently found renewed strength and courage to go on.

On hearing the sad news about the passing of my mother, the board of directors was sympathetic, supportive, and understanding. Having been previously aware of my mother's condition they told me that I didn't have to give the message after all under the circumstances. I accepted their prayerful support and understanding, but I decided nevertheless that I would rise to the occasion and complete my assignment, as I knew my mother, who was always my cheerleader, would have wanted me to do. I then handed it over to God and ventured out in faith, surrendering to the all-encompassing presence of God within me. And so I did my talk on Mother's Day, in honor of my mother.

Doing a tryout talk on Mother's Day with the death of one's mother only a day before is no easy task. Surprisingly, despite the sorrow and grief that I experienced, the talk went exceptionally well, and most people were amazed at the level of strength I displayed. The response from the congregation was overwhelmingly supportive, and in my grief I felt strangely motivated with an element of joy at the prospect of having a new church family and a new church home.

As I traveled to the airport to board my flight back to school, the president of the board of directors gave me his approval. "You can start packing your bags," he told me. That moment was indescribable . . . an interesting mix of joy for my success and accomplishment, and grief, lonesomeness, and sorrow at the passing of my mother.

I had surrendered my will to the will of God, and no longer would I have to choose between going back to Jamaica and going to St. Croix. Spiritual discernment had taken place, and the indwelling Christ presence had made my decision for me. My mother would be with me in my heart wherever I went. I later reasoned that my mother's death was confirmation that proved that I was at the right place.

I was ultimately offered the job in St. Croix as the first permanent full-time minister of that church, and I felt a sense of elation. Added to my elation was the fact that I was the third student out of twenty-nine to be placed in a church ministry at that time. Great results unfold when we allow the divine presence within to act on our behalf, making all decisions for us.

Love and Wisdom

> "Knowledge is full of labor, but Love, full of rest".
> Unknown Author

> "Wisdom is the ability to use knowledge and Love is the great harmonizing principle known to man" . . .
> Charles Fillmore

The qualities of Love and Wisdom play a very important part in creation as outlined in Genesis chapter one. Charles Fillmore states that the sixth day of creation is the bringing forth of ideas after their kind. In this step man is given authority and dominion over all ideas.

"And God said, let the earth bring forth living creatures after his kind, cattle and creeping thing . . ." (Genesis 1:24) "Cattle", according to Charles Fillmore, represent ideas of strength established in substance, and creeping things represent ideas of life that are more subtle in their expression, approaching closer to the realm of sense."

As man matures creatively, he realizes his oneness with God, being made in His Image and after His likeness. "So God created man in His own image, in the image of God, created He him; male and female created He them. And God blessed them, and God said unto them, be fruitful, and multiply, and replenish the earth, and subdue it: and have dominion over the fish of the sea, and over the fowl of the air, and over every living thing that moveth upon the earth." (Gen.1:24, 27, 28).

The application of wisdom in any situation is like pouring oil on troubled waters, and our experiences in life can be determined by the way we make use of love.

While I was in ministerial school, the power of love outplayed my fears to a great extent. Some people who probably took my quiet nature for weakness were quite surprised in later times when I suddenly found my voice. My interaction in the classroom progressed considerably after my first year in school, and my gradual awakening became evident. My self-confidence had improved considerably, and a light from within me began to emerge.

During the two-year period in ministerial school, it was a requirement to be interviewed by a licensing and ordination committee three times during the two-year period by two separate teams on each occasion. For some of us these were times of great anxiety, as we did not know what to expect.

The interviews were not centered on the display of intellectual knowledge, as we were mostly asked behavioral questions pertaining to attitudes toward ministry on a whole. What seemed of more importance was our ability to show competence in coping with complex circumstances and conditions in a church environment, and our ability to apply the principles of truth relevantly and appropriately.

Some of the questions were metaphysical in nature relating to the principles of Unity or the Bible, and some were just practical questions relating to ministry in the field. We sometimes over-prepared ourselves for the interviews, as we were seldom asked in-depth questions pertaining to our course work.

Although our instructors assured us that the interviews were nothing to fear, some of us were nevertheless intimidated by the experience. It soon became evident, however, that that the loving teams of ministers just wanted to help prepare us for ministry in the field.

In some cases we were asked questions which were geared to help uncover hidden agendas, most of which we were either unaware of or otherwise in denial about. It was amazing how the interviewers were guided to ask the right questions that helped to uncover them. The whole experience served to help us improve our self-awareness, and although some of us wished we could have completed the course devoid of them, we later proved the validity of the interviews.

There was one thing that some of us dreaded most of all during the process, and that was to be placed on "concern." Being placed on concern meant that both teams saw specific areas in our interactions that required our attention. This could range from self-consciousness to conceit, signs of insecurity, or it could just be an inability to handle trying situations in a positive way. When both teams were cognizant of the same irregularities, a second interview was in order, and this was the determining factor.

Being placed on concern was a taboo for most of us. Most people remained secretive about it for one reason or another. Some people, however, willingly shared it with the class with the intention of overcoming through prayerful and moral support.

Generally speaking, I myself do not do well under scrutiny, so naturally I was terrified after hearing about the licensing and ordination interviews. Had I known beforehand that this was a part of the process I might have changed my mind about ministerial school; but I was there by divine appointment so my job was to show up and trust the process.

This was going to be a very interesting process, I reasoned, but I knew that regardless of any obstacle I encountered, I could not and would not look back under any circumstances. I reminded myself, "No man having put his hand to the plow, and looking back is fit for the kingdom of God" (Luke 9:62).

St. Paul's message in Philippians 4:13 reminded me that I am richly endowed with the Christ Spirit within me. "I can do all things through Christ who strengthens me." I was also reminded that I had what it takes to obtain success and victory in 2 Timothy 1:7 "For God hath not given me a spirit of fear, but of power and of love and of a sound mind." Most of all, I found comfort in the promise in Philippians 1:6, "He which hath begun a good work in you, will perform it until the day of Jesus Christ." I held on to these promises and survived somehow with the power of love.

On the night preceding my first interview sleep eluded me, as I did not know what to expect. I prepared myself as much as I could physically, mentally, and spiritually. On the morning of the interview I slowly reached a point of full surrender and handed it over to God, affirming, "It is not I, but the Christ within that does the work."

As I went toward the interview room, I instinctively knew that the Holy Spirit was intervening, as I felt suddenly relaxed and mightily uplifted. I silently acknowledged its presence and entered the room confident and secure, affirming, "I am the light of the world and that light is shining in and through me right now." When I was asked to pray, I humbly handed the experience over to God, and my voice seemed to have echoed the reflections of my heart.

I felt the presence of God in the room, and each face reflected the light of the Christ within. In that moment there was no separation; we were all one in Christ. It was obvious that divine love had harmonized and conquered all feelings of fear, doubt, and anxiety, and instead there was a feeling of a deep connection with God, a deep connection with the experience, and a deep connection with everyone in the room. Everything fell into its rightful place, and I answered each question with precision and a calm assurance.

At the end of the interview I confessed that it was a big stretch for me, but God was my defense and my deliverer. He had seen me through. I gave thanks to the Almighty, and acknowledged once more the omnipotent, omnipresent, and omniscient God who will never leave us or forsake us when we put our trust in Him, when we work in partnership with Him. He will direct our paths.

On my second interview I was stretched beyond limit and drilled like a soldier. I was asked every imaginary question in the book. The questions were instantaneous and purposeful, and each answer seemed to have generated another question. Nevertheless, I found myself answering with precision and I stood my ground, refusing to be intimidated or thwarted.

Eventually, in exhaustion I faltered on a particular question. One of the team members, who would not accept my apparent surrender, purposefully rephrased the question, obviously testing my level of perseverance. I eventually reasserted myself and answered pointedly. At the end of the session I broke down and cried tears of joy. Finally, being filled with a sense of overcoming, I hugged each one of them, chanting over and over again, *"Thank You, God."*

I was later commended by one or two members of the team for standing up to the pressure, and they reassured me that I did very well. My prayer teacher who was present during the interviews also gave me her vote of confidence. "Marjorie," she said, "you know the principles of Unity so much that you can teach them." I felt very elated.

Looking back at the entire experience, I know that of myself I could have accomplished nothing, but with the presence of the Christ within, I was able to do my best. I am now convinced that love heals all discords, and when you take yourself out of the way, the Holy Spirit pours itself generously in and through you, filling your cup to overflowing.

The working power of love and wisdom has been enacted on many more occasions—too many to mention. On one particular occasion worthy of mention, I was given a traffic ticket for a driving offence. Unfortunately, I missed the court date and panicked upon the realization. After checking with the authorities I was advised to go to the courthouse a day or two later when missed cases would be processed.

I arrived at the courthouse early that day, but I had to exercise patience once more, having had to wait until all other scheduled cases for that day were processed. As my finances were low, I was filled with anxiety, unsure of the outcome. As waiting seemed forever, I eased my impatience with a silent prayer, earnestly asking God for patience and mercy.

In *The Revealing Word*, Charles Fillmore says, "Wisdom is the mental action based on the Christ truth within; the ability to use knowledge, while Love is the greatest harmonizing principle known to man".

Knowing that love is the great harmonizing force in the universe, I decided to cure my anxiety pangs with a visualization exercise while I waited. I envisioned myself strolling in a wonderful garden filled with the most beautiful flowers. A healing white light shone from above, penetrating my mind and my body, and I felt peaceful and calm. I took a deep cleansing breath, and pictured the light extending from me into the courthouse, filling the entire room, directed toward the judge. I continued to focus on the light of God, and saw the judge immersed in the light. I felt consumed with love and the Christ in me witnessed the Christ in him, and we became one. I felt myself relax, and knew that God was the case, and the judge, and there was absolutely nothing to fear. Silently I affirmed, "God is my defense and my deliverer. I have no fear."

Finally my name was called, and the nature of the case was announced. I stood upright and faced the judge with confidence, knowing that I stood on holy ground and nothing could hurt or disarm me. The judge stated the offence and asked me if I was guilty. I looked directly in his eyes, and with the love of God told him humbly and apologetically that I was guilty. "Do you know," he said, "that you are robbing the government of their revenue?" "Yes," I responded apologetically, "but it was a genuine oversight."

I was almost bowled over with surprise when the judge told me, "Your fine is one hundred Jamaican dollars." I did not trust myself to respond, thinking that my voice would betray my emotion. I found myself nodding instead, silently affirming "*Thank you, God!*" knowing full well that that fine was just as good as no fine at all. This was a huge blessing to say the least, as at that time a fine of that nature attracted a fee almost ten times more.

I left the room feeling like I was walking on air, and as I proceeded toward the cashier to pay my fine, the police officer, who was obviously dissatisfied with the outcome, exclaimed, "You got away with murder." I did not answer him, as he would not understand that there was a higher power in charge—not him or the judge, but God, the good, the omnipotent.

As I surrendered to the spirit of God within me, I experienced the power of love at work removing all seeming obstacles from my path, and I was overjoyed. Love is truly a great harmonizing force in our lives. "Love is the fulfilling of the law" (Romans 13:10).

The Sabbath

> "Not by might, not by power, but by my spirit says the Lord."
>
> Zechariah 4:6

> "In returning and rest shall ye be saved; in quietness and confidence shall be your strength."
>
> Isaiah 30:15

The next step in the creative process is called the Sabbath. The Sabbath is not necessarily a specific day or time of worship. The seventh day referred to in the bible signifies a time of completion. This is a time of silence or a time of rest. It is necessary to rest after any great task is accomplished. This is a time when we honor the divine presence within us by surrendering to its presence and power. Charles Fillmore states "The true Sabbath is that state of spiritual attainment where man ceases from all personal effort and all belief in his own works and rests in the consciousness that "the Father" abiding in me doeth His works. The Sabbath is kept any time we enter into spiritual consciousness and rest from thoughts and temporal things. Then we let go of the external observance of days, because every day on which we retire into Spirit and worship God is a Sabbath".

> "And the heavens and the earth were finished, and all the host of them. And on the seventh day God finished his work, which he made; and he rested on the seventh day from all his work. And God blessed the seventh day, hallowed it; because that in it he rested from all his work which God had created and made". (Genesis 2:1-3).

The Sabbath is a time of restoration when we release and let go, and allow the spirit of God to do its work in our lives. It is the most important part of the creative process, as nothing can be accomplished without the Spirit of God. God has a divine plan for all His children, and we have no idea what awaits us when we meet with Him face to face. Isaiah 30:15 states "In returning and rest shall you be saved; in quietness and confidence shall be your strength."

Rest and Renewal

The universe reflects a pattern of unfolding with a subsequent period of renewal. Although there seems to be an apparent death during winter, before long there is evidence of new birth when everything suddenly springs back into new life. "Except a corn of wheat fall into the ground and die, it abideth alone: but if it die, it bringeth forth much fruit" (John 12:24). "That which thou sowest is not quickened, except it die" (1 Cor. 15:36).

A time of renewal is necessary for humankind in all walks of life to heal our bodies, minds, and spirits and live life fully, and as co-creators with God, working without Him as our source is futile. We can never achieve any good thing without Him. He has all the answers. All the power and all the glory belong to Him.

The final step in the creative process in demonstrating Good is therefore to engage in a time of rest by trusting God and surrendering to His will and purpose for our lives. When we are driven by unforeseen circumstances and we have done all we can, it is time to turn it over to God. God, who is all-knowing, all-present and all-powerful, always sees us through our difficulties and miraculously comes to our rescue whenever we are open and receptive to the divine flow. God tells us that the battle is not ours. He is in charge not us, and until we acknowledge our powerlessness of ourselves, we will achieve nothing.

To achieve a restful state of being and enter into a realm of pure potentiality, there has to be a perfect balance between the faculties of thinking and feeling. During my ministerial training this state was enhanced by engaging in silent retreats lasting for about two days each. This ritual, which was a requirement, was a time when we did absolutely nothing but communicate with nature and listen to the divine self within. Most of us often chose remote and rustic places with modest accommodations intrinsically enhanced by nature and therefore relentlessly conducive to observing the silence.

As external activities of reading, journaling, listening to the media and verbal communication were forbidden our sense of awareness became heightened. We would simply meditate, sit or walk around leisurely and aimlessly, connecting with the affluence and reveling in the magnificence of the universe. With nothing else around to distract attention, the quiet is often so intense that it is easy to lose all sense of self. Overall, the intention of the retreat is to be emptied of self; our purpose to be free from earthly desires or agenda; to listen and connect with the Spirit of God, and to experience oneness with God and with all of God's creation.

With the peace and tranquility of the mind, human might and power, human opinions and judgment are relinquished, and the insights received through this surrender are amazing.

Usually, on our return to the classroom our faces would reflect the wonder of the experience, an enticing glow of peace that surpasses all understanding. These times of renewal naturally felt like a new beginning, the experience so exhilarating that we often felt fearless and courageous, filled with hope at the prospect of overcoming any challenge, ready to tackle and conquer them without reservation. As a result, our tolerance level greatly improved and we tackled our coursework with a new-found vigor and vitality.

Just as food nutrients are essential to health, so is a time of rest essential to our well-being. The writer of Ecclesiastics proclaims: "To everything there is a season, and a time to every purpose under the heaven". (Ecclesiastes 3:1). Balancing work, play, and rest is therefore very important to demonstrate our effectiveness at anything in life. In the Bible, as Mary and Martha interacted with Jesus, He demonstrated this truth to them. Both sisters represent two aspects of our being; Martha being a busybody, always finding work to do, and Mary constantly sitting lovingly at the feet of Jesus, obviously thirsty for healing love.

Mary must have achieved great inner satisfaction, which Martha obviously seldom experienced, probably because she did not take time from her responsibilities to even try. When Martha complained that Mary was not helping with the work, Jesus cautioned her, "Martha, Martha, thou art troubled over many things, but Mary has chosen the better part." Although both aspects of our being are necessary, there comes a time when balance between both states of being is absolutely necessary, and this can only be achieved by resting in God.

God Speaks in the Silence

God speaks to us in many different ways—through intuition, people, dreams or visions, the written word, music, animals or pets, and through nature, but ultimately, in order to hear from God we need to become still. "Be still and know that I am God" (Psalm 46:10). Ultimately, to surrender requires consent, or a yielding of the entire being. Newton Dillaway, author of the book *Consent* says, "Consent is not the fruit of a strained effort, but a quiet yielding of the entire being. Every part and particle is released from tension, from direction of the conscious mind, the better to be used by the great ocean of directive intelligence."

Elijah reached this state of consent in 1 Kings Chapter 19 when Jezebel had threatened his life. He was on the run after slaying the prophets of Baal, and he could find no respite. He became tired of fighting, and in exhaustion he fell asleep under a juniper tree. God was nevertheless always with him and provided for his every need. As soon as Elijah fell asleep, he felt the touch of an angel who told him to rise and eat.

When Elijah looked there was a cake baked on the coals and a cruse of water at his head. Elijah arose, ate and drank, and decided to lay down once more when the angel touched him a second time, "Arise and eat, Elijah. The journey was too great for you," she said. Again Elijah obeyed the angel, and then found the strength to journey for another forty days and forty nights, finally arriving at Mount Horeb.

There are some things in life that we of ourselves cannot do, and there comes a time when after doing all that we can, it is time to hand it over to God, who in all His glory and heavenly wisdom will guide us and give us the desires of our hearts. Elijah had reached the end of the rope, and he was ready to turn it over to God, who is always ready to give of Himself and made Himself available to Elijah.

Having reached the top of the mountain, Elijah took refuge in a cave. As he mentally settled himself he heard the voice of God, "What are you doing here, Elijah?" Elijah then got his long awaited opportunity to connect with God in the silence of his heart. "I have had it with the people of Baal," Elijah replied.

"They have worshipped other gods, slaying all my people, and now they want to take my life. I am so scared."

We cannot find God in a state of disarray, as God is not the author of confusion (1 Cor.14:33), and Elijah was about to prove this truth. God instructed Elijah to stand on top of the mountain, and when he did a great wind blew and smashed the rocks, but Elijah discovered that God was not in the wind. Then came a great earthquake, but neither was God in the earthquake. Then came a fire, but neither was God in the fire. Finally came the still small voice of calm, and when Elijah heard this voice, there was no mistaking it; he instantly knew that this was the voice of God. Elijah finally found out that God was right there within the silence of his own heart, and in awe he wrapped his face in a mantle.

This story suggests that Elijah was on a spiritual journey like most of us are. Although he was enthusiastic about God, he went about it in the wrong way, over extending himself, searching in the wrong places, being drained physically and mentally. But like Elijah, no matter how godly we are, we will never find God in a state of disarray. We need to surrender to the only power and the only presence, God the good, the omnipotent.

There was an easier way, of course; he could have surrendered to God from the start instead of trying to work things out on his own, but subconsciously Elijah needed the lessons for future goals, and the time in which to work things out. Consequently, his journey took him forty days and forty nights to arrive at Mount Horeb (a high place in consciousness). Once he arrived on Mt. Horeb, he finally surrendered to Spirit and became illuminated. Elijah then realized that he could not experience God from without, only from within.

The Gift of Silence

God had a divine plan for Elijah, but not until he had acclaimed his spiritual identity (arriving on Mt. Horeb, a high place in consciousness). Becoming empowered with this new "self-realization" he was now ready to carry out his divine appointment that God had set for him; first to anoint Hazel king over Syria, and next to give the baton to Elisha, who was to be his successor.

Like the Israelites who experienced many trials on their journey to the Promised Land, our journey to discover our divine purpose sometimes takes us through many winding roads and twisted paths. If we get frightened or discouraged and try to take matters into our own hands, we only miss the lessons and delay our good. We will never find the release and freedom until we surrender and hand them over to God.

Some things in life are beyond our ability to comprehend, and we may never understand the work of God in the universe or in our lives. We arrive at our destination whenever we are ready to be transformed, whenever we surrender to the all-knowing mind of God. Our responsibility is to be still, and we will receive from God, who works with and for us always. Jesus says in John 5:17 "My Father worketh hitherto and I work." God is always with us even during our trials, and he will assist us to arrive at that high place in consciousness where we are ready to receive. Once we arrive at this new place of awareness, we lift our vision higher, and having become open and receptive, the light of truth will shine forth from within.

The story of the prodigal son in Luke chapter 15 reminds us that God is with us always, even during our willful states, and when we acknowledge Him and surrender to His presence our blessings are forthcoming. Because of willfulness, the prodigal son found himself in a far country, separated in consciousness from his good, not because God held anything from him, but because he was separated from his good in thought. God is the only power and the only source, however, so the prodigal son, acting out of sense consciousness, did not have the right consciousness to maintain his riotous lifestyle, and he consequently ran out of substance.

When our backs are against the wall and things become too much for us to handle, we often surrender to God, remembering the many times God has come to our rescue. When we become still, acknowledge our human powerlessness, and surrender to the Spirit of God within us, we are instantly reconnected with God, the source of our good. So the prodigal son came to himself and humbly decided to return home and ask forgiveness. Because of the father's good nature, he greeted the son with open arms, clothed him, honored him by putting a ring on his finger, and celebrated his return with the killing of a fatted calf.

The will of God is to give us the desires of our hearts, but we first have to acknowledge God and give thanks, knowing that it is His will to give us the desires of our hearts. Next, we let go and let God, or become still in His presence. During the time of my graduation and ordination, with family and friends arriving to share in my celebrating, my own transportation became a necessity, as there were many loose ends to tie up. I prayed, affirming divine order, knowing that something good would manifest. Not being attached to the outcome, I finally put the matter at rest and surrendered.

A few months passed, and one day, to my surprise, a friend called to inform me that someone had donated a beautiful Ford Thunderbird to me. Although it was a couple years old, it was in perfect condition, and I was ecstatic and thankful.

All desires in life, whether for healing, relationships, or prosperity, are accentuated by surrendering to the stillness of God's purpose. During the summer of 2001, my mother, who was ill, constantly experienced many bouts of intense pain, so severe sometimes that she would cry out for help. My siblings and I did whatever we could do to help ease her pain and suffering, but we experienced many anxious moments.

Our faith was often challenged, and we felt quite helpless as we watched her suffer, unable to do anything. Despite these sudden bouts of pain, however, Mother nevertheless held on to her faith, displaying strength and courage beyond measure, and as soon as the pain subsided she would bounce right back each time as if nothing had happened.

One Sunday afternoon, I arrived home from church to find her writhing in pain. My sister and I both looked at her with a feeling of inadequacy. Being unable to do anything to help her ease the pain, we stood by, looking at her with a feeling of helplessness. After literally feeling her pain, I said a silent prayer asking God to intervene. Then a voice suddenly spoke to me. "You are a minister, do something." "There is nothing that I can do to make a difference," I silently argued. "Yes, you can," said the voice. Without further ado I went closer to her, took her hand in mine, joined hands with my sister, and then I began to pray.

As I began to focus my thoughts on God, thoughts of negativity invaded my mind. "There is nothing that you can really do to make a difference," I thought. Nevertheless, I continued to pray, still doubting and watching my mother's reaction from the corner of my eye. *Would my prayer make a difference?* I wondered.

The pain continued, and so did my doubts, but I was determined to drive the voice of negativity away, and like the father of the epileptic boy in the Bible, I prayed, "Lord, I believe. Help thou my unbelief." After a period of struggling with my carnal self, my exhaustion slowly gave way to a feeling of peace and serenity. I literally felt my mind and my body relax, and soon I began to feel empowered by a mighty presence within me.

For a brief moment I was lifted up to a higher dimension, and there were no more thoughts, only the experience of stillness far beyond my capacity to comprehend. I completely took myself out of the way, handed it all over to God, and waited in the silence. Suddenly, there was nothing to heal or understand, only the experience of the presence of God to be revealed.

In the quietness of the moment, my mother suddenly became still, threw her hands in the air in obvious relief, and shouted, "Thank You, God!" I subsequently had a feeling of exhaustion, yet also a peaceful feeling beyond my ability to fathom. We all sat in the silence afterwards, each absorbed in his own thoughts, each in awe of God's presence and power, giving thanks to God for this wonderful demonstration of His healing grace.

The benefits to be derived from surrendering to the presence and power of God were enacted on many more occasions, too many to recapitulate. Another one that stands out in my mind, however, is worth mentioning. After retiring from my garment manufacturing business one evening, I felt physically and mentally exhausted. As I prepared for bed that night, I felt so sick that I thought that I would not make it through the night. I was afraid to go to sleep, as I thought that I would die, but I was also afraid of not getting enough sleep, as I needed my energy the next day to complete an important assignment.

As I lay awake during the course of the night, anxious and fearful thoughts haunted me, and my prayers seemed futile. Around two o'clock that morning, however, I came to myself and decided that I had had enough mental suffering. I eventually surrendered to God and prayed, "God, you are in charge, not me. I now surrender to your divine will for my life. I rest in peace now, knowing that you are with me even unto the end." It suddenly did not matter whether I lived or died, and within an instant, I fell into a peaceful sleep.

The next morning I awoke at my usual time, around 6 a.m., feeling unusually energized and with an uncanny feeling that something mystical had happened during the night. I thought about the tiredness I experienced the night before, my extreme fear and anxiety that delayed my sleep, and I was puzzled. Something had changed.

As I sat in silence and prepared myself for my morning ritual of prayer and meditation, it all came to me in a flash. I remembered a distinctive dream in which I was cradled in the bosom of a huge man who carried me tenderly in his arms like an infant. With great care he laid me down in a garden covered with the greenest grass that I had ever seen. I felt safe, protected, nurtured, and at peace.

This dream was obviously of great significance, as my apparent healing and renewal that morning was a reality. It was evident that my surrender that night had substantiated my healing, as I allowed God's presence and power to take control.

Needless to say, my assignment for that day was completed effortless, and in record time. I proved once more that in becoming still God is able to transform even the most difficult situation into a blessing.

God is most active when all seems still. When we surrender to His power and presence in our lives, health of body, mind, and spirit, success and prosperity in affairs, peace and harmony in the environment, freedom from accident, and joy in living are all outer manifestations. God knows best, and He is the answer to all our desires, all our fears, and all our needs. "God is, therefore I am," He is the mission, the purpose, the gift, and the journey. God speaks to us always in the silence, but like Elijah we often miss out on the golden opportunities to experience Him, as we often look for Him in the wrong places.

We often miss out on our blessings, because they are not packaged the way we expect them to be, but God is always with us even though we may not be aware of His presence.

Using this process of creation helps us to:

1. Acknowledge God as the source of all good things.
2. Deny negation and affirm good, or separate the essentials from the non-essentials (darkness from the light).
3. Affirm and claim our good by declaring, "Let there be Light".
4. Use our God-given faculties of faith, imagination, will, understanding, judgment, love, and wisdom in creative ways to manifest good.
5. Let go, or surrender to the presence and power of God.

Although we are co-creators with God, it is ultimately God who blesses us with the increase. "I have planted, Apollos watered, but God gave the increase. So then neither is he that planteth any thing, neither he that watereth, but God that giveth the increase" (1 Corinthians 3:6-7).

In the quietness of this moment I take this time to become still. I focus my attention on the Christ Spirit within me my ever present source of all good things. In this calm awareness I acknowledge that the presence and power of God is instantly available to me and that the place on which I stand is holy ground.

Centered in Your presence, Almighty God, I lift my spiritual eyes to You, my creator and ever present source of help. In the sanctuary of my soul, I lift my mind and my heart to the limitless resources of Spirit. You are my fortress, my rock, my shield, and my hiding place. In You I live, move, and have my being.

Your love enriches my life moment-by-moment, day by day, and fills my mind with creative, prospering ideas. Your radiating light guides my choices and reveals my good. Decisions come to me more easily as I keep my attention on You, dear God. I am willing to let Your light shine within me, to know the right words to speak and the right actions to take.

You are the source of everything I need to live life fully. I gain new insights and inspiration that enable me to look beyond apparent lack to Your unending flow of goodness. In the silence of prayer I receive inner strength, peace, and faith.

Through my oneness with You, dear God, I am calm and confident. Each day I express more faith and receive more blessings. I know that You are always within me and around me. You are my support, my guide, my strength, and my inspiration. You are the strong and unshakable foundation of all life. With faith in You, I live each day with poise and confidence.

I pause right now to experience Your immense love pouring over me, renewing my mind and purifying my thoughts. I am aware only of Your divine presence in my life, and my gratitude for the joy of living. With a confident spirit I go forward to a life of happiness, security and abundant living.

Thank You, God!

PART III

16

Trusting the Process

"The more you recognize your blessings and express gratitude for the things you have, the more things you will have to express gratitude."

Zig Ziglar

"What the soul knows is often unknown to the man who has a soul. We are infinitely more than we think."

Kahlil Gibran

"So when the crisis is upon you, remember that God, like a trainer of wrestlers, has matched you with a tough ad stalwart antagonist—that you may be a winner at the great games."

Epictetus

We may read all the truth books in the world and seek all the spiritual help we can get, but the fact is nothing in the outer will actually change until the time is right—when we consent to be used by the process, or when we are ready to be transformed. Just as there is order in the universe, there is also order in our lives, and after the storm comes the calm. We need only to trust the process.

I learned how to trust the process when I began to experience a feeling of emptiness during my garment manufacturing business some years ago. Something seemed missing from my life, but I could not identify the cause of my spiritual inertia. My passion for God was still intact, but I could not identify the missing link. I continued with my spiritual practices, with regular periods of prayer and meditation, and continued to attend church and church-related activities, but nevertheless the spiritual high I once experienced seemed distant.

Although I constantly prayed for the light to be revealed, I found myself bombarded with feelings of uncertainty and what looked like unending gloom. I knew that God was with me, but I just could not find Him. I felt isolated and mentally separated from God, and I became restless. When I failed to demonstrate, I questioned God and myself. I wanted immediate answers.

Nothing lasts forever. There is always a lesson to be learned in each experience. The discomfort we experience on our journey can be viewed as a prerequisite to the awakening of our souls; consequently, we will continue to experience challenges for as long as it takes until we acknowledge God in the challenge and ultimately learn the lesson. My discomfiture and restlessness clearly indicated that a paradigm shift was in process.
J. Oswald Sanders, author of Spiritual Maturity wrote

> "The worst of God is that He does nothing." But God is most active when all seems most still. The working of God in nature is unseen but none the less effective. Under His invisible control the stars maintain their predestined courses and the restless ocean keeps within its appointed limits."

Despite the uncertainty of my future endeavors I continued desperately in an effort to find my balance, and although anxieties and fears continued to surface in my life, I was determined to conquer them and transform them into wonderful and exciting possibilities. Although I knew that with time God's perfect plan would unfold, I nevertheless found it difficult to trust the process, and so I continued to experience spiritual inertia and a great desire to find my true purpose. With my internal dialogue in conflict with my outer experience, I searched relentlessly for clarity and consolation.

In my quest to find an answer I reminded myself of the seeming inactivity of a caterpillar before it takes flight. "Nothing happens before the right time." Although the journey for the caterpillar seems long and tedious, the end result is an incomparable freedom. Obviously, my lesson in patience was still in progress, so I vowed to take a page from the caterpillar's book in cultivating trust. No matter how severe our circumstances are, God is always in the midst of everything.

God is always "closer than breathing, nearer than hands and feet." There is a story about a United States Marine who was separated from his unit on a Pacific island during World War II. The fighting had been intense, and in the smoke and the crossfire he had lost touch with his comrades. Alone in the jungle, he could hear enemy soldiers coming in his direction. Scrambling for cover, he found his way up a high ridge to several small caves in the rock, and he quickly crawled inside one of the caves. Although safe for the moment, he realized that once the enemy soldiers looking for him swept up the ridge, they would quickly search all the caves and he would be killed. As he waited, he prayed, "Lord, if it be your will, please protect me. Whatever your will though, I love you and trust you. Amen."

After praying, he was quietly listening to the enemy begin to draw close. He thought, "Well, I guess the Lord is not going to help me out of this one." Then he saw a spider begin to build a web over the front of his cave. As he watched, listening to the enemy searching for him all the while, the spider layered strand after strand of web across the opening of the cave. He thought "What I need is a brick wall, and what the Lord has sent me is a spider web. God does have a sense of humor." As the enemy drew closer, he watched from the darkness of his hideout, and he could see them searching one cave after another. As they came to his, he got ready to make his last stand. To his amazement, however, after glancing in the direction of his cave, they moved on. Suddenly he realized that with the spider web over the entrance, his cave looked as if no one had entered for quite a while. "Lord, forgive me," prayed the young man. "I had forgotten that in You a spider's web is stronger than a brick wall."

Sometimes we tend to forget the victories that God works in our lives in the most surprising ways. This remarkable story reminds us that God can turn even the most difficult situations into a blessing. Whenever we speak God's name through the consciousness of the Christ, we will experience His great power and love for us.

Sometimes we all face times of great trouble and the task of rebuilding some aspect of our lives. When the people of Israel faced the task of rebuilding Jerusalem, the great leader Nehemiah reminded them, "In God we will have success" (Nehemiah 2:20). God knows all our needs, and He will supply them according to His riches in glory (Phil. 4:19).

In the book of Ecclesiastics, the writer shares many amazing insights about the divine process and how he thinks we should live. There is divine order at work in everything, and God has a divine plan for our lives. Consequently, there are no mistakes in life, only opportunities to rise higher. God sees us not as failures, but as His children, constantly learning and growing. In Chapter 3 verse 9 the writer states, "That which hath been is now, and that which is to be hath already been and God reqiureth that which is past." Man, he concedes, is limited unto himself; God is in charge, and one's responsibility should therefore be to fear God, enjoy life, and learn from one's mistakes.

We should pray knowing that our breakthroughs will be made in God's appointed time, as God knows our needs even before we know them ourselves. "Before they call I will answer, and while they are yet speaking I will hear" (Isaiah 65:24). There is nothing we can do to speed up the process. The psalmist reminds us in Psalm 27:14 to be patient. "Wait on the Lord: be of good courage and He shall strengthen thy heart: wait I say on the Lord." Our responsibility is to trust God and acknowledge Him in all our ways, and trust Him. "He performeth the thing that is appointed for me" (Job 23:14).

When we concentrate on God's presence within us and not on our concerns, all our needs will be supplied. "Therefore take no thought saying, what shall we eat? Or what shall we drink? Or wherewithal shall we be clothed? (For after these things do the Gentiles seek:) for your heavenly Father knoweth that ye have need of all these things." (Matthew 6:31-32).

The process is continuous and so is the journey. Through many deaths and rebirths of the little self, life unfolds according to the divine plan. We will continue to learn and grow from our mistakes as we surrender to the will of God. Sometimes what seems like the end is ultimately a new and glorious beginning. Sometimes what looks like doom and gloom is a glorious new opportunity.

The mind is the vehicle through which we overcome doom and gloom, and perceive heaven or hell; good or bad. Our goal should be to awaken from the mind-set of negation. We arrive at a resurrected consciousness when the intellect is crossed. This is signified by Golgotha, the place where Jesus was crucified, in Matthew 27:33. According to Charles Fillmore's *The Metaphysical Bible Dictionary,* "Golgotha, the place where Jesus was crucified, represents the skull in Aramaic Jewish language. Consequently, Jesus the intellectual was crossed out so that the Christ may become one in all."

God is always with us during life's ups and downs, so we should always trust the process and watch God at work. During Jacob's challenge, he discovered that God was always with him and he declared, "Surely the Lord is in this place. This is none other than the house of God and this is the gate of heaven." Jacob demonstrated steadfastness on his journey, and although he had done wrong, he continuously acknowledged God. Eventually, he completed a very difficult journey, and what a great blessing that proved to be!

Our individual journey will continue for as long as is necessary, or until we are ready to be transformed. The journey might appear long, tedious, unpredictable, and frustrating, but the entire experience during the journey is nevertheless just as meaningful as the destination, because without the journey there is no reward. "We glory in tribulations also knowing that tribulation worketh patience; and patience experience; and experience hope". (Romans 5:3-4). Jacob had many hurdles to pass, but it wasn't until he had completed the entire journey that he realized the fullness of his blessings.

Challenges in life are a constant reality, and the process may even include a death of the old way of life, but through it all manifold blessings will manifest and the glory of the Lord will be revealed. "'The glory of this latter house shall be greater than of the former,' saith the Lord of hosts: 'and in this place will I give peace,' saith the Lord of hosts" (Haggai 2:9). As we learn to let go of the self, we too will experience the presence of God in all situations. When we let go and let God everything works for good (Romans 8:28).

We should all live our lives truly expectant of unlimited blessings as it is without doubt that we will be victorious. Despite all the challenges that face me from day to day, I am becoming increasingly aware of my abundant blessings, and looking ahead toward new and wonderful possibilities. The good news is that the process never stops, and no matter how often we fail, we can always try again and again and again.

17

Divine Providence

There comes a time when we have important decisions to make, and in our humanity trusting the process sometimes seems difficult. sometimes we are tempted to worry about things, but once our intention is clearly for the good for all mankind, the Spirit of God will lead us into the perfect opportunities, and what sometimes seems out of character usually works to our advantage.

Every experience and challenge is an opportunity for growth, but we have to be consciously aware of the presence of God in our daily lives as our provider, sustainer, friend, and counselor. In other words, we have to build our faith by staying in tune with the divine guidance from within and persevere despite the odds. There is always a light shining from within us, and God is always with us to make a way of escape, even though the way may appear dark and dismal.

I experienced this divine providence of God some time ago after closing my garment manufacturing business of many years because of a state of restlessness. Soon after my impulsive action, fear crept in and I became frantic when I was faced with dire consequences and financial instability.

Hope miraculously beckoned at my door when my sister and her family generously offered to share their home with me, free of charge or any type of obligation. This was a big relief, as my sister's home was comfortable and adequate to my needs.

I wasted no time in moving in, and I was warmly welcomed by the family and bonded easily with the entire household.

Shortly after moving in with my sister and her family, the blessings continued when I further landed a job selling computer paper for a relative who owned a paper manufacturing company. Although I had prior sales experience from my own business, integrating into the corporate world was a totally new experience, a new challenge and definitely a new chapter in my life.

This job was a divine idea in the mind of God, as it helped me to take care of my financial obligations as well as to clarify my intention on my spiritual journey. Unfortunately, I felt a sense of disillusionment, as the air of importance I had previously enjoyed as CEO of my own business was no longer valid, and in this new environment I had to reassert my past position as employer and controller and adjust my mind to accept my present status of employee and team player. To do this required a lot of discipline; I needed to go back to the drawing board and recondition my mind to accept things as they were in the present moment.

I was happy for the opportunity to be of service and to earn a living, and although the novelty of the corporate world was challenging and intimidating, my previous experience of owning and managing my own business equipped me well for my venture. From this perspective, I felt well prepared in the sales arena, but my imminent integration into the corporate world made me unsure and uncertain. In order for me to fit into the corporate world and remain spiritually authentic, I had to redefine my life's purpose and make adjustments to my lifestyle as well.

This I found most disconcerting. The world into which I had embarked was a big wide world with no boundaries, quite contrary to my little world, which I myself had formed, shaped, and defined. Now it was time for an integration of both worlds.

Not wanting to labeled "self-righteous," I tried to be flexible by becoming a part of the crowd, but there were times when I had to take a stand in defense of my values and beliefs. I was quite amazed at the differences that existed between the secular world and the spiritual world; what appeared to be the norm for some people was quite bizarre according to my former beliefs and customs. I suddenly realized that my world had been small, sheltered, and contained. Feeing bewildered and ill at ease, I was challenged to put my spiritual teachings to work in this new and challenging environment.

Unfortunately, as time went by, I felt myself slipping into oblivion as I gradually became more and more caught up with the material world, and my spirituality was seriously challenged. But I was determined not to conform to the society of "anything goes," so I prayed earnestly, asking God to intervene. "Lord, give me the faith to accept the things I cannot change, courage to change the things I can, and the strength to know the difference." I subsequently felt a power rising up in me, and I remembered the Apostle Paul's reminder in Philippians 1:6, "He which hath begun a good work in you will perform it until the day of Jesus Christ." With this reminder I was confident that I would be saved from slipping, that my spiritual foundation would remain intact, and that I would make the right choices.

Promises from God constantly surfaced and reinforced my faith. I was reminded of Romans 8:28, which states, "all things work together for good," as well as Ecclesiastics 3:1, which states, "There is a time to every purpose under heaven." My responsibility was therefore to be patient and trust the Divine presence within me.

In the meantime, it was time for me to choose. Would I serve my little self, the things of the world, or would I serve God? I instinctively remembered how Jesus stood strong in the face of adversity and temptations, and I instantly resolved to be strong and to try to follow in His footsteps.

Jesus was both human and divine, and therefore He was subjected to the wiles of temptations just as we are today. Among His many purposes was to demonstrate the challenges we might encounter on our spiritual journey, and to show us how to stand strong during trials and adversities and overcome temptations.

In Matthew 4:1-11, before Jesus went into public ministry He knew the great work God wanted Him to do and He had spent many days thinking and praying about it. Jesus was well prepared spiritually to complete His earthly mission but He had to prove that He was ready. He was therefore led into the wilderness by the Spirit of God where He was severely tested and tempted several times. Because Jesus spiritually connected and focused on the presence and power of God He displayed great strength however, and He overcame them all.

During the first temptation, the Devil thought that Jesus might have been hungry after being in the wilderness for forty days, so the Devil tempted Him with bread. "If you are the Son of God, command that these stones become loaves of bread." Although Jesus might have been hungry, He nevertheless resisted the temptation; He would not use God's great power to please Himself. He trusted His heavenly Father to take care of His needs. Jesus reminded the Tempter, "It is written: 'Man shall not live by bread alone, but by every word of God.'" This temptation failed, but the tempter soon thought of something else.

Each person going into public ministry often thinks of acquiring many followers, so the Devil took Jesus to the roof of a temple and tried to appease Him thus: "If you expect people to believe that you are really the son of God, you must show great signs. Now, jump off this roof and show us how God will protect you from getting hurt. In the scripture He has promised that His angels will not allow any harm to come to you."

Although the use of scripture is good, one does not gain from using the scriptures in selfish ways. Jesus also knew that scripture had power only when used from a consciousness of truth. Consequently, Jesus once again rejected the Tempter with the reminder: "Thou shall not tempt the Lord thy God."

Being in public ministry one can sometimes become distracted with worldly gains, so finally the Tempter showed Jesus all the kingdoms of the world and said to Him, "These great kingdoms are mine. I can give them to anyone I choose. I can give them to you if you bow down and worship me." Once again Jesus stood His ground and rejected the Tempter, "Get away you evil one, for it is written 'Thou shalt worship the Lord thy God, and Him only shalt thou serve.'" The tempter then left Jesus and troubled Him no more.

In my course of study, it has been revealed to me that the Tempter is not a person, but our own adverse thoughts. There are times when our authenticity is challenged, and thoughts of negation invade our minds, but when we speak the Word of God as recorded throughout the scriptures like Jesus, we too will drive thoughts of negation and temptation away from our minds.

In overcoming temptations, Jesus employed certain mental attitudes:

1. Jesus put God first.

Jesus might have been genuinely hungry, having fasted for many days, but nevertheless He did not give in to the temptation of sustaining Himself physically. He knew that the only real bread comes from God, the only power and presence in His life; He knew that God would supply all His needs, so

He consciously made His choice by putting God first, forcefully driving away all evil forces.

During life's challenges, it is not always easy to put God first, but Jesus did, and He told us that we also could do the things that He did. When faced with temptation, the human tendency is first to satisfy the self. Peter, who had previously confessed that he would die with Jesus, later failed miserably, denying having known Jesus at all.

According to Charles Fillmore, Peter represents faith, but not in its perfected state. Nevertheless, Jesus understands our humanity, and when there are signs of genuine remorse He readily forgives our trespasses. This was evident during His resurrection when Jesus appeared first to Peter and then to John.

2. Jesus quoted the scripture.

The scripture is inspired writings revealed to man by God and it is a very potent tool when it is used from the consciousness of truth. It has the power to open doors and shields us from trouble. Jesus used the scripture as His defense and the tempter instantly lost his fervor. "Thy word is a lamp unto my feet and a light unto my path" (Psalm 119:105).

3. Jesus used the power of the spoken word.

In the creation story in Genesis chapter 1, all things came into manifestation by the spoken word of God. "Let there be light" (Gen: 1:3). Similarly, in the first chapter of John, everything originated with the word of God. "In the beginning was the word, and the word was with God, and the word was God" (John 1:1). There is power in the spoken word of God. "The word was made flesh and dwelt among us" (John 1:14).

Words have the power to accomplish that which we please as stated in Isaiah 55:11. Jesus demonstrated this in the book of

Luke when He raised Lazarus from the dead. The first thing He advised the people to do was to take away the stone from the tomb. Secondly, He looked up to heaven and with a loud voice He called Lazarus back to life. Lazarus was then restored to life and Jesus further commanded the people to lose him and let him go.

"For the word of God is quick, and powerful, and sharper than any two edge sword, piercing even to the dividing asunder of soul and spirit and of the joints and marrow, and is a discerner of the thoughts and intents of the heart" (Hebrew 4:12).

My experiences in the corporate world were all a part of the process of decision making, and all my experiences enabled me to prove the providence of God. Having been blessed with the gift of free choice, I had the opportunity to go within for introspection, and having come to a crossroad in my life, I was forced to choose. Who would I serve, God or the world? Through it all I was able to reflect on my divine purpose, face my shadows, and confront them with confidence.

As I attuned myself to God in prayer, I made my choice with confidence, and the choices I made were filtered through my awareness of God as the very core of my existence. I learned to acknowledge God in every detail of my life, knowing that the wisdom of God was guiding me and directing my path. With this inner conviction I knew God had a divine plan for me, and I had a strong resolve that it was only a matter of time before I saw the light, which helped me to establish a balance between the relative and the absolute.

18

A Turning Point

A year or so after my experiences in the corporate world, I went on my way to ministerial school in Kansas City, Missouri. Before going off to receive my ministerial training, I had often had dreams about ministry, and I was very excited at the prospect of becoming a minister. Everything else, including my personal life, took a backseat as my divine purpose became increasingly clear. I affirmed that I would be the best minister there is, and promised myself that I would go wherever God sent me. I envisioned myself as a missionary or an evangelist. I wanted to help make a difference in the world.

After doing my tryout talk at the Unity church in St. Croix, I was subsequently offered the job as minister of that church, and with the recent death of my mother, I accepted the offer without reservation. The church anxiously awaited my tenure as their minister, and I made arrangements to assume the position as quickly as possible. This was a novelty for them as well as for me; I was going to be their first minister, and this was going to be my first ministry. We were both very excited.

Finally the day came when I was scheduled to take my flight from Atlanta, Georgia to St Croix, Virgin Islands, to assume my first assignment as a minister. My relatives in Atlanta sent me off with a blessing and their vote of confidence. There were no doubts in their minds that this was a divine appointment, and that I would be a successful minister. I too shared those sentiments, and deep within me I felt privileged and happy.

Despite this exuberance, however, I was secretly petrified and unsure. The future seemed vague and uncertain, and being so far away from my family and friends was intimidating. I nevertheless held on to my faith and affirmed, "God is my instant and constant companion, my rock, my shield and my hiding place, so I had nothing to fear."

As I boarded my flight, I acknowledged that my journey was surely an adventure in faith. I closed my eyes and silently prayed for guidance, strength, and faith.

On my arrival in St. Croix, I was met by a group of loving people who welcomed me with open arms. Previous feelings of anxiety, doubts, and apprehension quickly dissipated, and gradually I experienced a deep sense of belonging. I was even more reassured of divine order on arrival at my new home, as everything was in place and every detail taken into consideration. This was far beyond my expectation, and I was most appreciative. I could not desire anything more.

Looking out from the balcony of my new home, the oceanic beauty of St. Croix was captivating. There was a sense of magic in the air, and I felt an intimacy with the universe. A beautiful rainbow like I had never seen before, virtually visible from every angle, stretched out in a semicircular pattern in the sky above, reflecting its radiant beauty in the ocean below. I basked in the magnificence of the moment and silently acknowledged my blessings. I knew that this was a reminder that I was not alone, and there were many more blessings in store for me. On impulse, I once again closed my eyes and uttered a prayer of thanksgiving for God's abundance in my life.

That Sunday I gave my first message entitled "Spiritual Understanding." The response from the congregation was encouraging, and I felt once more that I had found a place in their hearts. With the doting attention I received, I was left with very little time to indulge in lonesomeness or alienation from my family, friends, and familiar surroundings. I knew that God had given me courage and strength to embark on this journey, and the warm reception I received from the congregation was evidence.

I acknowledged my courage in taking on this assignment, as I was ignorant about the culture of the United States Virgin Islands. But God had called and I had answered, and I felt a sense of security. I knew that I was in partnership with God, and there was nothing that faced me that He and I could not handle together.

I instinctively recapitulated the adventures of Abraham in the book of Genesis, and I remembered Abraham's obedience when God instructed him to leave his father's house to go to a strange land. Following after Abraham's footsteps was a tall order, I confessed, but I was willing to give it a try.

Abraham didn't just inherit his blessings. He justly inherited them. He obviously had his fair share of challenges, but he did not complain or lament. He surrendered to the will of God, because he knew that God was the source of all good things and he knew that God would provide. I decided to take a page from Abraham's book by trusting in God's divine plan for my life.

As challenging as this new experience was, I soon found myself loving it. My passion for ministry intensified, and it was obvious that the study group of over thirty years was about to evolve into a new status. My prior experience at the church and Sunday school in Jamaica soon began to pay big dividends, and planning a Sunday service and giving full length talks were accomplished with ease, having done this back home in Jamaica many, many times before.

The singing of Gospel songs and other appropriate secular music combined with other well loved and appropriate traditional hymns took the limelight. After a short while, a small choir formed from the small congregation of fewer than thirty people. I was in love with my ministry and the congregation, and divine ideas and inspiration on how to enhance our worship experience flowed generously. It seemed like everyone was in tune with God and with each other, and the volunteers served gladly and willingly. We were all in love with each other and excited about the future of our church.

There were a few inconveniences, however, that soon began to take effect. Not having a worship place of our own was one of them. A shared space with a kindergarten school was hardly adequate, and I often experienced a feeling of insufficiency at arranging and rearranging furniture and equipment, sometimes in the nick of time, just before our services began. This was obviously another lesson for me to exercise patience, and I asked God to guide me through it all. Nevertheless, I did the best that I could, praying for divine order and hoping that soon things would improve.

Christmas arrived and the church had its first candle lighting experience with a full time minister on board. Spirits soared high, and there was an air of expectancy. The New Years Eve service was well attended, and we all anticipated hope and looked forward to a new beginning; a productive, successful, and fulfilling new year.

At the beginning of the new-year, I continued to stress to the board of directors the need for an office space. Unfortunately, this request seemed premature by some and certainly not a priority at that time. I felt restless and unfulfilled, not being able to function and interact with the congregants effectively.

Stepping out in faith was a challenge for some people, as that meant increased expenses, and thus increased financial obligations. Hence it was a struggle for some to let go and make the transition mentally from a shared space to a private space or from the familiar to the unfamiliar. Consequently, things remained the same for a while and the move to a new place of worship was curtailed.

We continued our services under the existing circumstances for approximately six months, after which it soon became obvious that the honeymoon was over. Unrealistic expectations surfaced, and the family system was threatened because of personality conflicts.

I initiated board training with the help of the Association of Unity Churches, and the responsibilities of the minister and board members were emphasized. Unfortunately, this made very little difference, as things did not change much. Discontent began to brew for a variety of unrealistic reasons; my performance severely challenged, my personal life severely scrutinized and taken out of context.

One thing led to the next, and a division surfaced in the church as negative images circulated. I felt like an alien with a deep sense of sadness in my heart. Being judged prematurely and unfairly and not being given a chance to do what I had planned from my heart was most disconcerting.

I guess I must have given in to the effects of negation, as I soon felt defenseless and bewildered. It was difficult to minister to a congregation obviously opposed to my way of being, and as a result my performance was sadly affected.

Despite the many obstacles I faced, however, with the help and determination of the majority of the board members, we eventually succeeded in orchestrating a move to a new location, and a time was set for our move to ensue, followed by a grand celebratory affair.

Unfortunately, energies escalated during this time, leading to confusion. I felt very ill at ease, and it suddenly became increasingly difficult for me to fit into an environment where my performance was constantly under scrutiny and my leadership role of important decision-making was taken out of my hands.

I must take responsibility, however, and admit that with my lack of experience in handling such situations as a minister, I fell short, feeling completely challenged, overwhelmed, invalidated, and unacknowledged. I began to experience bouts of anxiety, scarcely seeing how I could possibly fit into an environment not conducive to my well-being. This unfortunate scenario began to affect my health, and I was advised upon medical examination to stay away from all work and work-related activities for an entire month.

This was a difficult and uncomfortable predicament, as it was the eve of our move to our new location and a function was already planned to celebrate our new church home, as well as to formally welcome me as minister of the church. But under the circumstances, my spiritual immaturity ill equipped me to partake in such grandeur with so many undercurrents underway. I could scarcely see how I could possibly remain intact and genuine without seriously compromising my health, so I thought it best to honor the doctor's decision and stay away.

I spent the entire month meditating, praying, and listening for divine guidance, and l was forced to make painful decisions. At the end of the month I saw it fit to hand in my resignation as minister of the church. As one can imagine, this decision had serious repercussions, and the members of the congregation responded with mixed feelings.

Soon after handing in my resignation, I began to feel delirious, and I was haunted with feelings of doubt and apprehension. Not only did I not know what I would do next, but I also began to feel a sense of failure and extreme guilt for being too impulsive and premature. I often wondered whether or not I should have persevered and exercise a little more restraint despite the challenges I faced. Knowing that nothing happens by chance, however, I acknowledged that there were many lessons to be learned from the experience, and I later affirmed that divine order was established, as what was done was done.

In looking back, I felt a great sense of sadness, and I felt duly short-circuited in my effort to be an effective minister. I had great plans for the church, but unfortunately, because of my impatience and lack of experience, I fell prey to negation and lost control of myself. The truth of the matter is that there were lessons to be learned not just for me, but for everyone concerned.

I began to face what seemed like the ending of another chapter of my life with apprehension and doubt, and I searched for an answer, finally coming to terms with my decision. I gradually took responsibility for my action, conceding that what was done was done, and affirming that all things work together for good. I ultimately pledged not to look back, but to look ahead with renewed faith and courage, trusting God to reveal all that needed to be revealed and heal all that needed to be healed. Going back to Jamaica was an option, but as much as I tried, I could hardly envision myself in Jamaica, at least at that time. I continued praying, asking God for strength and patience in waiting.

In January of the following year I decided to return to Jamaica in order to sever my ties with the Unity church in St. Croix. After a month or two I returned to St. Croix under different circumstances, this time on my own strength. I decided then that I would let go and listen for divine guidance. After three months of prayerful waiting, my inner voice told me that I had not completed my assignment in St. Croix.

After many setbacks, Unity on the Rock Prayer Ministry, a divine idea in the mind of God, was born and incorporated in August 2004. This idea was executed by four very dedicated souls who worked tirelessly to its fruition. As hopeful as we were, there were many anxious moments. Nevertheless, we learned to be content with what we had, trusting God as our all-sufficiency through it all.

There were times when my faith was severely tested, but each time I faltered, I often felt a deep conviction within me that something good was about to happen, and it never failed. Miraculously, I found the strength to persevere, eventually surrendering to the one presence and the one power of the universe—God, the good, the omnipotent.

The time came when my home became inconvenient for our meetings, so we began the search for an affordable and comfortable space. We prayed, surrendered, and waited. Quite unexpectedly one day, we found a shared space that was ideal for our meetings. Not only was the space adequate and affordable, it was also centrally located and all-inclusive. Everything that we could ever need was in place, including a copy machine, a fax machine, a refrigerator, a gas range, and adequate office furniture. The space was instantly available, and we wasted no time in moving in.

We offered daily meditations and a weekly prayer meeting, and our attendance slowly increased. Our time together was very rich and meaningful. We interacted freely with each other, sharing our joys, our sorrows, our fears, our anxieties, and our overcoming experiences. There was evidence of self-growth for each individual, and our lives subsequently improved.

Unity on the Rock continued to function as a prayer ministry, but pioneering a Unity ministry here on the island proved very challenging for a number of reasons. Most of all, I purposefully kept a low profile, not wanting to compete with the existing church that was still without a permanent minister.

I felt like Jacob in exile, away from my family, struggling to find my purpose. I even began to experience feelings of guilt, and I questioned my capabilities and my ability to execute my divine purpose, even blaming myself for having made the wrong choices.

Facilitating a radio broadcast was an option, and I probed the possibility, thinking that it would be a good way of getting the Unity message across. I affirmed divine order, and soon there was an affordable opening awaiting me at one of the radio stations. Without much hesitation and after seeking divine guidance, I launched into a weekly radio broadcast, "Into the Light," offering a full-length message and a meditation with one or two appropriate songs of praise. The response from the listeners was quite encouraging, so the messages were recorded and later sold as an added source of revenue.

Our weekly prayer meetings continued with the use of a prayer line. There were still times when I experienced a profound sense of failure, grotesquely unfulfilled in my mission and purpose. I felt like a butterfly entrapped in its cocoon with an uncertain future. Feeling spiritually disconnected, my sense of judgment sometimes seemed impaired and hope distant. Hoping desperately to find an answer to my dilemma, I often turned to the Bible and other spiritual books for guidance.

Author Charles Spurgeon warns us that discouragement can hit us in the hour of great success, before any great achievement, in the midst of a long stretch of unbroken labor, or when suddenly hit by "one crushing stroke." When this happens he says, "Be not dismayed by soul trouble. Count it no strange thing, but a part of ministerial experience."

Sometimes the best that we do does not seem good enough, and we go through an inner persecution, blaming ourselves for things that we sometimes have no control. Sometimes we set our standards so high that we neglect our humanity. Sometimes we focus on the outer work and disregard the inner work that is of greater significance.

Until we surrender to the presence and power of God within us and accept our humanity, we will continue to run around in circles and achieve nothing, eventually reaching the point of physical burnout and mental exhaustion, the result of which is spiritual disconnection.

Most of us on our spiritual journeys have the greatest intention. Most of us started our journey with great hopes, aspirations, and great expectations. We want to make a difference; we want to create maps; we want to integrate society, dissolve boundaries, and help to save humanity. This is all well and good, but "Except the Lord build the house, they labor in vain that build it." (Psalm 127:1). We of ourselves can do absolutely nothing, but with God we can do everything.

Elijah, in the Bible, an enthusiast, who loved the Lord beyond measure, eventually came to terms with this truth. Although he sustained a certain measure of success during his sojourn, yet he felt like a complete failure.

One has to wonder, what did Elijah expect? Many other prophets would have done anything to achieve his successes. He predicted a drought, and it was awfully dry for a period of three years. He challenged the priests of Baal to battle, and he won. He prayed for rain to cancel out the drought, and the rain came in torrents. Above all, Elijah utterly got the satisfaction of disgracing Jezebel.

With all of this to his credit, at his lowest point Elijah felt totally un-empowered, captivated with fear, self-doubt, and self-pity, and just about ready to hand in the towel. Elijah could not endure the emotional pain of life as it was any more; he would rather die.

Elijah eventually found himself at the mouth of a cave, swallowed up in his grief and misery. He was terribly afraid for his life, as Jezebel had threatened to kill him. Elijah was in a terrible state of depression. He had no place else to go, but it is said that "man's disappointment is God's opportunity," so God was able to reach to the depths of Elijah's spirit at the mouth of the cave.

God, who already knew Elijah's dilemma, nevertheless asked, "What are you doing here, Elijah?" He lamented that his disposition was because the people of Baal had forsaken God's covenants, thrown down His altars, and slain His prophets with the sword. Now he was the only one remaining and they were trying to kill him.

Instead of leaving that which he could not manage to God, Elijah took on everybody's responsibility, a feat that drained him to the ultimate limit.

Even though Elijah appeared to have failed, God saw him as a success. God knew that Elijah had great potential as a leader. There was further work for Elijah to do, but not until he saw the bigger picture.

We sometimes bite off more than we can chew, but God warns us over and over again that it is He who gives the increase. We should not be too consumed with outer circumstances. God is the problem solver. He will make a way when there seems to be no way. After Jesus chose his twelve disciples, as they prepared to go on their mission, He told them, "Whosoever shall not receive, nor hear your words, when you depart out of that house, or city, shake off the dust of your feet" (Matthew 9:14).

Our responsibility is to be, and not to do. Jesus told Peter, who wanted to know who would betray Him, "What is that to thee? Follow thou me" (John 21:22). God must have wanted Elijah to get down to basics, because He asked Elijah twice what he was doing there. God probably thought that Elijah was taking on much more than he could mange and burdening himself with things that did not concern him. Our responsibility is to do our part and leave the rest to God. The message is loud and clear. "Be still and know that I am God" (Psalm 46:10). "*When it seems like we are engulfed in a raging battle,*" Romans 12:19 cautions us, "'Vengeance is mine; I will repay,' saith the Lord."

No matter how severe things may seem, there is always hope through God. Elijah's case was a serious case of depression, but through it all he was reminded that he was not alone. Provisions were made for him each step of the way, and he received strength from God to continue on his journey. Even though Elijah thought he had failed, he was resurrected through the awareness of the presence of God within him. His journey had taken him from a cave to a mountain top. There seems to be a connection with these two states of awareness, as without the cave experience there would be no mountain to experience.

There is always a worthwhile lesson to be learned in our trials. First of all, no matter what we want to accomplish in life or how simple the task may be, we should always seek God's guidance first. Success in ministry is not measured by the amount of time or effort we exhibit, the zeal and enthusiasm we display, our paycheck at the end of the day, the number of souls we convert, or the size of our congregation. The reward is from within and not from without. It is God who gives the increase.

As long as we reach out to the divine presence, our divine purpose will be revealed. No matter how many accomplishments we may have had, the greatest to the least of us sometimes have had our moments of having failed miserably at one time or another. In his book *Biblical Wisdom for Daily Living*, author Peter Gomes reminds us of this reality as he says, "Failure is not to be viewed as the opposite of success, but rather the result of success."

Through God's promises, and encouragement from many inspired writings, I have developed a sense of compassion for myself and forgiveness of my perceived failures and inadequacies. I have subsequently found the courage to surrender to the will of God and join Paul in saying, "Therefore I take pleasure in infirmities, in reproaches, in necessities, in persecutions in distresses, for Christ's sake: for "when I am weak, then am I strong". My initiation is in progress and my flight imminent, as the peace of God fills me to overflowing. I know that my next assignment will be more fulfilling, more rewarding, and my success guaranteed. Even though we sometimes see ourselves as grasshoppers, God see us all as giants.

19

Embracing Change

Life is like a journey that takes us along many twisting and winding paths. If we fail to conform when changes are imposed upon us, we go against the flow, which may result in chaos and hardships. Changes can be uncomfortable, especially when they are imposed upon us, and we tend to become apprehensive mainly because of fear of the unknown. As a result, we may become fixed in our comfort zones, resisting the very change that is sometimes necessary for our growth and development. When we embrace change as a part of the process, the challenges will ultimately serve as stepping stones that lead us to our desired good.

We have what it takes to effect change, but we will never realize our goals unless we persevere, trust the divine guidance within us, and take the plunge forward even when the odds are against us. God, who is always with us, will strengthen us and help us to rise above our limitations. "For a just man falleth seven times, and riseth up again" (Proverbs 24:16).

Changes may be viewed as a death, but this is not all bad, as every death heralds a new birth or a new beginning. Each day is an opportunity for a new beginning. There is always something to amend, to forgive, or to do differently. In his book "Finding Yourself in Transition," author Robert Brumet writes

> "The external new beginning may occur before or after we feel ready for it; it may be expected or unexpected. And yet as we pray for guidance and divine order, trusting in God at work in our life, the New Beginning will occur exactly the right time and in the right way."

Our lives like the universe unfold in divine order, and changes are sometimes necessary to initiate a better way. Nothing lasts forever. After winter the calm, warm spring brings sunshine and hope. There is a divine connection between the universe and our lives, and there is always a promise of hope and sunshine after many dark periods in our lives.

In Nelson's Complete Book of Stories, Illustrations & Quotes, Robert J. Morgan writes

> "Every hero of Scripture needed new beginnings. Adam and Eve, after they ate the forbidden fruit; Moses after he killed the Egyptian; David, after his adulterous relationship; Elijah after an emotional breakdown in the desert; the disciples after Good Friday. And maybe you."

How to Initiate Change

If we are fearful of change, we will never accomplish anything and we will remain in a state of fixation that is not profitable. To be stagnant is to die. We initiate change when we trust the process, when we are open and receptive. There is nothing to gain by being complacent. If we need to learn to swim, for instance, we need to first go in the water. Next, we stretch out on the water, paddle our feet, and swing our arms. When we go forth with the flow and relax, the rest becomes easy.

Throughout our lives there will be ups and downs, but we cannot enter into a new sense of awareness until we shed our old awareness. ("Be ye transformed by the renewing of your mind, that ye may prove what is that good, and acceptable, and perfect, will of God" (Romans 12:2.)) We transform our minds by accepting changes as a part of the process, getting out of our comfort zones, and acting. By being open to change we have the opportunities to learn new skills, to advance intellectually, and to grow spiritually. In order to advance and grow, we need to set realistic goals, step out in faith, and God will do the rest for us.

Looking back over my life, I have made many strides, stretching myself immensely. Going overseas to live in the United States for two long years and enduring the cold for two winters was a big change in my life. Accepting a ministry in the United States Virgin Islands, where I had not been previously and where I had no friends, family, or relatives was another big and adventurous move for me. But each time the end result has been such a great feeling of joy that makes me stronger, wiser, and more resilient. "Cast thy bread upon the waters: for thou shalt find it after many days" (Ecclesiastes 11:1).

20

Choices

On our journey to the mountain top as spiritual aspirants we are faced with many challenges and ultimate decision-making. What each day is like is entirely up to us. We are the sculptor of our own lives and we have the opportunity to do the shaping.

Our choices have consequences, as each choice we make shapes our every experience and ultimately, our world. For instance, if we awaken late in the mornings, we know that we may be late for work, and if we are constantly late for work, we stand the chance of losing our jobs. Likewise, if we chose to skip our meals, or if we eat the wrong foods, we stand the chance of developing an ulcerated stomach.

Free choice is our God-given right. We begin making them the moment we awaken each day. While we live in a free society, we have the freedom to choose what time to awaken each day, what foods to eat, what clothes to wear, which way to drive, how fast to drive, our occupation and our religion, which schools to send our children, our friends, our homes and so forth.

As we engage in our daily activities, life happens, and sometimes circumstances seem beyond our control, but how it affects us depends on our ability to endure. Naturally, we have a choice either to sit and brood over what might have been, or to accept the things that we cannot change and learn to make the most of them.

The wonderful news is that despite the choices we make, or despite the way we react to adversity, there is always an opportunity to transform unpleasant situations into a blessing simply by changing our original concept of them.

When we put God first in our lives divine order unfolds, leading to success and spiritual fulfillment. God gives us free choice, however, so that we do not become automatons. Nevertheless because God is principle, and principle is law, we are bound to the law, and therefore accountable to the law of cause and effect. We are free to put our hand in the fire for instance, but when we get burned, it is completely our responsibility. It is a known fact that fire burns, and God would never convey messages of negation to us.

On their way to the Promised Land the Israelites learned the importance of making wise choices. They were given the gift of free choice, but unfortunately they violated this privilege, experiencing all manner of hardships. In Joshua chapters 23 and 24, the Israelites lived in Canaan for many years and enjoyed the land that God had given them. The journey they traveled must have been very challenging, as they suffered many trials along the way. Nevertheless, they persevered, and Joshua was wonderful in helping them to stay focused.

Having reached Canaan, they were very happy indeed. It was well worth the journey, as they learned many lessons. Now that they had reached their destination, they were about to make sure they lived their lives according to the divine plan.

There were still challenges that faced them, however; the heathen people were still a force to reckon with. But the lessons they learned through their trials and errors should have been enough to help them handle adverse situations in a wise way, or at least so they thought.

Joshua was now one hundred ten years old, and no longer could he lead the Israelites against the heathen people who still lived in the land, but Joshua knew God would help the Israelites. Now that Joshua was about to die, he wanted to talk to his people one more time. He sent messages throughout the land calling all the people and their elders to meet with him. All the people came, for they loved and honored Joshua. They never refused to obey him. Together they remembered all the wonderful things God had done for them.

And so, Joshua spoke to them for the last time.

> "Be very courageous," he told them "and be sure to keep all God's laws that Moses wrote in the book. There are still heathens in the land, but you must drive them out. Have nothing to do with them. Do not bow down and serve their gods. Do not marry with them. If you do this, God will bless you tremendously. If you disobey, great trouble will come to you."

Joshua reminded the people how God had been with them since the days of Abraham, how He blessed Abraham by leading him to Canaan, promising him that the land would belong to his descendants, how God had rescued their fathers who were slaves in Egypt by sending Moses and Aaron to lead them out, and how God had led them across the sea with the Egyptians drowning in pursuit of them.

As Joshua spoke, they nodded their heads. They heard about Abraham, Isaac, and Jacob. They knew how God had led the Israelites out of Egypt. The people's hearts began to beat faster when Joshua reminded them of the wonderful things that God had done during their own lifetime. He reminded them of the words of the Lord, which said, "I brought you across the Jordan and gave you victory over all your enemies. Now you have a good land of your own." The people knew that the words of the Lord were true. God had done a great deal for them. They were emotional.

At last Joshua said, "Today, you must chose whether you will serve the Lord God, or worship other gods, but as for me and my house, I will serve the Lord." And the people answered, "We will serve the Lord and obey his commands."

Joshua knew that he could not live much longer. Because he wanted the people to remember their promise after he was gone, he wrote their promise in a book. Then he set up a great stone under an oak tree. After Joshua's death, this stone reminded the people of their promise to God and to Joshua.

Soon after this meeting Joshua died, and the people continued to serve the Lord as long as there were elders in their tribes who knew the great works God had done for the children of Israel. God had instructed them to drive the heathen out of Canaan, and when they fought against them, God helped them. Their neighbors were actually afraid of them because God was with them. Although the Israelites wanted to keep their promises to God, it was not always easy for them.

And so a time came when the Israelites stopped fighting. Perhaps they wanted to rest and enjoy their new land. Perhaps they took a short rest before going back to battle, not realizing that the work was a continuous process. Consequently, they became relaxed and complacent, and soon became friendly with their idol-worshipping neighbors. Their children intermarried with the heathen people, and they began worshipping idol gods as well. Everything fell completely out of order. As a result, the people suffered for breaking their promise to the Lord.

What the Israelites didn't know is that the journey never ends. We should be always vigilant in our efforts to live from the awareness of God's presence, and He will guide us always into making wise choices. Challenges do appear, and sometimes it seems as if we are tested, but when our lives are grounded on divine principle we cannot go wrong. "To whom much is given, much is required" (Luke 12:48).

When our lives seem out of order and we are not demonstrating good as we did before, it is time to go back our center and examine our purpose; it is time to go back to our source and choose God. The journey is continuous, and the challenges help us to stretch and become stronger. We need to remain focused by putting God first in everything, acknowledging Him in all our ways, and He will direct our paths. "No man can serve two masters: for either he will hate on and serve the other; or else he will hold on to one and despise the other. You cannot serve God and mammon" (Matthew 6:24).

As long as we live in this world there will be challenges, but Jesus told us we might overcome our challenges simply by following after His footsteps and making the right choices. We can make wise choices when we turn within to the indwelling Christ and allow God to make them for us.

The journey of the Israelites toward the Promised Land is constantly enacted in our lives over and over again, and we lose our way at times, getting distracted, becoming unruly and disobedient. Although we may know the truth like the Israelites did, we sometimes get complacent, letting our guards down, allowing temptations to get in our way, and neglecting our spiritual responsibilities, the consequence of which is limitation and mental struggle to accomplish that which is good. The good news, however, is that we always have an opportunity to start afresh. "Be ye transformed by the renewing of your mind that ye may prove what is that good, and acceptable, and perfect, will of God". (Romans 12:2).

21

Ask, Seek, and Knock

> "Ask and it shall be given you; seek, and ye shall find; knock and it shall be opened unto you."
>
> Mathew 7:7

As we live daily, asking, seeking, and knocking becomes a part of our everyday experience, but there is a spiritual way of doing this. When we are guided by our intuition we will be guided about when and how to ask the right question in our quest for our desires.

Asking, seeking, and knocking all involve action, both passive and active. It is about doing as well as being. It is not about begging and pleading. God, the giver of all good things, knows our needs even before we do, and He has already supplied them. Whatever we receive physically from others is in essence a gift from God, who is the source of all things.

To ask, seek, and knock is to establish a consciousness of God with the constant practice of prayer and meditation and the study of God's holy word. "If ye abide in me and my words abide in you, ye shall ask what ye will and it shall be done unto you" (John 15:7). When we have the consciousness of God, it will be established that God is unfailing and unlimited supply, and in reality everything that we desire. Experiencing God as omnipotence, omnipresence, and omniscience should be our ultimate goal.

Ask

God is always available, ready and willing to supply our needs, but we need to cultivate the habit of asking. "If any one you lack wisdom, let him ask of God, that giveth to all men liberally, and upbraideth not; and it shall be given him" (James 1:5).

Sometimes our prayers are not answered because we ask for wrong and selfish reasons. "Ye ask and receive not because ye ask amiss that ye may consume it upon your lusts" (James 4:3). In asking we should seek to glorify the Father that His will be done in us.

The correct way of asking is not to beg and plead, but to ask in the name of the I Am. "If you shall ask anything in my name I will do it" (John 14:14). It is not necessary to toil or strive for what we need, rather we should state our requests, and thank God in advance for the manifestation. "Be careful for nothing, but in everything by prayer and supplication with thanksgiving, let your requests be made known unto God." (Philippians 4:6).

Above all, we should ask in faith, and then let it go. In her book *Lessons in Truth*, author Emily Cady says "Do not look for signs and wonders; but just be still and know that the very thing you want is flowing in and will come forth into manifestation either at once or a little farther on." She continues

> "Even if at first you are not conscious of having received anything from God, do not worry or cease from thanksgiving. Do not go back of it again for the asking, but continue giving thanks that while you waited you did receive and that what you received is now manifest."

The kingdom of God within us is a consciousness of abundant good manifested in divine ideas. In Mark 10:15 Jesus likened the kingdom of God unto a little child. "Suffer the little children to come unto me and forbid them not, for such is the kingdom of heaven" (Matthew 19:14). Little children trust their parents completely, and Jesus is reminding us that as His children He expects us to adapt a childlike attitude in trusting Him for all our needs.

Seek

We should never go to God only for material gains, nor should we be laid back in our prayers. "Labor not for meat which perisheth, but for that meat which endureth unto everlasting life" (John 6:27).

It is by seeking God first, and not the things of the world, that we receive all that we need. "Seek ye first the kingdom of God and His righteousness and all these things will be added unto you" (Matthew 6:33). To seek God first is to acknowledge God as the giver of all good things, and to be assured that all our needs will be met. We should therefore focus on the presence of God within us, and not on the outer manifestation of material gains. When we are vigilant in our spiritual work and earnestly seek the Divine Presence, we will find the answer to our prayers.

Desires from the heart are in reality God's desires for us. God knows our needs even before we ask. "Before we call God answers and before we speak God hears." The answers we seek and the manifestation of our desires will unfold at the right time, but we must be open and receptive. Daily prayer and meditation should be our aim, and God will supply all our needs according to His riches in glory (Philippians 4:19).

Knock

Knocking is the final step of the process and involves action. To knock is to be in full preparedness. "Whenever the student is ready the teacher will appear." When we have done all we can on our part and our genuine desire to experience God is evident, the door will be opened, and all other things will be added unto us.

When I applied to the Unity Ministerial School in the year 2000, one of the requirements was to earn 240 credits, most of which had to be completed at Unity Village in Missouri. One week of classes at the school would earn us forty credits, so I had to make several trips to Unity Village in order to qualify with the required credits. In retrospect this was an adventure in faith, as my finances were inadequate after the closure of my business.

One day while I was in meditation, I received divine guidance to call the director of the international ministries and ask for help with my tuition expenses. I was delighted when, without hesitation, the director generously agreed on behalf of the school, offering to assist me with both my accommodation and tuition expenses.

I subsequently began my training at Unity Village in Lee Summit, Missouri, and within a two-year period I successfully completed and graduated from the Personal Development program. The journey of a thousand miles begins with a single step, and the first step in my adventure in faith was now complete. Asking, seeking, and knocking certainly worked in my behalf, validating scriptural promise.

22

Persistence

Life happens and misfortune has no color, shape, or form; people get sick and die; loved ones commit crimes and are incarcerated; homes are destroyed because of natural disasters; people lose their lifelong savings due to bad investments and fluctuations in the stock market; families break apart; people die of broken hearts; people are disappointed in love; people get wrongfully accused and are persecuted; and the list goes on and on. These are the realities of life, which by are by no means isolated or restricted to anyone of any particular race, ethnic group, or social standing. Misfortune has no prejudice and strikes indiscriminately, un-foretold. Persistence enables resilience which makes us strong as misfortune strikes.

Humankind has a fighting spirit within. We are made to withstand the most severe misfortune. No matter how severe our circumstances are, there are always choices to make and new opportunities to explore and overcome. The life of a human being can be compared to that of a tree. The roots of a tree represent our faith. The trunk, branches, and leaves symbolize our intellectual and emotional faculties, and the fruits of the tree symbolize our ability to create new life and to affect the lives of others. The strength of a tree is in its roots. Trees are solid and grounded. The most admirable trait of a tree, however, is its resilience. Some trees thrive through all seasons. It has been proven that many trees can withstand windstorms traveling at speeds of sixty miles per hour or more, and most of all a tree can live to be over two hundred years old! For a tree to be grounded, it needs to be attached to its life source—the soil. Within all mankind is the power of resistance. We were made to withstand forces of nature, and the human spirit is made to withstand even the worst-case scenario, but like the tree we have to be grounded in spiritual discipline, utilize our spiritual faculties, and turn our faces toward the light of God. Deuteronomy 20:19 states "For a man is a tree of the field."

There is a story of a simple butterfly that once had a lesson to teach an author. After clearing bush in the mountains for several hours, the author decided to take a lunch break while enjoying the beautiful scenery of a rushing stream with woods all around him, as well as a near-by canyon.

After biting hungrily into his sandwich, his concentration was broken by a persistent bee buzzing around his head. He felt tormented and threatened by the stinging sound, and he waved off the bee, but each time the bee returned. After awhile, the author decided to swat the bee to the ground and step on it. Unfortunately, to his amazement the bee returned in full force and renewed its attack.

In his fury, he ground the insect into the sand with all his weight—all 210 pounds. Thinking that he had gotten rid of the bee, he returned to the log to finish his lunch. He could not believe his eyes when he noticed movement in the sand near his feet. The bee was desperately dragging itself out of the dirt.

Intrigued by the persistence of the bee, the author bent over to watch. The bee's right wing seemed intact, but the left one looked "crumbled like a piece of paper." Despite it all, the bee stretched and tried his wing, moving it slowly up and down. It ran its legs along the length of the damaged wing, trying to straighten it. The bee groomed and doctored itself as well as it could, trying to recover from the assault.

Finally the bee tried using its wings, but the left one seemed hopelessly crippled. As a veteran pilot, the author knew much about wings, so he bent down to observe the bee and concluded that it would never fly again. The bee, however, had a different plan. It kept working its wings furiously in an effort to fly. Still on his knees, the author watched as the bee attempted to fly. It reached an elevation of about three feet, but unfortunately crashed back to the ground. Undeterred, the bee tried again and again and again, each time gaining a little more strength, sometimes flying erratically in different directions.

At last the bee took off, buzzed over the stream, and was gone. The author later reported that he was so stunned at the resilience of the bee that it took him some time before he could get off his knees.

Many great men and women through persistence have displayed great resilience, tapping into the one and only source of power and strength within them—God, the good, the omnipotent, overcoming setbacks, failures, and defeats. Abraham Lincoln is one of those people who exercised great persistence even after many setbacks and failures. Not accepting defeat in any of his life's circumstances, he never stopped until he became victorious. Experiencing failure after failure, Lincoln did not give up, and he eventually went on to become a great president and to be called "A Man for the Ages." He inspired many people of all generations to never give up, and he encouraged them to believe in their dreams.

The good news is that all humankind is capable of exercising the same potency in overcoming, as every person has the potential to achieve success. To achieve a desired goal, however, one should be vigilant in its pursuit, acknowledging God as the source of all good and praying without ceasing.

Jesus told a parable in Luke chapter 18 that explained the importance of praying without ceasing.

> "There was a certain judge in a city who neither feared God nor regarded man. Now, there was a widower in that same city who went to the judge seeking justice from her adversary. The judge repeatedly ignored the widow's request, but the widow was persistent. She didn't mind the constant resentment and insults she endured from the judge, and she would not stop asking until her request was granted. This was her right, and she would not stop going to him until he heard her and granted her justice.
>
> The judge soon began to see the widow's trend, that she was determined. He didn't want to be continuously bothered by this widow, so he said to himself, *"Even though I do not fear God or regard man, I will get this widow away from bothering me. I will give her what she desires and be rid of her."*

Jesus reminded us that if this unjust judge, not fearing God or regarding man, could give in to this widow's perseverance, how much more will our heavenly Father who loves us so much answer our frequent and persistent requests?

Like the woman in this parable, many of us are persistent, sometimes for years, in an effort to accomplish a desired goal. We engage actively in our work despite many challenges along the way, praying time and time again, and doing whatever we can humanly do to achieve our desired goal. Because we believe in our dreams, we persist in our efforts to achieve, and consequently no cold-shoulder, insult, discrimination, or fear can stop us from achieving our desired goals. The breakthroughs usually come sooner or later, often unexpectedly; whenever we are truly expectant, but are unattached to the outcome. We know that God is our supply, and we expect only good, but we do not focus our attention only on the result. Instead, we focus our attention on God, who is in essence "all things." Sometimes the result is not exactly packaged the way we expected it, but more often than not, it comes in a perfect way.

Ultimately, it pays to be persistent, but it is also very important to have the right intentions behind our persistence. Persistence with the right intention has many rewards.

1. It keeps us centered

Persistence does not change God it changes our limited awareness of self, putting us in tune with the mind of God. God wants to give us the desires of our hearts, but belief in the myth of separation often delays our good. The more persistence we become in affirming our divine potential the more our spiritual awareness will increase . . .

2. It breeds optimism

Deep within us is a spirit of optimism which comes to the fore with an attitude of persistence. This is because God is always on our side, and He wants to give us the desires of our hearts.

In 1 Kings 18:1-16, Elijah demonstrated his optimistic nature by praying persistently for rain when there was no rain in Israel or the nearby countries for over three years. There was no grass on the hillsides, and the fields looked like wastelands. The farmers could not raise crops, and the people suffered from hunger. Even though there was no sign of rain, Elijah displayed a deep optimistic spirit as he prayed persistently for rain.

Ahab, king over Israel, was sure there would never be rain until Elijah announced it. Elijah advised Ahab to go on top of the mountain, because the famine was over and soon there would be rain. Ahab looked up in the sky and there was not a rain cloud in sight. Nevertheless, he did what Elijah told him to do.

Elijah got to the top of the mountain, and with his servant watching him he knelt down and prayed earnestly, asking God to send rain upon the earth. Next, Elijah sent his servant to look toward the sea for any sign that it might rain, but the servant reported nothing. Elijah continued praying nevertheless, each time sending his servant to look for any sign of rain. After praying for the seventh time and sending his servant to look for rain, finally the servant reported seeing a little cloud about the size of a man's hand rising out of the sea.

Elijah became very optimistic. He continued to fast and pray even though there was still no rain. Soon, however, the sky became dark, and the rain began to pour in torrents. The thirsty land drank in the fresh water and the brooks overflowed their banks.

That little cloud the servant saw out at sea represents Elijah's faith, (compared to a grain of mustard seed, which we know has great potential). Jesus said in Matthew 17:20 "If you have faith as a grain of mustard seed you shall say unto this mountain, 'Remove hence to yonder place' and it shall; and nothing shall be impossible unto you. Howbeit, this kind goeth not out but by prayer and fasting." Elijah certainly worked this principle and manifested rain by his optimistic attitude and constant prayers.

We all have the power to demonstrate whatever we want, but a lot of discipline is required to release negation. In his book, *Beyond Fear*, author Don Miguel Ruiz says, "To bring on the rain you must transform your point of view and become one with the rain and the atmosphere. When you are in harmony with their vibration anything can happen."

3. It breeds discipline

A persistent attitude helps to initiate spiritual discipline and facilitate unwavering trust in God. God is all-knowing, all-powerful and all-giving, and when we learn to hand over all our cares to Him we cultivate patience and ultimately, hope. "Let patience have her perfect work, that ye may be perfect and entire, wanting nothing" (James 1:4).

God, the giver of all good things, will never leave us or forsake us. May Kupferle writes in her book *God Will See You Through,* "Take time to be quiet, to be still and contemplate the truth that God's love is right there with you and His light is shining through your mind revealing all that you need to see and know. Listen within and let God's wisdom gently turn your thoughts over and over until the questions become answers, the doubts become newborn faith."

4. It sets the tone for success

Winston Churchill wrote

"Heights by great men reached and kept
Were not attained by sudden flight,
But they while their companions slept,
Were toiling upwards in the night."

We were all meant to succeed. As children of God we have unlimited resources right within us, but first we must believe in our divine capabilities and act with determination and persistence. Recently I watched a program on television called "Made," where young people took on many challenges that at the onset seemed insurmountable.

The process of metamorphism intrigued me, and I watched in awe the level of discipline that was required in most cases. The manifestations were amazing! A tomboy transformed into a beauty queen, an overweight girl turned into a trim and exquisite dancer, and an excessively overweight and highly undisciplined young man lost weight, eventually winning a karate competition! I was speechless when I watched him break two pieces of board all at once with the power of his mind.

Most of the contestants found themselves at the verge of quitting during the process. The discipline of relentless training was unequivocally arduous and too overwhelming, but winners are not quitters, and quitters are not winners, so they persevered, and though they did not all win the competitions, the lessons and the discipline they learned were unequalled.

As I watched the process involved, I became absorbed in admiration, and I realized that they all possessed one thing in common, which was the foundation of all their efforts—a deep abiding faith in their ability to succeed, a profound strength and a sheer determination to succeed. They all wanted desperately to achieve. No one wanted to fail.

5. It makes us resilient.

"If at first you don't succeed, try and try and try again." Many of us were drilled with this rhyme in school, and what a blessing it has been to most of us! It has guided us throughout our lives and encouraged us not to give up. It doesn't hurt to try, as nothing beats a failure but a trial.

Persistence helps us to become resilient, reinforcing our faith in believing that the power of God within us makes all things possible. The more we try the more tolerant and resilient we become. If our belief is firm as a rock, we will succeed ("Upon this rock I will build my church; and the gates of hell shall not prevail against it" (Matthew 16:18).); if it is shaky like sand, it is no doubt that we will fail. It is always our fears and doubts that prevent us from achieving. God already knows our needs even before we ask, and before we call He answers.

We are all spiritual warriors. There is a fighting spirit within us that knows no boundaries, no barriers, no defeat, no fear or regret. It is the presence of God that comes to our rescue the moment we reach out to Him. The comforting, guiding presence of God encourages us to rise above all seeming challenges, and we find strength and courage to press along in faith. We all have the power of God within us to do and to be, but we must persevere resolutely in faith, even when it seems at times that all odds are against us. All things are possible with God, but we must assist God by working the principle and believing.

While I operated my garment business some time ago, I had many drawbacks. I had the choice either to persevere with persistence or I had the choice to give up and be doomed to failure. As I was determined to succeed, I forcefully adopted a persistent attitude, and after overcoming many trying periods of doubt, uncertainty, and setbacks, my resilient spirit would not be thwarted and I prepared my samples for the sales market. Each moment of defeat seemed to spur me on, and somehow I mustered the courage to step out in faith after moments of introspection and regrouping.

The time came for me to show my samples, but my enthusiasm quickly turned to disappointment, as I was often redirected. I often felt so humiliated and defeated during those moments thinking that my samples were not up to scratch. All I wanted to do was cry, but my feeling of insufficiency was usually short lived. Beneath my disappointment and intense frustration was a spirit of sheer determination; I would not give up, I confessed. And so I pressed on.

Eventually after many trials, I got my first order. This was hardly a substantial order, but nevertheless I was elated. Soon after everything began to fall in place, and within a short time I had to expand my business to accommodate the sales. My brand name "Jamaica Krush," soon became a household name in Jamaica, and my success was eminent.

Soon after conquering the wholesale market, I began to visualize myself owning and operating a retail store as well. I envisioned displaying a fantastic and successful fashion line enhanced with occasional fashion shows.

Step-by-step everything I visualized came into fruition, and I progressed unrelentingly, often experiencing an air of importance. I felt a great sense of accomplishment at my creativity despite my informal entrepreneurship skills, and most of all, at my resilience. The return from my endeavor was even more encouraging and promising, and I felt greatly blessed at the approval and satisfaction of my clients.

It is always good to be persistent in life as there are always challenges to overcome and perfection and growth to be achieved. I was able to prove this truth during my ministerial training when negation and inadequacy threatened my self confidence. Being determined to transform my weakness into strength, I did everything I could humanly do to change my adverse thought pattern. I devoted more time to prayer and meditation, constantly affirming my good, and it wasn't long before the light of truth began to dawn. Slowly, but surely, the transformation became evident and I was on my way to experience victory. It was not an easy journey. There were many hurdles to pass, and there were many doubts. I felt like quitting the program on many occasions, but something deep within me compelled me to hold on. This was the desire of my heart; I had come too far and I would not allow myself to give in to defeat.

The more I visualized my ordination, the more energized and encouraged I became, so I pressed on. When I finally accomplished my goal it was with such elation! I proudly thought I had earned it and consequently deserved it, and no one could take it away from me. I felt strong, confident, and powerful, and yet at the same time deeply humbled. The process had worked itself out and the hardships and discomforts that I endured were worth every moment.

6. It creates a sense oneness with God

Persistence allows us the opportunity to build a deep relationship with God. In the heart of persistence is the depth of optimism, grounded in the goodness of God; in love, hope, courage and faith. When we make God the main focus of our lives and pray without ceasing, we will achieve the desires of our hearts. Self-awareness increases, and there is an ultimate feeling of oneness with the divine. In this state of awareness the exegete declares, “It is not I, but the Father within that does the work.”

One should aim at balancing patience, persistence, optimism, and most of all expectancy without being too focused on the result. In other words, when we believe in our divine capabilities and leave the rest to God unlimited blessings unfold.

Let us now turn our attention within us for a moment of prayer and meditation.

“I center my mind in the light of God’s love and peace, and I become aware of His presence and power filling every part of my being with love, peace, and joy. I affirm, ‘God’s light guides me, God’s love strengthens me, and God’s power makes my way easy and successful.’

As a child of God, I call forth the gifts of God within me, and I experience abundant good in every area of my life. Through the mind of God within me, I know and understand all that is before me. I make wise choices and I experience success in all things.

In the quietness of this moment I give myself now to You, Almighty God. I am patient and calm, assured that You are my ever present help in every need. New doors of opportunity are opened to me now, and I am expectant. In this peaceful awareness I release all concerns to You, and I trust in Your divine will to establish all that is right and orderly in my life. My mind is poised and my heart serene, for I know that the spirit of God works in all and through all to bring forth great possibilities in my life.

I now place myself and all those for whom I pray in Your care and keeping. Wherever I go, whatever I do, the Spirit of God is always loving me, guiding me, comforting me, strengthening me, and protecting me. Thank you, God for answered prayer. Amen.”

PART IV

23

The Dynamics of Ministry

Ministry is serious business, and pioneering a Unity ministry comes with many challenges. Ministry is about embracing the physical, psychological, social, and spiritual dimensions of individuals and offering hope for healing of the whole person. Although we are one in spirit, we differ culturally, ethnically, socially, and economically. Consequently, the leader of a successful ministry requires spiritual maturity and skills to deal with complex situations as they arise.

Prior to entering the field of ministry, I heard many mixed messages concerning church protocol and the dynamics of ministry, some of which were quite intimidating. In my naivety, I thought that my temperament would make me an exception to the rule. I consequently envisioned a peaceful environment free of conflict and fleeting emotions. I was convinced that I would only foster cohesiveness and harmony and make a difference. How wrong was I! I later proved that a successful ministry comes with an openness and willingness to heal at various different levels.

Before venturing out in the field, most of us wondered what our ministry would look like and how our closely held dreams would materialize. From this place of anticipation we were spurred on in the field of ministry, preparing ourselves mentally, spiritually, and emotionally.

The prospect of entering ministry for the first time comes with an air of excitement, awe, and expectancy. No one knows the dynamics of ministry until they experience it for themselves. This is the time when most of our hopes and dreams will be realized, but most of all this is a time of healing.

Following the Examples of Jesus

Jesus was just in all His ways, and although He practiced non-resistance in the most trying cases, he was tempted, persecuted, and crucified, though for a good reason. Through it all, He became our way shower and redeemer. Had He not been crucified, there would not have been a resurrection and the great opportunity for us to experience redemption. This proves that Christ-likeness does not necessarily thrive only in peace and material comfort. It is only through challenging situations that the soul is strengthened and success achieved.

It is evident from the life of Jesus that He neither judged nor condemned anyone. Rather, he saw "good" in all. An outstanding example of the compassionate spirit of Jesus stood out for me in Mark 9:38-40, when the disciple John complained to Jesus that someone who was not one of them was casting out demons in His name. Jesus was very forthright with John when He replied, "Forbid him not, for there is no man, who shall do a miracle in my name that can lightly speak evil of me. For he that is not against us is on our part."

This response from Jesus tells me that they are different routes to heaven and once the intention is to glorify God rather than self, God validates them all. We all have different viewpoints as individuals; we speak different languages; we come from different cultures, we have different likes and dislikes but we all share the individuality of Spirit, or the Christ within.

Jesus also had a way of dealing only with matters of significance. He cautioned us to stay with the matters at hand and not to gossip, judge, or criticize others, but to focus on the Christ within. In other words, no matter whom we are or what our circumstances are, we all have the Christ potential within us.

In John 21:20-22, when Peter questioned Him as to who would betray Him, Jesus answered, "What is that to thee? Follow thou me." In other words why meddle in affairs that do not concern us? Judging others is God's responsibility not humankind's. Our responsibility is to follow Jesus. If we would only try to embody these teachings of Jesus we would be much further ahead spiritually, and we would not be too hasty to condemn or judge our brother or sister.

The apostle Paul, the most devout of Christians had more than a fair share of trials and persecutions, and yet he stood his ground, acknowledging his weaknesses and using them as stepping stones. I asked myself who am I, then, to be spared the ups and downs of ministry?

Building Community through Ministry

Although we all share the individuality of the Christ, we also have personal character traits that make us unique and different from each other. As a result, the minister has to be spiritually aware so as to integrate these differences and let them work together for the good of the whole.

God made us in His image and after His likeness, and therefore each of us is an important part of creation. Although we are individualized expressions of God, we are nevertheless one with God, one with each other, and one with the universe. Therefore each of us plays an important part in creation. As we share the love of God with others, we take time to listen and pray with those in need of support. Our lives affect each other, so we should commit ourselves to a world of community through the practice of good fellowship and love for one another.

In his book *The Little Soul and the Sun*, Neale Donald Walsh uses a children's parable to demonstrate that each person is a lighted being, and therefore a necessary part of creation. In this story, although the little soul was aware of being the light, it didn't know how to express the light.

According to Walsh, God told the little soul "You are like a candle in the sun. Oh, you're there all right. Along with a million, ka-gillion other candles who make up the sun. And the sun would not be the sun without you. Nay, it would be a sun without one of its candles . . . and that would not be the sun at all; it would not shine as brightly." And that's the truth; we were all meant to shine together to make up a grand design of one powerful light. We all complement each other when we share our individual gifts with each other!

Unconditional love and acceptance of self and of others is what we need most in ministry. We live in a time when our need for connecting is stronger than ever. As some of us move from place to place every so often, we sometimes feel isolated and lonely, not being able to connect with our families, who are usually miles away from us. When our needs are not met, the minister helps to provide various opportunities for people to connect. A sense of community helps to pull us out of this isolation. This helps to improve our physical and emotional well-being.

To experience success in ministry, stability, integrity, personal maturity, and awareness must be ensued.

Responsibilities of a Minister

Having a loving consciousness of service to others and an understanding of the world and the people we serve as we go out into the field are some of the responsibilities of a minister. There can never be too much preparation emotionally, mentally, and morally, as this helps in fostering good human relationships in ministry.

Next we go to God in prayer asking for clarity, surrendering to the process, knowing that we are not alone. We then set the stage with workable techniques, focusing our attention on our vision for ministry, gathering worthwhile information from our mentors, classmates, and all those who have gone before us.

A pastoral minister should support individuals spiritually, helping them to discover their Christ potential. The ultimate work, however, rests with each individual, as knowledge from within is revealed at the appointed time. It is often said, "When the student is ready, the teacher will appear." "Howbeit when he, the spirit of truth, is come, he will guide you into all truth: for he shall not speak of himself; but whatsoever he shall hear, that shall he speak: and he will show you things to come" (John 16:13).

Although skills and knowledge are important, the minister's presence and consciousness are even more important. The minister should be authentic, vulnerable enough to facilitate trust and at the same time strong enough to instill discipline and order.

As the demands of ministry increase, the minister should spend quality time enhancing his or her spiritual life by practicing the presence of God constantly. Jesus showed us this need during His time on earth; He constantly went to the mountains to pray. "In these days he went out to the mountains to pray, and all night continued in prayer to God" (Mark 3:7).

We can never feel the pain and struggle of another, but as the minister pours himself or herself into being with the burdened person, he or she learns how to show empathy and compassion. Ultimately, the minister learns how to erase negative behavior patterns by demonstrating unconditional love.

A minister should work toward empowering people by:

1. Encouraging them to be themselves, and showing them that they too can make a difference in their lives as well as the lives of others.
2. Encouraging them to move out of their comfort zones by breaking old patterns and saying yes to new opportunities.
3. Helping others to discover their spiritual gifts.
4. Providing training.

A minister's job can be very demanding, but otherwise very rewarding; it can also be a very lonely experience, as people's expectations of the minister are usually quite high. Nevertheless, one has to strike a balance and show up according to the divine plan.

The Healing Aspect of Ministry

Practicing ministry in the field has been a very healing experience, and the practical teachings of Unity have equipped me well for this experience. One never stops learning, and the experience has taught me how to examine many aspects of myself, my strengths and my weaknesses, and to take responsibility for whatever surfaces in my life. I have also learned the power of forgiveness; how important it is to let go and let God.

Ministry is not only about healing others; it is also about healing self. It is about being open to embrace one's shortcomings without fear of losing one's power or vulnerability. It is about striking a balance between the absolute and the relative.

In our effort to experience the light, we first have to acknowledge the darkness. Being the light is a wonderful experience, but we expand and grow only by acknowledging our shortcomings and forgiving each other's misgivings. We need to acknowledge our dark side in order for the light to shine through. Ultimately, everything works for good, and whatever discomfort we experience in ministry is indicative of a necessary healing. One has to be open and receptive, and most of all surrender to the all-knowing mind of God, and challenges will then become our stepping stones. 1 Peter 4:12 says

> "Beloved think it not strange concerning the fiery trial which is to try you, as though some strange thing happened to you, but rejoice inasmuch as ye are partakers of Christ's sufferings; that when His glory shall be revealed ye may be glad also with exceeding joy."

Ministering Through Trials

Times of upheaval and uncertainty among Christian churches are not uncommon, and the minister has to set an example by exercising love, strength, faith, and patience in order for healing to take place. In the Bible St. Paul modeled this example when on one of his missionary journeys he received disturbing news from Corinth that there were some serious conflicts within the church. When he left Corinth he had left a seemingly strong and healthy following. Now he had to think of ways to settle the conflicts from afar. Paul wrote stern letters to the people, urging them to come together as one body in Christ.

Church growth involves team effort, which requires commitment, dedication, and determination not just from the minister, but from everyone. St. Paul implored the people in the church at Corinth that Christ should be first and foremost in everything. He reminded them that the Christ couldn't be divided, as the mind of Christ is the only mind there is. He encouraged them to stay focused in one accord despite outer distractions.

> "Now I beseech you, brethren, by the name of our Lord Jesus Christ, that ye all speak the same thing, and that there be no divisions among you; but that

> ye be perfectly joined together in the same mind and in the same judgment"(1 Corinthians 1:10).

Paul's model is a good example for Christian fellowship, and it reminds us that although there are ups and downs in ministry, everything works for good when we are guided by the Christ's principles. There will always be oppositions, differences of opinions, and outer disturbances, but Paul showed us how to focus our attention on the prize to be won—peace and happiness in the realization of the Christ presence within.

Paul's examples of humility are truly essential tools to experience and demonstrate the Christ Spirit within. Nevertheless, he confesses in his humanity that he is capable of erring just like anyone else, and that the journey of a Christian leader is no easier than the journey of a follower, as temptations do come to the best of us. Paul's distinction, however, comes from his willingness to take responsibility by acknowledging his mistakes and starting all over again. In 1 Cor. 15:31 he says, "I die daily."

Paul admits that living the Christian life is not an easy road to victory. To stay focused when temptations arise takes a lot of strength. It is always a struggle, and overcoming it requires the qualities of self-assertiveness, self-restraint, sound judgment, a strong determination, and the will to succeed.

> "For that which I do, I allow not: for what I would, that do I not, but what I hate, that I do . . . I find then a law, that, when I would do good, evil is present with me. For I delight in the law of God after the inward man: But I see another law in my members, warring against the law of my mind, and bringing me into captivity to the law of sin which is in my members" (Romans 7:15, 21-23).

Practicing ministry as a female Unity minister has its fair share of challenges in the island of St. Croix. People in the

Caribbean are mostly traditional in their religious beliefs, and Unity's non-traditionalism and spiritual practices and beliefs are often challenged, criticized, and confused with other religions.

Many people are also of the fixed notion that a minister should be male in gender. Consequently, a female minister, especially one that appears young, attractive, and modern generates a lot of speculation and skepticism. As one's authenticity is often questioned, one therefore has to employ a deep level of spirituality in order to combat such notions.

I once visited a traditional church here on the island where all ministers in the congregation were asked to identify themselves by raising their hands. I raised my hand and it became obvious that I was deliberately overlooked. In his remarks, the minister made it clear in no uncertain terms that a woman's place is not behind the podium as a minister, but in other subordinate roles.

I left the church that day feeling sorry for the minister, whose ego had allowed him to be cold, calculating, and insensitive. I thought about Jesus' examples of humility, and His ability to express and demonstrate love and compassion in the most trying circumstances, and wondered which one of His examples was being portrayed in this minister's attitude. This incidence left me wondering about our intention as ministers, and how much work we still have to do in order to perfect the teachings of Jesus.

We are all children of God made in His image and likeness, but with the privilege of free choice we are also capable of erring. Erring is not all bad, however, as it allows us the opportunity of introspection, leading to further awareness and transformation.

Ministers are supposed to be God's chosen people who have a responsibility to lead the flock. They are nevertheless fallible just like anyone else. To be Christ-like is to be honest, acknowledging our shortcoming and our limitations. It is very important to be authentic and true no matter how often we fall short. God is always merciful to us. The apostle Paul was one of the most outstanding Christians who displayed the most humble and sincere characteristics. He often wrote about how difficult it is to be a Christian!

Jesus, God's chosen son, displayed His humanity on more than one occasion, which proved that He was real. During the raising of Lazarus, He expressed His humanity and *He wept* (John 11:35). He also expressed His humanity when He became angry at the people who used the temple for the wrong purposes. "And Jesus went into the temple of God, and cast out all them that sold and bought in the temple, and overthrew the tables of the moneychangers, and the seats of them that sold doves" (Matthew 21:12).

In the creation story, God created us perfect. "So God created man in His own image, in the image of God created he Him" (Genesis 1:27). Yet we are very far from the image of perfection. "There is none righteous, no not one" (Romans 3:10). These two statements are an interesting dichotomy. We were made in the image and likeness of God, who made us perfect, but unfortunately, because of wrongful living, we have not lived up to that state of perfection. "Thou wast perfect in thy ways from the day that thou wast created, till inequity was found in thee" (Ezekiel 28:15). We all aspire to live the perfected life, but in our humanity we go up and down the ladder of perfection.

My journey as a Unity minister has had its fair share of challenges, and like Paul, I continue in the struggle, dying daily to my little self, knowing that love is the answer. It has become increasingly clear that my experiences in St. Croix relate to a healing and transformation of my soul, subsequently leading to clarity of mission and purpose through various challenges. As the journey continues, I am grateful that through it all I am cultivating spiritual understanding and learning to exercise divine wisdom.

"And my speech and my preaching was not with enticing words of man's wisdom, but in demonstration of the spirit and of power: That your faith should not stand in the wisdom of men but in the power of God". (I Corinthians 2:4-5).

24

From Darkness to Light

"A new womb will come forth from the tomb of darkness."

Na'im Akbar

"Every new situation we face in life sends us back into the womb of darkness. Like an embryo we must go through changes to become whole, healthy, and complete. We may feel lonely, confused, or frightened. In reality we are growing, developing, evolving."

Iyanla Vanzant

"To everything there is a season, and a time for every purpose under the heaven: A time to be born, and a time to die; a time to die and a time to pluck up that, which is planted; A time to kill and a time to heal; a time to break down and a time to build up; A time to weep and a time to laugh; a time to mourn and a time to dance; A time to cast away stones, and a time to gather stones together; a time to embrace and a time to refrain from embracing; A time to get and a time to lose; a time to keep and a time to cast away; A time to rend and a time to sew; a time to keep silence and a time to speak; A time to love and a time to hate; a time of war and a time of peace." (Ecclesiastics 3:1-8)

No matter how dark the road may appear, the light of God, which is always shining, can be experienced at any given moment. A life filled with sunshine and roses alone would soon lose its flavor, and so the darkness serves its purpose, which is to deepen our appreciation of life.

Challenges are intimidating, but as there is no resurrection without a crucifixion, we likewise cannot experience victory without a challenge. Ultimately, every experience in life works for good. Not only do challenges give us the opportunity to step up on the ladder of self-realization, but they also give us the opportunity to achieve "Christ consciousness," becoming one with the Christ and one with all of God's creation. The giver of the gift, God, is the true inexorable substance from whom every perfect gift comes, and when we are resurrected in consciousness we become one with substance, or one with the gift. In this realization we call forth whatever we desire, and it is done unto us.

Nevertheless, a spiritual crisis can be a very disconcerting experience, especially after a long period of spiritual connectedness and belonging. In her book *Mysticism*, Evelyn Underhill says, "The dark night is really a human process in which the self, which thought itself so spiritual, so firmly established upon the super-sensual plane, is forced to turn back, to leave the light, and pick up those qualities which it had left behind."

Sometimes difficulties arise not to hurt us, but to awaken our spiritual potential and to lead us into greener pastures. If we should get discouraged, we would only miss the grand opportunity to experience a rebirth of our souls, and ultimately a resurrected consciousness. God never leaves us during times of adversity. He is with us in every experience and wants to give us the best.

Just as there is darkness and light, there are also two sides to everything in life: a positive and a negative. Both sides, however, are just opposite ends of the same stick. To find the solution to our challenges in life is to find a balance between these two variables. The writer of the book of Ecclesiastics believes that all our experiences in life are for a divine purpose, and consequently there is a time for everything under the sun. Each day is a new day to change old ways and experience the light of God through new beginnings. Our aim is to arrive at a place of "self-realization" even in the midst of trials and tribulations, where we see God in everything. "We glory in tribulations also; knowing that tribulation worketh patience; And patience experience; and experience, hope" (Romans 5:3-4).

Sometimes challenges seem insurmountable when we face failure, disappointments, sadness, and tragedy, and sometimes we feel spiritually disconnected, as our prayers seem futile. This seemed to be my experience some time ago, when after completing six years in the field of ministry facilitating radio broadcasts, workshops, and worship services I found myself further and further from inner satisfaction. My personal life seemed empty and unfulfilled; my family and my friends distant. As the answer seemed elusive, I sat each day waiting and hoping that the dark night would end. A lack of spiritual connectedness made me question my original beliefs, and I found myself completely in the void, anxiously awaiting a reconnection with the Divine. In her book *Anatomy For the Spirit*, Carolyn Miss says "Waiting and becoming is the symbolic meaning of being called to ordination—that is, allowing the Divine to awaken part of your spirit that contains the essence of what you are capable of contributing to others as well as to yourself."

Despite the feelings of emptiness, I had a great resolve that I would eventually find myself, and the dark night would end. I tried to unleash my encaged emotions and make a distinction between the real and the surreal inwardly—through prayer and meditation—and outwardly through writing. Through this medium I was able to redefine my original intention and mission, ultimately bringing parity between my inner and outer worlds while waiting with expectancy for divine instructions on how to proceed.

Cultivating the Will to Succeed

Nothing happens before the right time, and it sometimes takes a period of time for the soul to find release from pain and mental struggle. Sometimes in our humanity we may become willful and seek a particular outcome to a situation, but we need to pray for patience and surrender to the will of God, as God in His wisdom knows best and sees a better way for us always. "'For my thoughts are not your thoughts, neither are your ways my ways,' saith the Lord" (Isaiah 55:8).

The way out of all mental, emotional, and even physical pain is to lift our thoughts higher to the presence and power of Christ within us. Of ourselves we can do nothing. It is the Christ within us who does the work. Cultivating the will to succeed requires patience, strength, faith, and courage. With sheer determination and will to succeed, the battle will be won.

Job, who was a righteous man, experienced this type of mental struggle when in his distress, he declared

> "Behold I go forward, but He is not there; and backward, but I cannot perceive Him: On the left hand where He doth work, but I cannot behold Him: He hideth Himself on the right hand, that I cannot see Him: But He knoweth the way I take: When He hath tried me, I shall come forth as gold" (Job 23:8-10).

Even though it might seem difficult to make a spiritual connection with the divine presence during our challenges, it is important not to neglect our prayer times. We need to persevere in our difficulties with a sincere effort to find the peace of God within us. There is no situation in our lives that the spirit of God cannot conquer or transform, but we need to surrender to God's presence within us and know with deep abiding faith that we shall overcome. As difficult as things appeared, Job persevered through it all, never failing to acknowledge God. Eventually, Job won the battle, and God blessed him more abundantly than before.

When we acknowledge our powerlessness as Job did, this is a signal that we are approaching our day of resurrection. It means that God is weaning us off the dependence on outer things so that He can show us a better way. It means that God is calling us higher, but we need to spend more time with Him in the silence, trusting His divine plan of good for us.

Looking back over my life since I entered the field of ministry, I have had many challenges. Past experiences of demonstrating Good in an instant sometimes seemed distant, staying focused sometimes difficult, and sometimes even God seemed out of reach and even non-existent.

Many wonderful things have materialized in my life nevertheless, but my spiritual goals seemed nowhere in sight. Although I felt spiritually disconnected, I was still convinced that there had to be a bigger picture, and so I tried desperately to hold on to my faith, knowing that soon the dark clouds would disappear, and I would once again rise above all my challenges.

I continued in my effort to find my balance, but challenges continued to confront me one after the other, warning me that my healing work was still in progress. One morning I awoke with a dizzy feeling that warranted urgent medical attention. As prayer has always been my defense, I was never one to visit the doctor's office, but on this occasion it became evident that my prayer connection had been short-circuited, and it became necessary for me to integrate my spirituality with some form of physical therapy, in this case to seek medical attention.

I headed toward the doctor's office somewhat overwhelmed by my feelings, apprehensive, and confused. I was taken aback when my diagnosis revealed highly elevated blood pressure. This was certainly a wake-up call, and I took responsibility for what showed up, becoming more conscious of my daily routine, vowing to listen to my body, and to do whatever I could to keep my health and spirituality in check.

A few weeks following my health diagnosis, I traveled to Atlanta, Georgia to visit my siblings and to facilitate a workshop. As we shopped in the mall one day, we decided to have our blood pressure checked by an automatic machine. The band around my arm kept expanding and expanding. *This must be an error*, I thought. I started it over and over again, but there was no mistake. My blood pressure registered 201/134. My sister being a registered nurse, went wild with panic. With a reading like that she could hardly believe that I had energy to walk. She insisted on taking me to the emergency room, as she sensed trouble, but I assured her that I was all right. She later resorted to administering some home remedy, promptly making an appointment for me to see the doctor the following day.

By then my blood pressure had reduced somewhat, but it was still dangerously high. The doctor was alarmed at my high blood pressure reading, did an electrocardiograph, and immediately put me on medication (something I never thought I would ever need).

I spent Thanksgiving Day in Georgia, and immediately after returning to St. Croix, I continued to have dizzy feelings. By then other accompanying symptoms surfaced—frequent urination, blurred vision, and excessive thirst, so once more it became necessary to pay another visit to the doctor's office. After outlining my symptoms, the doctor who decided to test my blood sugar was in for another shock, as my glucose reading was so high that it went off the scale. Unfortunately, my worst fear was confirmed. I was a diabetic!

The doctor advised me to go to the lab to take a blood test and return to see him at his office the following week regarding the result. The day following my test I received an emergency call from the doctor's office. My glucose reading had registered seven hundred!

The doctor was puzzled. "With a reading like that you should be in the hospital receiving insulin," he told me. I assured him that I felt fine, but he advised me to check into the emergency room if there were any signs of weakness. I never did, as I did not have any such feeling.

I went to see my doctor the following week, and it was confirmed that I had type 2, diabetes. I took the news with a calm demeanor, affirming wholeness and perfection and seeing myself whole and well.

After a few months of trying to see the good in the situation, I saw clearly that this was indeed a wake-up call, as I had definitely taken my health for granted. Since then I have become much more aware of my body's needs and functions, and I saw the importance of adequate diet and exercise in my daily routine. I continue to give God thanks each day that through His grace and mercy I sought medical attention at the appointed time, and that my health was not completely jeopardized.

The spiritual journey is long and challenging at times, and healing of mind, body, and spirit is necessary in order to progress spiritually. Although I became more health conscious, my spirituality continued at low ebb, and although I do not profess to be in the category of a saint by any means, I firmly believe that my discomfiture is the result of some form of purification. Evelyn Underhill writes in *Mysticism,* "Psychologically, then, the 'Dark Night of the Soul' is due to the double fact of the exhaustion of an old state, and the growth towards a new state of consciousness."

During the many challenges I endured, I gradually began to see the light when I decided to surrender to the will of God. The lesson for me was to trust and wait. Nothing lasts forever, and nothing happens before the right time. When everything seems despondent and desolate, suddenly new life bursts into bloom, and everything changes in an instant—without warning. The warm spring comes after the cold winter. This was the consolation and the prize; an end, a new beginning, and a new me!

25

Strength in Weakness

No matter how many times we have endured trials and challenges, as long as we are physically alive there will always be a need to exercise strength, as there is always something to overcome mentally, physically, or spiritually.

Challenges help us to develop our spiritual muscles; they enable us to become stronger. Strength, according to author Charles Fillmore in *The Revealing Word*, is "the energy of God; freedom from weakness; stability of character; power to withstand temptation; capacity to accomplish. Strength is physical, mental and spiritual. All strength, originate in Spirit."

Sometimes we tend to shrink away from certain tasks thinking that we are too weak, but that is the very reason why God chose us for those tasks. Instead of the wise and the noble filling the front line of God's army, we find the foolish, the weak, and the despised. This is because God wants to make His strength perfect in our weakness. God can and will turn around any difficult situation into a blessing.

Looking back over our lives, most of us have been overwhelmed at one time or another with situations we never thought we could handle, and we often wonder how we ever handled them. The truth is—we didn't. God did, through us. The reason we become overwhelmed is that we of ourselves do not know how to stand against trials, but God within us does. In 1 Corinthians 1:25-28 Paul writes

> "The foolishness of God is wiser than men; the weakness of God is stronger than men. For ye see your calling brethren how not many wise men after the flesh, not many mighty, not many noble are called. But God has chosen the foolish things of the world to confound the things which are mighty; and base things of the world, and things which are despised, hath God chosen, yea, and things which are not, to bring to naught things that are."

All our overcoming experiences are attributed to the strength of God within us. Of ourselves we can do nothing. We need to know when to do and when not to do, and we should never lose awareness of the omnipotent, omniscient, and omnipresent God; we should worship Him and Him only should we serve. All the glory belongs to God, who in His goodness gives wisdom and power liberally to all men.

The ego is the biggest barrier that separates us from our good. Without the help from God we are bound for failure right away. King Uzziah in the second chapter of Chronicles learned this reality in a harsh way. "And he made in Jerusalem engines, invented by cunning men to be on the towers, and upon the bulwarks to shoot arrows and great stones withal. And his name spread far abroad; for he was marvelously helped, till he was strong" (2 Chronicles 26:15).

Having become successful, Uzziah developed a haughty spirit thinking that he had achieved his successes on his own merit. As a result, He disregarded God and burned incense in God's temple, a ritual that was reserved only for priests. "But when he was strong, his heart was lifted up to his destruction; for he transgressed against the Lord his God, and went into the temple of the lord to burn incense upon the altar of incense" (26:16).

God is love, and He does not inflict punishment on his children. God has nothing to do with the pain we feel as result of willfulness. When we miss the mark we punish ourselves according to the law of cause and effect, which is perfect and just. If we know that fire burns, for instance, and we deliberately put our hand in the fire, we have no one to blame for the burn we receive but ourselves for our carelessness. Similarly, Uzziah paid a price for his willfulness and disobedience when he developed leprosy, a self-punishment for burning incense on the altar of the Lord. "And Uzziah the king was a leper unto the day of his death and dwelt in a several house, being a leper; for he was cut off from the house of the Lord" (2 Chronicles 26:21).

In Judges Chapter 6, Gideon presented quite the opposite scenario. In contrast to Uzziah, Gideon was very humble, and because of his humility God worked in and through him—despite the disobedience of the Israelites—to strengthen him in all that he did.

After the children of Israel were delivered into the hand of the Midianites for seven years, they cried unto the Lord, who sent a prophet to deliver them. An angel of the Lord appeared to Gideon and told him that the Lord was with him. "The Lord is with thee, thou mighty man of valor" (Judges 6:12). But Gideon didn't understand. If God was with him, why were there so many calamities in their lives?

Gideon was doubtful. God, however, commissioned him to save the Israelites from the Midianites, reassuring him that he should have no fear because He would be with him. Gideon still doubted that the Lord was really with him, and in his humility Gideon besieged God, "O my Lord, wherein shall I save Israel? Behold my family is poor in Mannaseh and I am the least in my father's house."

Once again the Lord reassured Gideon that His presence within him was all that he needed in order to be successful.

Gideon nevertheless continued to ask God for further signs, and after receiving them he was finally convinced that God was really with him.

The Midianites were finally defeated, and the men of Israel who witnessed this victory praised Gideon, besieging him to be their ruler. In his humility, Gideon acknowledged that he of himself did nothing, but that it was the power of God working in and through him that made them victorious. "I will not rule over you, neither will my son rule over you: the Lord shall rule over you" (Judges 8:23). Gideon constantly acknowledged God as the only power and presence in his life, and he was successful in battle despite the disobedience of the children of Israel.

As we cross rivers and overcome battles, we should always give God the glory. Whenever we acknowledge God as the giver of all good things and surrender to His presence, we will find the strength within to continue on our journey and accomplish mighty things.

We can do nothing without God. We develop our faculty of strength when we learn to wait on God. "But they who wait upon the Lord shall renew their strength; they shall mount up with wings as eagles; they shall run, and not be weary; and they shall walk and not faint" (Isaiah 40:31). When the people of Israel were faced with the task of rebuilding Jerusalem, the great leader Nehemiah reminded them, "In God we will have success!" (Nehemiah 2: 20).

In another example, David, who was grounded in spiritual love, displayed both spiritual and physical strength and disarmed the formidable Goliath, convincingly defeating him in battle. In 1 Samuel 17:47, David said to Goliath, *"And this assembly shall know that the Lord saveth not with sword and spear: for the battle is the Lord's, and He will give you into our hands."*

No one is exempt to seeming failure and the subsequent experience of weakness, even when we do our best. The apostle Paul, who was a profound Christian, had his moments of weaknesses as well. In 2 Cor.13:9-10 he relates, "And he said unto me, "My grace is sufficient for thee: for my strength is made perfect in weakness." Therefore I take pleasure in infirmities, in reproaches, in necessities, in persecutions, in distresses for Christ's sake: for when I am weak, then am I strong." There is always a blessing attached to our moments of weaknesses, and should we become frightened or discouraged, we would only delay our good and lose the blessing.

To develop strength in weakness requires:

- Patience

"Wait on the Lord, and keep his way, and He shall exalt thee to inherit the land" (Psalm 37:34).

- Humility

"If my people which are called by my name shall humble themselves and pray, and seek my face, and turn from their wicked ways: then I will hear from heaven, and will forgive their sin, and will heal their land" (2 Chronicles 7:14).

- Trust

"Trust in the Lord with all thine heart: and lean not unto thine own understanding. In all thy ways acknowledge Him, and He shall direct thy paths" (Proverbs 3:5).

By the grace of God I am learning to surrender to the process, and I watch in awe as my inner strength takes precedence over my weaknesses. I bless the many challenges that face me each day, as through it all I get the opportunity to develop my spirituality and exercise my God-given strength. "Not by might, not by power, but by my spirit says the Lord."

26

Why Worry When we Can pray?

> "Worry is a small trickle of fear that meanders through the mind until it cuts a channel into which all other thoughts are drained."
>
> Anonymous

> "Worry is putting question marks where God has put periods."
>
> John R. Rice

> "Worry is the interest we pay on tomorrow's troubles."
>
> E. Stanley Jones

Some people worry at the drop of a pin—whether things are good or whether things are bad. Worry, however, changes nothing, and most of the time what we usually worry about seldom happens, anyway.

Prayer is the antidote for worry, so why worry when we can pray? "When these things shall come upon thee, if thou will call upon the Lord and obey His voice, then the Lord will turn thy captivity and have compassion on thee" (Deut. 30:1-3).

Worry is sometimes inevitable as we go through our human experiences, but God is always with us; God understands our weaknesses; He is working with us, not against us.

> "There hath no temptation taken you but such as is common to man: but God is faithful, who will not suffer you to be tempted above that ye are able; but will with the temptation also make a way to escape, that ye may be able to bear it" (1 Cor. 10:13).

Whatever we dwell on will become a reality in our lives, and thus the more attention we give to challenges the bigger and more overwhelming they will become. If we concentrate on hardships and limitation, that is what we will experience. However, if we concentrate on the presence of God within us, we will experience an abundance of every good thing in our lives. "In all thy ways acknowledge Him and He will direct our paths" (Proverbs 3:6).

We should not worry, because God is always there for us. He is the only presence and the only power in our lives, and He is always willing to bless us with good. To experience His presence, however, we need to desire Him and seek Him with all our hearts. "My God shall supply all your needs according to His riches in glory" (Philippians 4:19).

Worry is actually wrong thinking (of the mind) and wrong feeling (of the heart). We tend to worry only because we falsely believe that we are separate and apart from God. This unfortunately results in hardships and all types of limitation. No matter who we are, or what we have done, the truth is God is within everyone, equally present, and we can never be separated from Him except through our minds. "In Him we live, move, and have our being" (Acts 17:28).

We do not have to ask others to do the work for us, nor do we have to look in distant places for our good. It is right within our very reach. "Neither shall they say lo here, or lo there, for behold the kingdom of God is within you" (Luke 17:21). We gain access to this divine presence any time we choose through constant prayer and meditation.

We all face challenges from time to time, but they do not last, nor do they have power over us. Despite our many trials, God never leaves us or forsakes us, and when we seek Him there is always a blessing in store for us.

A very encouraging story is told about James Cash Perry, who it is said came from a long line of Baptist preachers. He grew up with deep convictions, and he was unwaveringly honest. He never smoked nor drank, and he was a hard worker. It has been told that in 1929 when the Great Depression hit, Perry found himself in crisis. He had made unwise commitments and they turned out sour. Perry began to worry about them, and soon he was unable to sleep. He developed a painful case of shingles and was hospitalized. His anxiety only increased in the hospital, and it seemed resistant to tranquilizers and drugs.

His mental state deteriorated. He later said, "I was broken nervously and physically, filled with despair, unable to see even a ray of hope. I had nothing to live for. I felt I hadn't a friend left in the whole world; that even my family turned against me."

One night he felt so oppressed he didn't think his heart would hold out, and expecting to die before morning, he sat down and wrote farewell letters to his wife and sons. He did live through the night, however, and the next morning he heard singing coming from the little hospital chapel. "Be not dismayed whate'er betide *God will take care of you.*" Entering the chapel he listened to the song, to the scripture reading, and to the prayer. "Suddenly," he said, "something happened. I can't explain it. I only call it a miracle. I felt as if I had been instantly lifted out of the darkness of a dungeon into warm brilliant sunlight."

All worry left him, as he realized more fully than he had ever imagined just how much the Lord Jesus cared for him. From that day, J.C. Perry was never plagued with worry, and he later called those moments in the chapel "the most dramatic and glorious twenty minutes of my life."

During challenging times, we need to trust God, and He will work things out for us. On the way to the Promised Land when the Israelites faced numerous challenges, Moses reminded them that God was with them and He would see them through their difficulties. "Do not be afraid. Stand firm and see the salvation of the Lord, which He will accomplish for you today. For the Egyptians whom you see today you shall never see again" (Exodus 14:13-14). This truth was enacted over and over again during their journey as long as they did what was required of them and served the Lord.

Throughout the entire Bible are God's promises that God is with us always, even during the most trying circumstances. "Lo I am with you always, even until the end of the world" (Matt. 28:20). Matthew reminds us that if God provides for the sparrows, even more so will He provide for His children. "Take no thought what you shall eat or what you shall drink for your heavenly father knoweth that you have need of all these things. But seek ye first the kingdom of God and His righteousness; and all these things will be added unto you" (Matthew 6:31-33).

God is always with us. He understands our weaknesses, our pain, and even our inability to pray when things seem insurmountable. It is always certain that the dark clouds will disappear, and God's presence and blessings will once more become a reality. "Likewise the Spirit also helpeth our infirmities: for we know not what we should pray for as we ought: but the Spirit itself maketh intercession for us with groanings which cannot be uttered. And He that searchest the hearts knoweth what is the mind of the Spirit, because he maketh intercession for the saints according to the will of God" (Romans: 26-27).

Worrying is actually counter-productive. It actually breaks down our bodies and makes us vulnerable to all manner of diseases. Treating the symptoms of worry does not remove the cause. To eradicate worry in its entirety is to remove the cause, and the cause of worry is actually wrong thinking and wrong feeling. Therefore, to remove it is to deny that unforeseen consequences and conditions have power over us and affirm God in the situation.

Sometimes we may not have control over what happens to us, but we do have control over our thoughts. Deepak Chopra says in *The Seven Spiritual Laws of Success*

> "We cannot try to have a positive attitude, but our attitude will change if our choices are appropriate. The choices will produce a change in thought. Every thought is a memory, or a desire; an interpretation or a choice. We are infinite choice makers and interpreters. If we choose conscious choice-making from a deep level, then we can create what we want."

We should always endeavor to entertain thoughts that are inspiring, uplifting, and productive, and we will subsequently reap after their kind. The apostle Paul agrees with this truth in Philippians 4:8.

> "Whatsoever things are true, whatsoever things are honest, whatsoever things are just, whatsoever things are pure, whatsoever things are lovely, whatsoever things are of good report; if there be any virtue, and if there be any praise, think on these things."

Turning now to God during times of uncertainty I focus my attention on Thee O God, and what peaceful thoughts fill my mind! Your presence fills me with hope, peace and strength. When I am engulfed in fear and worry the encouraging promises of Jesus give me hope. In this moment of surrender,

Your love heals me, strengthens me, and liberates my entire being. I feel free from all tension and stress, as I cast all my cares on You.

Attuned to your presence, dear God, I find the answers I seek. I know what to do and I have the courage to do it. I keep my mind and heart centered in You, dear God, and I lift my vision above any thoughts of lack or limitation knowing that with you all things are possible. Thank You God, for this marvelous realization of Your divine presence within me, which is the answer to all that I seek. Amen.

27

Talks on Healing

The most devout Christian sometimes experiences times of uncertainty. My mother was one of them. She was a survivor in more ways than one. Not only was she capable of demonstrating supply in times of need, but she also demonstrated healing as she conquered life-threatening illnesses.

Healing takes place at different levels. One can be healed physically and yet not spiritually. Unfortunately, physical healing does not last if one doesn't have the consciousness to maintain it. Spiritual healing, however, is a deeper concept in which there is a total surrender of the soul to God, and one accepts whatever the outcome may be, even death. In the book *Healing Words*, Larry Dossey, MD states

> "During illness the quiet way of being we've been examining flows from one's true center. It is focused, authentic, genuine, and accepting of any outcome. It is not self-conscious and contains no pity for the 'I' who is sick. It is not contaminated by fear of death and contains no fear or guilt."

During my second year in high school my mother was hospitalized because of an illness. I guess my older sisters thought that I was too young to be told the nature of the illness, but deep down I knew it was something serious. Her absence from home while she stayed in the hospital was greatly experienced, and our home felt empty without her.

Prayers from my family and friends were fervent, and there were many anxious moments as we awaited her return home. Finally, the time came when she returned home, and we were thankful to God that her healing was in progress.

Many, many years after my mother's healing experience, she faced yet another challenge. This happened soon after I finally made it into ministerial school which, for me was a very big achievement and an outstanding demonstration of faith. Not only was I going to live in a country with severe cold conditions, but I was previously daunted with fear, as I had never been to college ever before.

Having survived the first term, I was overjoyed. I felt a sense of achievement. At the end of the second term I was even more ecstatic. My term evaluation was satisfactory, and I would be able to go home for the Christmas holidays. Reconnecting with family and friends would give me an opportunity to unwind and recharge my batteries so that I could return to school refreshed and energized. How I looked forward to this time of renewal!

My exuberance was only short-lived however, as a couple days prior to my departure I received a telephone call from my sister with what appeared to be the worst-case scenario about my mother's health. She had been ailing for some time, and she had now been diagnosed with cancer. I was devastated, and being away from family and friends did not make it any easier.

Finding myself in a state of denial, my irrational mind told me that the diagnosis must be wrong. This was my mother. *Only some people got cancer*, I thought. People who have cancer eventually died and I could not and did not want to think that not only did *my* mother have cancer, but she could also eventually die from cancer.

My mother was a good person who lived a Christian life, and I questioned why she would get cancer. I searched for the answers, secretly wondering what my mother did to deserve this. I hated to even entertain such a preposterous thought, and I quickly changed my trend of thinking, conceding that my mother had done absolutely nothing wrong.

I chose not to question God, trusting that through her illness His works would be made manifest. And so I prayed for spiritual and physical healing for my mother and understanding and faith for myself, hoping that despite the outcome my mother would be at peace with herself, with everyone else, and with God.

All things considered, I went home for Christmas that first year of my ministerial training, trying hard to exemplify a positive attitude and a courageous spirit as a minister. It wasn't until then that I finally heard the truth about my mother's previous illness many years ago. At the age of forty-four, my mother had been diagnosed with cervical cancer. She was miraculously healed after receiving surgical treatment, and she went on to live another forty years. That information was like music to my ears, and my deflated spirit was somehow mended, being confident that history would repeat itself.

As a consequence of my mother's illness, the entire family went home for Christmas. We had a grand family reunion, which was quite a treat, as we had not all been together for quite some time. That Christmas was my best Christmas ever, and I felt that the rest of my siblings shared the same sentiment. We spent quality time with each other and with our mother, communicating with her at a deep level, and I could tell from my mother's calm demeanor that she treasured those moments and felt loved and nurtured by us all.

My mother was calm and peaceful, and although the unanimous decision was not to divulge the doctor's diagnosis to her, she must have guessed that something was amiss, as this was the first time in many years we all had come together to celebrate Christmas with her and with each other all at the same time. The doting attention she received and our appreciation of each other was surreal, and as a result of her illness we received many gifts:

1. Our interaction with each other improved.

We connected with our mother, with each other, and with God at a much deeper level. Our communication greatly improved, as we were more open and honest, listening more intently and speaking less. We exercised understanding and compassion, accepting and appreciating each other without blaming or fault-finding.

2. Our prayer times accelerated.

We realized that everything was in God's hands, so we learned to trust by focusing on the power and presence of God. My mother never stopped praying despite the writhing pain she felt. There were times when, in her humanity like Job, she questioned God, but she knew that God was with her always.

Her peaceful attitude reflected the state of her soul, and it was obvious that she was at peace with God, with herself, and with everyone in our family. Unfortunately, I was not around to hold her hand and look in her eyes at her passing, but my sisters told me about the peaceful look on her face as she passed, that she looked like an angel.

3. We learned to appreciate life and to live one moment at a time.

We did whatever we could to support and assist her in her needs, and we left the rest to God. Mother never took anything for granted. She appreciated each new day and tried to make the most of it. She read extensively, kept up with current happenings, and savored each moment. She enjoyed her friends and her family, and took time to smell the roses.

4. Most of all, we learned to trust God.

We acknowledged God as creator and sustainer of all life. We knew that His divine plan is always at work and it is always good. God was in charge, and we prayed for strength to accept whatever the outcome would be.

Despite our positive outlook and our proclaimed faith and acceptance of the manifestation, there were moments when I strived to come to terms with the reality of the situation, and my soul searching continually surfaced, often wondering why my mother, who was such a profound Christian, would get sick and suffer so much pain and discomfort prior to her passing. In my quest to justify my mother's illness, I rationalized that there must be a bigger purpose to our suffering that we cannot see, and consoled myself that God is mysterious and His ways are perfect and just.

Despite this acknowledgment, however, I had many questions; I rationalized within the sphere of my own limited reasoning, secretly questioning if there could possibly be any relevance in equating holiness with health, and wondering if illnesses could possibly be a result of spiritual malpractice or shortcoming. But there are more questions than answers, as there have been countless cases of sinful people who have never experienced a single health-related issue all throughout their lives.

The mystery of the Divine will then continue to intrigue us, as this assumption has absolutely no base on which to stand! In John 9:2-3 when the disciples asked Jesus, "Master, who did sin, this man or his parents that he was born blind?" Jesus answered, "Neither hath this man sinned nor his parents: but that the works of God should be made manifest in him."

There is always a divine plan at work and a purpose for everything in life, and the passing of Lazarus in the gospel of John revealed many such truths. When Lazarus died, many of the Jews were skeptical of Jesus. They had many questions. "If Jesus opened the eyes of the blind, why couldn't he prevent this man from dying?" they asked. But Jesus had an agenda. He already knew their thoughts, and He wanted to demonstrate the power of God by calling Lazarus forth from the tomb right before the very eyes of the Jews.

Jesus also prepared both Mary and Martha for the ensuing miracle: It was Mary's belief that Lazarus would be raised at the resurrection, on the last day, but Jesus enlightened her by telling her "I am the resurrection and the life: he that believeth in me, though he were dead, yet shall he live: and whosoever liveth and believerth in me shall never die" (John 11:25-26).

Sometime later when Jesus told the people to take away the stone from the tomb, Martha cautioned Him that there might be a stench, as Lazarus had been dead for four days. Jesus also said to her, "Said I not unto thee, that, if thou wouldest believe, thou shouldest see the glory of God?" (John 11:40).

There must have been a divine purpose for the death of Lazarus, as when Jesus first heard of the death of Lazarus, He told His disciples, "I am glad for your sakes that I was not there to the intent ye may believe" (John 11:15). After the death and resurrection of Lazarus the purpose of Jesus was fulfilled, as many people came to believe in Jesus.

This message helps to reinforce our belief there is a divine purpose in every dark period of our lives, even death, as God is all-present, all-powerful, and all-knowing. We should therefore be confident in embracing all circumstances, knowing God knows best and all things work together for good (Romans 8:28).

Faith and Healing

Faith is an important ingredient in our lives, but the working of our faith is even more important. Myrtle Fillmore, cofounder of Unity, demonstrated the working of her faith at the age of forty when she was told that she had tuberculosis, a diagnosis that the doctors thought was incurable. In her quest for wholeness, she was divinely led to a spiritual conference that was to change her life forever. She was told during a lecture that as a child of God she could not possibly inherit any sickness or disease. She held on to this truth and believed it with all her might, affirming, moment-by-moment, that she was whole and perfect.

Believing that her body had intelligence, she often spoke to the organs, tissues, and cells of her body, praising them for having served her well and asking forgiveness for her unintentional abuse. Her healing process subsequently began, and within a couple of years, not only was she completely healed of her condition, but she also continued to live for another forty years.

Through her quest for wholeness, Myrtle Fillmore's faith in the goodness of God led her to a remarkable healing experience. She ultimately discovered the truth that human beings are divine, and that illnesses, or diseases, are considered a part of a natural order and not a sign of ethical, moral, or spiritual weakness. Myrtle Fillmore's self-discovery not only helped with her own liberation, it also initiated the liberation of millions of people throughout the world with the birth of Silent Unity, a profound prayer ministry that began as a consequence of her healing over one hundred years ago. Myrtle Fillmore's healing proves that God is in charge in health, sickness, and in death, and He works in mysterious ways, His wonders to perform.

During my mother's illness, the healing story of Myrtle Fillmore presented to me a divine outworking of God's divine purpose, and through her example of faith I was enabled to regroup and rekindle my faith in the power of God to restore health. I acknowledged that with God all things are possible, not just for some people, but for all people.

After my family's reunion at the time of my mother's illness, I returned to school after the Christmas holidays and engaged in a prayer marathon, often going to the prayer chapel at Unity Village, praying fervently for a divine outcome to my mother's illness. As a new light of understanding began to dawn, I began to see my mother in a different light; love, admiration, and respect for her flooded my entire being. Knowing that she constantly lived a life of prayer and demonstrated her faith in believing, I had no doubt that this time would be no different from the first time she was healed. I had a strong resolve that she would do it again a second time around, and the more solace I sought, the more the grace of God beckoned me into complete acceptance. After a while, it didn't matter if the healing was physical or not; I knew that the grace of God was my sufficiency, and His grace would be made perfect in my weakness. I trusted that through it all my mother's spiritual healing would be realized and she would be able to confess as Paul did in Philippians 1:21: "For to me to live is Christ, and to die is gain."

I had faith that the many prayers offered on my mother's behalf would be heard. I was filled with hope and handed over all my fears and anxieties to God, who is all-knowing, all-powerful and always present. I was open and receptive to the lessons to be learned, and I envisioned my mother infused with God's light and peace that passes all understanding.

God is the Only Power

Illnesses and pain have absolutely no power over us except the power that we give to them, and whatever we focus our attention on will increase and grow. In Matthew 28:18 Jesus said, "All power is given unto me in heaven and in earth." If healing is required, we therefore need to focus our attention on the Christ within us and not on the existing problem. Nothing in the outer world can harm, deter, or frighten us. God is the only power and the only presence in our lives. There is absolutely no other power. "Greater is He that is in you than he that is in the world" (1 John 4:4). Drawing from the examples of Jesus, we have the power and authority to deny sickness and pain and claim healing by focusing on the presence and power of God. "He that believeth on me the works that I do shall he do also; and greater works than these shall he do; because I go unto my father" (John 14:12).

God sees us whole and perfect. "Thou art of purer eyes than to behold evil" (Hab. 1:13). We should therefore endeavor to make health our business, practicing it faithfully and patiently as we breathe and think, striving to maintain a healthy mind-set, and feeding ourselves with the Word of God, despite the appearance of pain and sickness. When we focus our attention on health, it will respond gracefully to us; when we feed on the Word of God, we will become more self-conscious, and pain, suffering, and sickness will not threaten us. Paul Ferrini says in *The Silence of the Heart*

> "Pain is not your enemy, but your greatest friend. It brings you back to the body. It brings you back to the breath. It brings you back to the wholeness of your experience. It is the mind in which healing and integration are always happening."

28

Freedom through Forgiveness

"For if ye forgive men their trespasses, your heavenly Father will also forgive you."

Matthew 6:14

"He who cannot forgive others breaks the bridge over which, he must himself pass."

Anonymous

"The weak can never forgive. Forgiveness is the attitude of the strong."

Mahatma Gandhi

"He who forgives ends the quarrel."

African Proverb

"Love is an act of endless forgiveness, a tender look, which becomes a habit."

Peter Ustinov

"Forgive us our trespasses as we forgive those who trespass against us . . ."

Jesus

"Forgive seventy times seven,"

Jesus

"If a man strikes you on one side of your face, turn to him the other side."

Jesus

"With love we learn forgiveness, and with forgiveness, compassion."

Alan Cohen

"Humbleness, forgiveness, clarity and love are the dynamics of freedom. They are the foundations of authentic power."

Gary Zukav

Father, as I come into your presence in this moment, I relax my mind and free my thoughts. I let go all concerns of the past and for the future knowing that negative conditions have no power over me or my life. Through the power of God within me I release people, places, and things that no longer serve me.

Through your forgiving love, O God, scars, wounds, and hurts are made whole. All un-forgiveness in me and toward me, all intolerance and injustice are completely blotted out. Through Thy redeeming love I am washed clean, rising above all human appearances, all material bondage.

In a spirit of surrender, Almighty God, I acknowledge you as Father, mother, counselor, healer, and friend. I am assured that your presence is within me and without me, and that there is no condition in my life that Your presence cannot heal, and nothing hidden that the power of God cannot reveal.

In the quietness of this moment I come to You an open vessel, open to receive my good. Immersed in this mind of Christ, I let go of all concerns of the past and for the future. I am free from doubts, fear, anxiety, and any condemnation of self and others, as the forgiving love of God frees me from all mistakes of the past or present. Create in me a clean heart and a new spirit, O God.

In this moment I welcome the strength and assurance that come from being one with Your forgiving Spirit, O God. I have faith in You to guide and support me with wise and loving counsel in all that I think, all that I say, and all that I do. I am open and receptive to new ways of seeing, thinking, and being.

All suggestions of limitation or unhappiness are erased from my mind. Centered in the mind of Christ, I am free in mind, body, and spirit. I rest in your promise: "Son, thou art ever with me, and all I have is Thine." I now hand over all my cares, my desires, and all my concerns into your loving hand, and I go free.

I now claim my divine inheritance, the riches of your kingdom. Peace, love, and joy abide within my consciousness. Thank you God, for Your love that heals in every way, and for your truth that sets me free. We thank You, God, for hearing us always and for hearing us now. We pray in the name and through the power of Jesus the Christ. Amen.

One of the many virtues of living a Christian life is the ability to forgive yourself and others. It gives us the opportunity to free our minds, hearts, and spirits from condemnation from ourselves or others. Forgiveness helps to filter negativity and give us the opportunity to see ourselves as we truly are. Sometimes being the target of an injustice is a great blessing; it virtually helps us to release resentment, pain, and sorrow from the past. With forgiveness comes freedom, as we evolve to a higher consciousness, blessing someone else and also receiving a blessing in return.

Practicing forgiveness is not an easy process. Although forgiveness is vital to our well-being, most of the time we find it difficult. It may take years to accomplish, especially when we have been deeply wounded. Some of us hold unforgiving thoughts all throughout our lives not realizing the harm that we cause ourselves. In his book *Goodbye to Guilt*, Gerald Jampolsky writes, "The ego looks at forgiveness with a split mind. It counsels us to forgive, but don't forget. It really is a double message that says don't forgive completely; don't forget the past or you will be vulnerable." But this is the furthest from the truth. The ego often deceives us, making us think that we are powerful in the face of un-forgiveness, but un-forgiveness only makes us virtually weak and unaccomplished.

There is absolutely nothing to gain from entertaining an unforgiving spirit. Un-forgiveness will result in all types of negative emotions, such as fear and resentment that block us from experiencing the goodness of God in our lives. When we hold on to thoughts of un-forgiveness, the only one affected is ourselves, not the person we're unwilling to forgive.

Many of us find ourselves stuck in certain negative situations, and our lives seem stagnant only because of un-forgiveness. The term forgiveness means *to give for*, or to give "good" in return for what seems evil, to restore relationships between others and us, and between God and us. When Peter asked Jesus how many times we should forgive our brother who trespasses against us, Jesus said, "not seven times seven," but "seventy times seven" (Matthew 18:21-22). This means that forgiveness should be a continuous practice.

Lessons in Forgiveness

The very nature of God is to forgive, and God expects us to forgive also. In the Old Testament, the Israelites were governed by the old laws that held an eye for an eye and a tooth for a tooth mentality. Although this precept had its place in history, we have since then evolved into a new awareness with the arrival of the New Testament. With the New Testament came Jesus, and with Jesus came *grace* and Truth. God is love, and

He is the only power and presence in our lives, but the love of God cannot be experienced when fear exists in our minds.

It is interesting to note that in the Bible some of the people who appeared to have sinned most were always the ones closest to Jesus, not because Jesus loved them more than anyone else, but Jesus loves us more when we acknowledge our transgressions and display a sense of humility. Consequently, Peter, who ashamedly denied Jesus just before the resurrection, was the only name singled out at His resurrection. Jesus understood the pain and grief Peter suffered after his denial of Him and wanted to reassure him that he was forgiven.

During the Sermon on the Mount, Jesus taught His disciples a model prayer in which the act of forgiveness was outlined. "And forgive us our debts as we forgive our debtors" (Matthew 6:12). This tells us that unless we first practice forgiveness, God cannot forgive us. Forgiveness of self, of others, and forgiveness from God are like a two-way street. They go hand in hand. We cannot have one without the other. As we give, so we also do receive.

Jesus also emphasized the need to forgive others in a parable in Matthew 18:23-35. There was a certain king who took account of his servants. The king commanded one servant, who owed him ten thousand talents, to be put in prison—him and his family—and ordered that all that this man had be sold so that he could pay his debt. The servant filled with remorse pleaded with the king for mercy, "Just have some patience with me and I will pay you all." The king was moved with compassion and out of the goodness of his heart forgave him of all his debt.

Soon afterward, the man forgot the kindness shown to him by the king and demanded that his fellow servant, who owed him a hundred pence, be cast in prison because of his inability to repay him his loan. Although the fellow servant pleaded for mercy he nevertheless took him by the throat and cast him into prison until he could pay. The king, who was very displeased at this act of un-forgiveness, denounced the unmerciful servant and delivered him to the tormentors until he could pay his original debt.

This parable demonstrates the perfect outworking of God's laws. We are all servants subjected to the law, and our transgressions place us in debt to the law. We all fall short and consequently need to give an account for our transgressions, which are many. "Do not be deceived. God is not mocked; for whatever a man sows that he shall also reap" (Galatians 6:7).

The good news is that the grace of God is always at work in our lives, and we can seek forgiveness and be free from our transgressions any time we desire. Forgiveness or spiritual release is a dual action that operates through the law of love and grace and a willingness to forgive others.

Forgiveness for most of us can be a difficult journey, but with God's help it can be done. It is a life-long experience that we need to practice constantly as we face the challenges of life. When we learn to forgive we accept responsibility for our freedom and happiness knowing that we can hurt not a single one but our own selves. We can feel the peaceful presence of God when we take one moment at a time, giving and forgiving instead of getting and blaming.

We may not know how to forgive, and we may not want to forgive, but when we exercise willingness to forgive, the healing process will begin. When we open ourselves to receive guidance from God, we will begin to go the extra mile and see Good in all situations. Whenever we stop focusing on the little self, we will discover that we are not separate and apart, but one with each other, all capable of making mistakes. As we learn to give more of ourselves, receiving will become easy and we will see the benefits of letting go of guilt, condemnation, and blame. True forgiveness allows us release from guilt and fear, and allows us to experience heaven on earth.

True Acts of Forgiveness

In the book of 1 Samuel, David, a little shepherd boy, killed Goliath and enabled Israel to defeat the Philistines, and his fame grew as a result. Saul, feeling threatened by David's popularity and successes, tried on numerous occasions to kill him, but David, who was "God's beloved," showed us the power of forgiveness, as he forgave Saul.

Saul was unsuccessful in his attempts to kill David, because David constantly walked with God and was therefore highly favored by God, and the Spirit of God was always with him, protecting him. Despite Saul's resentment of him, David still loved Saul and proved his love by cutting off a piece of Saul's garment while Saul slept.

Because David was constantly in tune with God, he was very blessed, and his forgiving nature made him very successful as king over Israel. No wonder it has been recorded that long after David's reign, the Lord acknowledged David, as He bestowed certain blessings on his descendants, "for David, my servant's sake."

Some time ago, Victor Gauminga, a World Vision project coordinator, demonstrated how forgiveness could build bridges of peace and love and remove mountains of challenges, uniting people in a spirit of love and peace. Victor wanted to get rid of water-borne diseases in his home village, Laime Chico, and developed a plan for building a pipeline to supply the villagers with clean, drinkable water from a source that was a distance away. Unfortunately, this plan would run through a rivaling village, Laime San Carlos, where the people had a long lasting feud with the people from Victor's village. When the people of Laime San Carlos heard about this plan, they vowed to destroy any such pipeline that ran through their village. Consequently, the whole plan was bombarded.

In spite of their hostility, the people in Victor's village, knowing that there was no church in Laime San Carlos, decided to promote an evangelistic effort there. This proved both difficult and dangerous, as not much attention was received from the rivaling villagers. Four people responded, however, and became believers in Christ. Those four people were spiritually nourished by the people from Victor's village, and so they went on to witness to others in their community. Gradually, a church was formed in Laime San Carlos.

The good news is that the very man who had originally opposed the pipeline plan became a Christian, and after seeing how wrong his attitude had been, asked forgiveness, eventually cooperating with the project.

Five years after, clean drinking water flowed through dependable pipes to the people of Victor's village, to those of the originally opposing village, as well as two other nearby villages. Recently, it has been reported that there are now growing churches in all four districts.

Forgiveness Brings Peace

My mother's willingness to forgive others has left an indelible print in my life, and each time I find it difficult to forgive, I remember her forgiving spirit. Her simple acts of forgiveness never failed to build bridges of love and initiate peace. This attitude was truly commendable, and I tried to emulate her on many occasions.

My mother's tolerance level was frequently tested, and in her humanity she often displayed strong emotions in defense of her rights, but she was firm and downright outspoken, unafraid to call a spade a spade. Family, friends, and neighbors who often crossed boundaries with her quickly saw another side to her, as she often gave them a good tongue lashing, but her anger would subside as quickly as it started, and soon all would be forgotten. She seemed to react in the moment, but she was also one of the most forgiving people I ever knew. She never held onto a grudge. If she was wrong, she would be the first to acknowledge her mistakes, make amends, and reconcile the differences, and if she was not the one at fault, she would be open to work things out amicably.

I have had many great challenges throughout my lifetime, and I must admit that in some instances it has not always been easy to forgive, but I have learned that in order to move forward in life, there has to be forgiveness of self or others. My experiences since my ordination and while living in St. Croix have been quite rewarding, yet there have been numerous issues that necessitated the ultimate need for forgiveness. It has not been an easy road as dreams have been shattered; promises have been broken, and feelings of disillusionment, remorse, and inner persecution have all surfaced.

Ultimately, all things work together for good, and I therefore hold onto the truth that God sees us whole and perfect. God is always with me, and there is nothing in the world to separate me from His love, "Thou art of purer eyes to behold evil" (Habakkuk 1:13). Through it all, I have learned to reconcile my differences by ultimately taking responsibility and examining my own shortcomings. In most instances I reasoned that because I felt the pain, the responsibility was on me to enforce the necessary changes.

I therefore persevere in my effort to free my mind, knowing that the Spirit within aligns my thinking with a grander plan, and even though painful emotions, such as failure, sadness, sorrow, and loss will continue to surface, they actually have no power over me. By endeavoring to maintain a peaceful state of mind, there is a grand prize to be won—the realization of an *"untouchable"* me, the Christ within.

Forgiveness opens the door to unlimited possibilities and brings us freedom and peace that passes all understanding. When it seems difficult for us to forgive, it is time to surrender to the Father and confess, "*Father, I am in fear. Let me by the power of the Holy Spirit see rightly.*" God's presence will then surround us, and He will remember our transgressions no more.

29

Amazing Grace

Because of the belief in the myth of separation, we experience all manner of hardships in our lives. God as Principle is eternal, unchanging, and unlimited. God's laws are also perfect and just; whatever we sow, we also reap. God's love is limitless, and no matter how often we transgress the law, God never ceases to extend His forgiving love through grace, which is an extension of the law of cause and effect. "Love is the fulfilling of the law" (Romans 13:10). Therefore, God's love must be unconditional.

Because God is all-good, grace works to ensure that the law benefits and blesses us. Jesus said in John 1:16-17 "And of his fullness we have all received, and grace for grace. For the law was given by Moses, but grace and truth came by Jesus Christ."

Grace is not something that we earn, nor does it come only to the good. As children of God we are all deserving of God's grace. It is freely given to all God's children, but we have to seek it. God's grace moves through the most complex circumstances in life. It strengthens us when we feel too weak to continue, embraces us when we feel alone, energizes us and sees us through our sorrows, and fills our lives with purpose and meaning.

There are definite consequences when we miss the mark, but we can be redeemed through God's grace, which is not an escape from the law, but an extension of the law. Jesus made it clear in Matthew 5:17, "Think not that I am come to destroy the law or the prophets: I am not come to destroy but to fulfill."

God's love works in and through all situations as grace to cancel our debts to the law so we can start all over again. When we feel that we have done our best in unforeseen situations and nothing seems to be going right, there is no need to struggle. Through the death and resurrection of Jesus, it is possible for us to overcome our human weaknesses and rise to a new awareness in truth. "Behold the lamb of God which taketh away the sins of the world" (John 1:29). Charles Fillmore states, "He (Jesus) became the way by which all who accept him may 'pass over' to the new consciousness. That which died on the cross was the consciousness of all mortal beliefs that hold us in bondage—such as sin, evil, sickness, fleshly lusts, and death, which He overcame" (ECF 153).

Grace Supersedes the Law

No matter what our circumstances are, God's law, which is perfect and just, works always to establish order and bring forth good. This was enacted in 2nd Samuel 1:12-25 through David, God's beloved, who because of lust arranged to have Uriah killed in battle so he could wed his wife, Bathsheba.

Because God is good, however, the law, which is perfect and just, worked to establish order in David's circumstances, and David was subsequently given the opportunity to repent through God's grace with the help of Nathan, who made David aware of his transgressions by telling him a story.

> "A rich man and a poor man," Nathan told David, "were neighbors. The rich man had many flocks and herds, and the poor man had only a pet lamb. One day the rich man had company. Instead of killing

> one of his own sheep, he killed his neighbor's pet lamb and roasted it for his guest."

Sometimes our egos stop us from acknowledging our mistakes and block us from our good. David allowed his lust for Bathsheba to block his sense of awareness, and acted from 'sense consciousness' (judgment inspired by the five senses), being unaware of the harm he had done. He expressed anger toward the rich man, agreeing with Nathan that the rich man should be punished.

When Nathan told him that the story was about him, David became very remorseful. Even though he was in denial, when confronted with the truth David had no other choice than to acknowledge his mistake. David humbly took responsibility for his wrong doing, even agreeing that he deserved to be punished.

David remembered from past experiences how rewarding his walk with the Lord had been, and as there were consequences for not honoring God's laws he decided to take responsibility for what he had done, fasting, praying, and confessing that he had sinned against the Lord. As a result of his sincerity and his humility, David was forgiven.

David regrettably crossed the line, and despite the fact that he was God's beloved, according to the law of cause and effect, divine order had to be established, and although David was forgiven, he still was held accountable for his transgressions.

In a metaphysical sense, David represents love, but his infidelity proves that he did not represent love in full expression, consequently when love takes the form of lust, no lasting fruit can be produced. As a consequence, David's first child by Bathsheba died.

The fruit of lust had to die to bring forth the fruit of love, so in order for David to be reconciled with God and experience the true love of God, he had to get rid of his lust or, sense consciousness, and seek forgiveness.

The law worked finally worked on David's behalf to restore order, and through fasting and prayer, David was able to purify his thoughts, which resulted in a feeling of compassion toward Bathsheba. When we humble ourselves before God, acknowledge our mistakes, deny negation and surrender to the awareness of God's love, we ultimately experience God's love through grace . . .

We live by grace when we live in love and wisdom. To live by grace is to live in wisdom, and to live in wisdom is to know God in the most intimate ways; to be open to the divine direction and inspiration we receive in our quiet moments with God.

David later proved that the love of God transcends all situations when the fruit of wisdom—Solomon, David's second son—was born. Metaphysically, this story tells us that anything that is born outside of love cannot survive. God is love, and we come nearest to Him when love is uppermost in our consciousness.

Saving Grace

Many of us have fallen short many times in our lives, and by acknowledging our mistakes we have been redeemed by the saving grace of God over and over again. In most cases we are never the same as something within us dies, but out of that perceived death, good often manifests. This was the case of John Newton, whose life changed so drastically that he shared an amazing testimony in the words of the song, "Amazing Grace," which most of us all know so well.

During his early years, John Newton's life lacked conviction. He lived a reckless life as a trader of slaves. After experiencing many mishaps at sea, including having one of his crewmen swept away during a storm, he began to see another way of existence.

Sometime after Newton got married, he unfortunately suffered a stroke. This was the beginning of Newton's call to serve the Lord. Newton finally became a convicted believer, and through the grace of God was ordained into the ministry. Sometime later, Newton wrote the popular song, "Amazing Grace," that continues to bless many people.

Sometimes we may feel cursed, believing that some mistakes in life seem too great to be reconciled. But God's grace is like an anchor in the storm. Nothing can destroy us as long as we hold on to the anchor. No matter how trying our circumstances are, the grace of God is always available to support, comfort, and bless us in our trials. No matter how weak we may feel, God is always able to strengthen and deliver us through grace.

Just before my acceptance to ministerial school, I went through a stormy period in my life, and God's grace came to my rescue several times during my time of preparation.

Although I had worked hard to establish a very successful business, I was ready and willing to make a sacrifice, as my greatest desire was to become a minister of religion. Living a Christ-centered life became my aim, and the more I practiced living from my Christ center, the more invigorated I became. The passion I previously experienced from my business was duly replaced with the utmost joy in sharing the goodness of the Lord with others. I looked forward to the unfolding of a new chapter of my life.

Unfortunately, my financial situation was in ruins. I owed the bank more than I could afford to pay! This dilemma was of great concern to me, as I did not have enough money saved to take care of my needs or maintain myself, much less to pay for my tuition at ministerial school. Nevertheless, I had a great resolve that this was a divine calling, so I kept my faith and waited earnestly for divine intervention.

My financial situation was not the only barrier; I didn't have the adequate academic requirements to enter the ministerial school. In spite of these obstacles, I prepared myself by completing all the prerequisite courses, and I initially graduated from the Personal Development program, acquiring the required credits for ministerial school. There were still more bridges to cross however, as I didn't have a bachelor's degree.

As I pondered my predicament, I shared my concerns with a very good friend and minister from the Unity school, the late Rev. Maurice Williams, who visited the Unity church in Jamaica. He encouraged me never to quit. "Just keep seeing yourself as a minister," he said. I took his advice and quickly felt empowered by his vote of confidence, affirming that God was in charge and He would see me through. I continued to convince myself that being a minister was God's divine plan for me and that it would happen, but I still had my doubts!

Despite all my professed faith, my financial situation continued to plague me. One day while in meditation I received divine guidance to write a letter to the bank asking for mercy. I promptly acted on my divine guidance, and from my heart I wrote to the bank, asking for lenience in repaying my loans. To my surprise, the bank acknowledged my letter and invited me to see the manager. With a feeling of relief I prayed, thanking God for divine order in the situation, and quickly made an appointment.

I made it to the bank on the day of my appointment feeling very optimistic. The manager listened intently as I poured out my heart to him, and I was taken by surprise when he told me, "Don't put this on your head, Marjorie. Just pay us whatever you can." God had poured out His saving grace upon my situation and relieved me from financial pressure, and I was overjoyed. I had no preconceived notion regarding the outcome, but I must confess that this demonstration was much more than I anticipated. The way to complete my ministerial training was beginning to unravel, and I was convinced once again that God was with me and everything was in divine order. Nothing could stop me now from achieving my goals. I silently said a prayer of thanksgiving and left the manager's office feeling on top of the world.

Experience teaches wisdom, and sometimes with each breakthrough comes an equivalent challenge. Still, the challenges ultimately become our stepping stones, as they help us discover who we are in relation to God. Someone once said, "Austerity is like a strong wind; it tears away from us all but the things that cannot be torn, so that we see ourselves as we truly are."

There were times during my preparation for ministerial school when I felt defenseless and powerless, unable to stand on my own, but I was determined to conquer the pitfall of negation that continuously surfaced, and so in an effort to rescue myself, I was forced to take an inward journey to the far reaches of my soul, and draw from that un-depleted source of living water.

I continued to prove that the grace of God overrides all challenges when I subdued my fears and surrendered to the all of God. And so that summer, as I continued to seek God as the answer, another miracle happened to assist me in my quest to enter ministerial school. The admissions team from the school made an allowance for all international students who didn't have a bachelor's degree. I would be accepted after all, without the required minimum of a bachelor's degree! This was absolutely and undoubtedly the work of God, the biggest and best demonstration of answered prayer that I had ever experienced, and I was elated, to say the least. I was further convinced that the light of God was shining on my path, and nothing could stand in my way.

Turning within to a quiet place, I now center myself in the presence of God, and I place myself and all that concerns me into the loving hand of God. Any difficult situation is now transformed into a blessing, and I am comforted and assured that only good can come to me. I let go of any fear, doubt, or anxiety and I experience a new sense of freedom. Even in the face of doubt and anxiety I am continually blessed by the grace and love of God. I am joyful and energetic, strengthened and peaceful.

I am assured that the forgiving love of God knows no bounds. I now live each day with poise and confidence, forgiving myself for all mistakes of the past or present. I acknowledge everyone as loving children of God living also in God's grace. I relax and let go, being sustained by the flow of God's goodness. As God's love and His grace become a reality in my life, I am blessed and I am a blessing. Thank you, God. Amen.

30

A Time of Hope

> "Every valley shall be exalted, and every mountain and hill shall be made low: and the crooked shall be made straight, and the rough places plain: And the glory of the Lord shall be revealed, and all flesh shall see it together: for the mouth of the lord as spoken it."
>
> Isaiah 40:4-5

A situation often appears hopeless when we have exhausted all options and human resources, but because of the saving grace of God, hope is a mainstay for many of us. As long as there is life, there is hope.

We sometimes experience a sense of hopeless because we often seek quick solutions to difficult and complex challenges, and until we surrender our willfulness to God's will, sometimes we can experience hardships for years. We should never give up however, as with God all things are possible. God is absolute and unchanging good. He is our Father and our mother, always willing to comfort and bless us, but we must seek His guidance. He is always on our side. He will supply all our needs. He wants us to be healthy, happy, prosperous, and successful.

> "What man is there, of you, whom if his son asks bread will give him a stone, or if he asks fish will give

> him a serpent? If you then, being evil, know how to give good gifts unto your children, how much more shall your father which is in heaven give good things to them that ask him?" (Matthew 7:9).

During the Babylonian captivity in the book of Ezekiel, God demonstrated to the Israelites—who had lost their way because of disobedience and willfulness—how hope could be reestablished among them, eventually returning them to a peaceful environment.

As their relationship with the Lord deteriorated, they lived in an up and down rebellion against Him for four hundred years during the kingdom era, continually paying the price. Finally, judgment came in the form of a military conquest. God showed them that all was not lost, however. Through the prophet Ezekiel, God showed them that there was hope.

Ezekiel the prophet was among the first set of exiles taken to Babylon eleven years before Jerusalem was destroyed. He was called to prophesy in an extraordinary vision in the fifth year of exile when he said the heavens were opened and he saw visions of God. This overpowering experience convinced him that God was with him. In his visions, Ezekiel received insights about God's dissatisfaction with the people of Judah for their faithlessness.

After the fall of Jerusalem, Ezekiel's messages to the exiles brought a message of comfort and a promise of return to their land. In a vision, God showed him a valley full of dry bones. The bones were so dry that they must have been there for a very long time. These bones represented the Hebrew exiles, whom were living in captivity in Babylon.

The Hebrew people must have considered their situation hopeless. They thought that their God had abandoned them forever. Ezekiel must have wondered what hope there was for God's chosen people. When God asked Ezekiel if he thought the bones could live, Ezekiel meekly responded, "Only God knew." Ezekiel knew that the situation was in God's Hand, and that with God all things are possible.

In his vision, God told Ezekiel to prophecy, to speak to the bones and instruct them to listen to God's word. God said he would cause breath to enter into the bones and they would live again (Ezekiel 37:4-5). When Ezekiel prophesied to the bones, the bones assembled into skeletons, and muscles and skin covered them. The bones, however, did not have breath in them, so God further told Ezekiel to prophesy to the wind, or the Spirit. The four winds then breathed life into the assembled bodies, and the dry bones were transformed into a living, breathing army (Ezekiel 37:8-10).

Spirit is used to describe the vital force of a person, so the spoken word can be referred to the Holy Spirit. God told Ezekiel to prophesy to the wind, or spirit, and life was put back into the bodies. By affirming the power of God in our lives, by keeping our minds free from all judgments and discrimination of self and others, we will ultimately experience illumination, transformation, and self-realization.

Ezekiel was impressed with the transformation he saw in the valley. This was a sign from God that the Hebrew nation would be restored and the exiles would be able to return home.

> "Then He said unto me, these bones are the whole house of Israel: behold they say, 'Our bones are dry and our hope is lost: and we are cut off from our parts . . . And I shall put my spirit in you and ye shall live, and I shall place you in your own land: then shall ye know that I the Lord have spoken it, and performed it,' saith the Lord" (Ezekiel 37:11, 14).

The Babylonian captivity represents a departure from spiritual consciousness or a departure from our true state of being. When we live in "sense consciousness" (apart from God) we find ourselves in the foreign land of Babylon (confusion) which results in mental captivity—a state of lonesomeness, frustration, and hardships, as demonstrated by the Israelites. As living in this atmosphere is not conducive to our welfare, we yearn to go back to our true state of being (Jerusalem; a place of peace).

Ezekiel's job was to help the Jews rise to a higher consciousness. During challenging times, Ezekiel reminds us to trust in God. Elizabeth Sand Turner, author of *Let There Be Light*, writes

> "In times of distress we need just the consciousness that Ezekiel symbolizes. He will come forth to instruct us and guide us so that we may have the strength to lift up our eyes to God. In the upward sight lies our ability to meet a hard condition in a spiritual manner."

Because of God's promises, we have the power of the Holy Spirit within us to change all negative conditions into a blessing. When we learn to meet challengess in faith, we will rise from hopelessness to hope or from sense consciousness to spiritual consciousness. Making our way back to spiritual consciousness requires discipline, as well as the perpetual cleansing of the mind.

31

Restoration

Let nothing disturb thee,
Nothing affright thee;
All things are passing;
God never changeth;
Patient endurance
Attaineth to all things;
Who God posseth
In nothing is wanting,
Alone God sufficeth

Saint Theresa

In the beginning, according to the first book of Genesis, there was darkness upon the earth. God separated the darkness from the light by calling forth the light, and then there was light. Through His spoken word, God showed us how we too can transform negative situations in our lives by calling the Word of God forth into the light. Actually, the spoken word is the light. So by affirming the power of God in any difficult situation we call forth the light.

As God's laws are perfect and just, there are definite consequences for willfully neglecting our spiritual responsibilities. The good news, however, is that when we surrender to God and acknowledge our powerlessness, we are saved through grace (Ephesians 2:5). No matter how many times we fall short, there is always an opportunity to heal and grow by acknowledging our mistakes and starting over again.

We have the opportunity at all times to rise higher in consciousness by letting go and letting God. The more we apply the truth to our lives, the more conscious we will become, and the more freedom we will experience. Author and poet James Dillett Freeman says in his book *The Case for Reincarnation, "God does not make us fixed, he makes us free."*

Our journey is never completed, as challenges do arise from time to time, and living the perfected life requires discipline. Great effort is therefore necessary to persevere and rebuild our lives. Elizabeth Sand Turner writes in *Let There Be Light* "The period of Restoration symbolizes our return to Spirit and our efforts to maintain a spiritual consciousness. During a time of trial (exile), we turn to God and our release eventually comes. However, it is one thing to gain a spiritual blessing, such as freedom, but quite another thing to maintain it."

The Jews had a similar experience. When they were given permission by the Persian king Cyrus to return to their homeland in Jerusalem, only a few wanted to return. The older Jews who were transported to Judah in 597 B.C. were too old, and as they had grown accustomed to the life in Babylon, they chose to remain behind. Consequently, only the spiritual minded, as predicted by the prophets of the eight and seventh centuries B.C., were willing to take the journey back to Judah to start a new life.

Those Jews who decided to take the journey were astounded when on their arrival in Judah they found Jerusalem in shambles. The poorer class of Jews, who had remained in Judah, was complacent, so the responsibility rested on the newcomers to rebuild and establish a religious life. There were numerous challenges facing them. The surrounding people resented their return and constantly tried to war with them, giving them no peace.

The pure Jews of Judah resented the Samaritans because they were a mixed race, so when the Samaritans offered to help them rebuild the temple they refused. As a consequence, the Samaritans decided to sabotage their efforts. Discouraged by the interference of the Samaritans, the Jews sank into despair, delaying the completion of the temple.

Similarly, whenever we make a commitment to live the spiritual life we are sometimes bombarded with thoughts of negation and feelings of doubt and uncertainty. When we are faced with challenges, we tend to lose our perspective, energy, and focus, often sinking into despair. Whenever we persevere in our efforts to achieve our desired goals, however, help usually comes from God in one form or another.

As we strive to live the spiritual life, the prophets Haggai, Zechariah, Isaiah, Obadiah, and Malachi, who all played individual roles in rebuilding the temple, do have a message for us. They encourage us to be steadfast and vigilant; to persevere in trying times and to set our priorities right, as victory is always at hand. Despite all the challenges that faced the Jews, the prophets exercised immense strength in leading the people in the direction of their good.

Haggai

Haggai reminds us that if we neglect our spiritual responsibilities, we will fail to realize our good. When we are focused, clear, and single-eyed with a sense of purpose, we can transcend distractions that delay our progress on the spiritual path. He reminds us of the importance of focusing on the presence of God within and not on outer things. "Is it time for you, O ye, to dwell in your ceiled houses, and this house lie waste? Now therefore thus saith the Lord of hosts; Consider your ways. Ye have sown much, and bring in little; ye eat, but you have not enough; ye drink, but ye are not filled with drink; ye clothe you, but there is none warm; and he that earneth wages earneth wages to put it into a bag with holes. Thus saith the Lord of hosts; Consider your ways. Go up to the mountain and bring wood, and build the house; and I will take pleasure in it, and I will be glorified saith the Lord" (Hag 1:4-8).

Zechariah

Zechariah began his prophetic work in the same year as Haggai, and continued for several years longer. He reminds us that we need to eliminate fear from our consciousness and employ spiritual discipline and determination as our spiritual tools. "And it shall come to pass, that as ye were a curse among the heathen, O house of Judah, and house of Israel; so will I save you, and ye shall be a blessing: fear not, but let your hands be strong" (Zec. 8:13).

Elizabeth Sand Turner says in *Let There Be Light* "When we are disobedient to God's law it seems as if we are cursed, in that hardships of all kinds overtake us. But when we turn again to Him, a blessing is forthcoming. To eliminate fear from the mind and be strong in faith and works is the course before us."

Zechariah believed in living from a high moral and ethical standard, and he reminded the people that in order to reap their blessings, they needed to live up to their highest ideals. "These are the things that you shall do; Speak ye every man the truth with his neighbor; execute the judgment of truth and peace in your gates; and let none of you imagine evil in your hearts against his neighbor; and love no false oath: for all these are things that I hate, saith the Lord." (Zech. 8:16-17). Haggai and Zechariah's messages inspired the Jews so that they continued to work on the temple, completing it within four years.

Isaiah

Isaiah's main concern was the neglect of the Sabbath. His messages were filled with inspiration and hope, but he emphasized the importance of upholding high spiritual ideals. He explained the meaning and benefits of a spiritual fast, which are to deny false conditions and affirm the truth. This kind of fast, he said, is much more acceptable unto the Lord than to refrain from food and repent in sackcloth.

> "Is it such a fast that I have chosen? a day for a man to afflict his soul? is it to bow down his head as a bulrush, and to spread sackcloth and ashes under him? wilt thou call this a fast, and an acceptable day unto the Lord? Is not this the fast that I have chosen? to lose the band of wickedness, to undo the heavy burdens, and to let the oppressed go free, and that ye break every yoke? Is it not to deal thy bread to the hungry, and that thou bring the poor that are cast out to thy house? when thou seest the naked, that thou cover him; and that thou hide not thyself from thine own flesh?" (Isaiah 58:5-7)

We should set aside specific times to commune with God, and our desires should always be to glorify Him. When our intentions are honorable, the Lord will attend to our prayers and He will hear our cry. We should cleanse our minds daily from negation and concentrate only on God. When we engage in this form of spiritual cleansing, our light shall spring forth and our healing shall be realized. "Then shall thy light break forth as the morning, and thine health shall spring forth speedily; and thy righteousness shall go before thee . . . Then shalt thou call, and the Lord shall answer; thou shalt cry, and he will say, Here I am" (Isaiah 58:8-9).

Obadiah

Obadiah stresses the dangers of living a sense-centered life. There is nothing to gain, as without God we are nothing. We cannot exist by ourselves, and there are definite consequences when we try to live without God. "Though thou exalt thyself as the eagle, and though thou set thy nest among the stars, thence will I bring thee down, saith the Lord" (Obad.1:4). At the same time, Obadiah reiterates the benefits to be derived from living a God centered life. "But upon Mount Zion shall be deliverance, and there shall be holiness; and the house of Jacob shall possess their possessions."

Malachi

Malachi reminds us that living from an ethical standpoint is very rewarding, and it is in giving that we receive. Malachi criticized the priests and the entire religious system for their indifference to their religious responsibilities. He believed that the Lord would execute judgment on them according to their ways. Malachi was more concerned with their inability to pay the dues of the Temple.

> "Even from the days of your fathers ye are gone away from mine ordinances, and have not kept them. Return unto me, and I will return unto you, saith the Lord of hosts. But ye said, Wherein shall we return? Will a man rob God? Yet ye have robbed me. But ye say, Wherein have we robbed thee? In tithes and offerings. Ye are cursed with a curse: for ye have robbed me, even this whole nation. Bring ye all the tithes into the storehouse, that there may be meat in mine house, and prove me now herewith, saith the Lord of hosts, if I will not open you the windows of heaven, and pour you out a blessing, that there shall not be room enough to receive it" (Mal 3:7-10).

Malachi had a final word of encouragement for the righteous. “They shall be mine, saith the Lord of hosts, in that day when I make up my jewels; and I will spare them, as a man spareth his own son that serveth him” (Mal. 3:17). Charles Fillmore says in *The Metaphysical Bible Dictionary*, “All real and lasting wealth and happiness are based on unity with God. Malachi will tell you this, or you can prove it for yourself after you have spent years in material experiences.”

Nothing worthwhile in life is achieved without great effort and determination, so there were still a variety of social and economic problems and a variety of others challenges that interrupted the building of the second temple in Jerusalem, and the walls of Jerusalem were still in ruins. Some of the Jews who remained in Babylon were comfortably well off, so when a deputation from Judah sought help, Ezra and Nehemiah—two outstanding Jews—answered the call to serve.

Ezra and Nehemiah

Ezra brought with him the priestly code, which is a “strict observance to the Sabbath.” This was a means of establishing order and enthusiasm among the people.

Ezra’s enthusiasm to the observance of religious laws together with Nehemiah’s outstanding leadership ability aroused a new national spirit that moved the Jews to continue their work on the temple. Many forms of opposition continued to surface, however, and there were many setbacks that confronted them, but Ezra and Nehemiah—who both believed in the cause—persevered, and despite it all the walls of Jerusalem were finally completed.

The population of Jerusalem gradually increased, and Nehemiah introduced religious forms of worship. According to Charles Fillmore, Nehemiah signifies, “that in us which inspires us to higher and better things. He represents, too, the boldness and the courage that set about the rebuilding of a character weakened by sin." There were other hindrances that surfaced, but Nehemiah insisted upon proper observation of the Sabbath and enforced stringent rules pertaining to intermarriage. Together, both Nehemiah and Ezra did a great job in establishing community and strengthening Judaism.

According to Charles Fillmore in *The Revealing Word*, "spiritual marriage represents the union of two dominant states of consciousness." An inter-marriage then would suggest a mental opposition between spiritual consciousness and sense consciousness, which results in conflict. The Sabbath is a time of rest, when we come apart for a while and find rest for our souls. Whenever we become too bombarded with the cares of life, we often find little time for rest and consequently experience conflict in our thoughts.

The period of Restoration in the Bible is of great significance to our spiritual life. Sometimes trials, challenges, and discouragement come in the form of oppositions from virtually all angles, challenging our connection to the divine Source, delaying our good. Daily prayer and meditation are very necessary tools to combat daily distractions and overcome temptations. When we stand up for what we truly believe, and despite the appearances persevere with faith and courage, we will be victorious. The good news is that there is no limit to trying. We can always try again and again and again. Our next effort may very well be our best effort ever.

32

The Road to Overcoming

> "To Him that overcometh will I grant to sit with me in my throne, even as I also overcame, and am set down with my Father in His throne" (Rev. 3:21).

There may be many different perspectives to the book of Revelation, but it is nevertheless filled with hope and inspiration to the despondent who encounters obstacles on his or her spiritual path. It tells us that despite the challenges that face us in life there is always a way to overcome.

The road to spiritual attainment is not an easy one for truth seekers; there are many trials along the way, and our life's experiences take us along challenging paths. The challenges we encounter are at times self-inflicted, and although they may be overwhelming, there is always hope once we become consciously aware of our oneness with God. Charles Fillmore writes in *Keep a True Lent*, "Spiritual power, mastery and dominion are attained by the over-comer."

We exercise dominion when we discover who we are and recommit ourselves to the Christ consciousness. As we celebrate our overcoming experiences, we should focus mainly on the victory and less on the challenges. "And I saw a new heaven and a new earth: for the first heaven and the first earth were passed away; and there was no more sea.

And I John saw the holy city, New Jerusalem, coming down from God out of heaven, prepared as a bride adorned for her husband. And I heard a great voice out of heaven saying, Behold, the tabernacle of God is with men, and He will dwell with them, and they shall be his people, and God himself shall be with them, and be their God. And God shall wipe away all tears from their eyes; and there shall be no more death, neither sorrow, nor crying, neither shall there be any more pain: for the former things are passed away" (Revelation 21:1-4).

As long as there is life there will be challenges. Overcoming a mental struggle after a long and tedious journey can be a very wonderful experience. As we all as individuals have valuable lessons to learn, we sometimes struggle for years to find the good in a situation. God is always calling us up higher, but nothing will unfold until we are ready to receive our good.

In Genesis chapters 25-35 Jacob allowed his mind to control him, as he tricked his brother and deceived his own father for material gains. Because of Jacob's wrongdoing, he went through a mental struggle to find release, ultimately finding good in the situation.

Jacob was encouraged by his mother, who loved him more than his brother Esau, to trick his father, who was blind with old age, and pretend to be Esau. He served Isaac a meal of stew and received Esau's birthright. When Esau found out that Jacob had taken his blessing he was irate; he wanted to kill him.

In fear of his life, Jacob had to flee. As a result, Jacob became a fugitive, on the run from Esau. It was not long before reality began to set in, and Jacob began to feel remorseful. He had gotten the birthright of his brother, but the aftermath of his gain was too great a price to reconcile. The journey for Jacob was long and tedious, and he felt alone, haunted with many wandering thoughts. Why did he allow his conniving mother to coerce him into deceiving his father and stealing from his brother? Would Esau ever forgive him? Would he ever see his father again? Jacob was truly concerned.

God is love, but love is the fulfilling of the law (Romans 13:10); consequently according to the law of cause and effect no wrongful deed go unpunished. Jacob was therefore punished according to the law of cause and effect, but when there is genuine repentance from us the grace of God works to transcend the law, offering us optimum release.

Jacob ultimately had the power of God to reverse his transgressions and change his life around by the renewing of his mind. On his way to Canaan he was completely overwhelmed. When he heard that Esau was chasing after him with an armed force, Jacob turned to God for refuge. Amazingly, God was always with Jacob even though he did not know it. Feeling completely subdued and uncertain of his future, Jacob became mentally exhausted, and so he decided to rest for a while. Choosing a stone for his pillow, he wrapped his cloak around him and before long he fell asleep on the ground.

Tired from his journey, Jacob became very still and instantly fell asleep. In that moment of stillness he had a very unusual spiritual encounter. During his sleep Jacob dreamt that he saw a ladder that reached up to heaven. Beautiful angels were going up and down the ladder, and God was standing at the top. Jacob heard God's voice telling him that he would give him and his descendants the land on which he lay, and that his descendants would be as many as the dust of the earth. God told Jacob that through this his family and all people of the earth would be blessed. God also promised Jacob that He would be with him and protect him wherever he went, and most of all, that He would never leave Jacob until this promise was fulfilled.

There is good in everyone, and no matter how great our transgressions are the forgiving love of God is constant and everlasting. God forgives us always, but we must seek forgiveness by taking responsibility for our actions. There is always an opportunity to start all over again.

Jacob awoke from his dream and instantly knew that God was with him. He felt much lighter. At least it seemed like hope was not lost. Filled now with hope, Jacob began to experience a change in consciousness. As a mark of recognition, he consecrated the stone he used as a pillow by pouring oil on it. He then called the place "Bethel," which means "the house of God." Feeling uplifted and encouraged, Jacob made a promise to God. If God would bless him by protecting and providing for him always and allowing him to go to his father's house in peace, he would acknowledge Him and serve Him as his God, and furthermore he would give back one tenth of whatever he received from God (Gen. 28:20-22).

Being energized with the promise that God was with him, Jacob continued on his journey, arriving near his uncle's home in Haran. Here he met the beautiful Rachael, his uncle's daughter who took him to see Laban, her father. Jacob instantly fell in love with Rachael and agreed to work for Laban for seven years, after which time he would marry her.

It is said that unfair games play twice, and Jacob was about to prove this theory. As was customary in those days, the first daughter had to be the first to wed, so after waiting seven years to marry Rachael, Jacob first had to marry Leah, Rachael's sister, and then wait another seven years before he could marry Rachael.

The time came when Jacob finally married Rachael, and he became very rich. Having been exiled for a period of time, Jacob thought it was now time to go back home. Laban, however, who had become successful with Jacob's help, wanted him to remain, but Jacob had another plan. Unbeknownst to Laban, Jacob departed with his family and belongings.

When Laban became aware of Jacob's departure he was enraged. Immediately, he set out in pursuit of them. By the time he caught up with them, however, his anger had subsided, as God warned him not to hurt Jacob. They reconciled their differences and then parted in peace.

Forgetting the past can be a very long and difficult road for many people, but the power of release is right there within us. Sometimes when we decide to turn over a new leaf our past often gets in the way, haunting us with feelings of blame and guilt, and we consequently suffer mental agony, finding it difficult to make that final release. In order to receive forgiveness from God, we first have to forgive ourselves, or others, and until we give ourselves permission to let it go, we will continue to suffer the mental anguish of our past. Ultimately, our suffering will last for as long it takes, until we give ourselves permission to let go.

Consequently all was not over with Jacob; he still had another hurdle to pass. He still wrestled with his guilt from deceiving his father and stealing his brother's birthright. He had not entirely let it go. He constantly thought of Esau and dreaded the idea of a confrontation, so he prayed, asking God to protect him. Just to be on the safe side as they journeyed, Jacob decided to divide his family in two groups, sending one ahead so that if Esau attacked, at least one set would be safe. He also sent a peace offering of sheep, oxen, camels, and other animals to his brother. With the majority of his company gone ahead of him, Jacob had some time to himself to reconcile his wounds.

Once we surrender to His presence and power in our lives God never fails to turn our sorrow and pain into joy and happiness and the discomfort one endures in the struggle cannot be compared with the blessings to be realized at the overcoming.

As Jacob slept that night, a strange thing happened to him. At the break of dawn he wrestled with a man of God, who said to him, "Let me go, for the day is breaking."

The wrestling continued between Jacob and the man of God, but Jacob was determined to conquer. He would not give up. In a moment, Jacob saw a glimpse of light, and that was all he needed to press on. With sheer determination Jacob said to the man of God, "I will not let you go until you bless me." The man of God was impressed with Jacob's strength, determination, and desire for freedom. Jacob went through a severe test and he prevailed. "What is your name?" the man asked him. "Jacob," he answered. "You will now be called Israel," said the man (meaning a prince of God), "because you have power with God and man."

Jacob had prevailed and was now ready for change, hence his change of name from Jacob to Israel. After this final overcoming experience, Jacob named the place "Peniel," because he had seen God face to face.

Jacob wrestled with his own thoughts over his past and suffered mentally with feelings of isolation, guilt, and shame. Having reached the pinnacle of the experience, Jacob eventually saw reason from the perspective of truth and surrendered. As Jacob's awareness of God grew stronger, it became easier for him to release the past.

Because of Jacob's sincerity, humility, and his willingness to surrender, God was willing to see Jacob through the darkness. God is everlasting and unconditional love, and He wants us to experience His love always. Carolyn Myss says in *Anatomy of the Spirit*, "Confession is symbolic of purging all that is not honorable within us. It heals the damage we create by the misuse of our will power."

Jacob's story teaches us that no matter what we are going through, the presence of God is always with us, and He does not hold us in bondage to the law. We have the power within us to change any unforeseen circumstance in our life, but we have to be ready and willing to take responsibility. We have to consent to being transformed by the renewing of our minds, and God's forgiving grace will always be our sufficiency in all circumstances.

After a long period of guilt and remorse Jacob finally surrendered to his Christ-self, and he became victorious both spiritually and materially. Jacob made the transition from being a trickster to being highly favored by God, demonstrating that there is good in everyone regardless of past actions.

The journey for Jacob was long and tedious. He struggled immensely in his mind for a release from his wrong deed, suffering great hardships and mental and emotional pain. He was ready and determined to be transformed, so he persevered in his struggle, finally conquering all his fears and experiencing victory.

The gifts that Jacob sent to Esau represented a peace offering, or a change of consciousness. We often experience a feeling of immense joy when we overcome a mental struggle, let go of a destructive habit, achieve success, or forgive ourselves or others. Whenever we free ourselves from mental bondage, we open ourselves to the abundance of the universe, our lives take on a new meaning, and like Jacob we rejoice, knowing that we too have prevailed unquestioningly.

After Jacob received his blessing from God, he was free indeed. There was no more fear in his domain. He could now face Esau, or what seemed like his enemy, squarely. Knowing that he had control over his own thoughts, actions, and feelings, Jacob realized that the past, or Esau, had no power over him.

The time eventually came when Jacob saw Esau face to face. He was surprised and relieved when Esau ran to greet him, throwing his arms around him kissing him, indicating that the past was behind them and all was forgotten. This was the undeniable proof that the power and presence of God was with him always. Jacob's blessings were now a reality.

Both Jacob and Esau then parted in harmony after their peaceful reunion, and Jacob continued on his way with his family to Haran. Rachael died on the way, leaving a tiny baby called Benjamin. Jacob was also happy that his father was still alive, and he was even more grateful for the many blessings from God.

Jacob's overcoming experience is real to life, and proves that there is always hope for us through the love of God. Like Jacob, we face daily struggles that seem to engulf and alarm us, but when we reach out to God and acknowledge our powerlessness, He will rescue us from our fears. We are never alone.

Although Jacob had done wrong, God was with him nevertheless, because the nature of God is to love us unconditionally. Jacob experienced a mental separation only because of his own guilt, but God was always with him. Because Jacob acknowledged his mistake, however, he was ready and willing to take responsibility and initiate change.

The dream that Jacob had with the ladder reaching up to heaven with angels ascending and descending represents his struggle to release his past. Although Jacob tried tirelessly and earnestly to focus on the presence and power of God within him, his humanity constantly surfaced, resulting in mixed states of consciousness. Eventually, Jacob persevered and he won the battle with God's help.

It is not always easy to overcome challenges, as doubts, anxiety, and fear constantly get in the way and we question ourselves. *Am I worthy? Is God true to His word? Will things really change?* When we persevere in our faith, pray without ceasing, and reach for our highest ideals, God will come to our rescue and give us the desires of our hearts; we will eventually overcome.

As the light of understanding dawned on Jacob, he used his challenge as his stepping stone, and he anointed it with oil to signify his gratefulness for the challenge. Through it all, not only did he develop a personal relationship with God, but he reaped great rewards, as he learned to trust in God and prove the wonderful working power of God within him.

Jacob's final overcoming experience happened on his way to the finish line. This happened just before the break of day. Transformation was at hand! Jacob was determined that he would not let the challenge go until he found the blessing in it. "I will not let you go until you bless me," Jacob said. The man of God saw that the light was dawning. Jacob was coming unto his own, so he released Jacob and blessed him, "because he had power with God and with men, and had prevailed."

At last, Jacob experienced mental freedom, and the challenge no longer prevailed. He totally released it and turned it over to God, and the guilt and shame he once felt were gone. Jacob was now ready to put the pieces back together and get on with his life. Having released the past, Esau no longer was a threat to him. God was the only presence and the only power in his life, and nothing could stand against him. Esau was no longer a threat, as Jacob had relinquished his fear of Esau, taking back the power he had entrusted to him, and Esau had no other choice but to conform. "Love is the fulfilling of the law" (Romans 13:10).

The term "struggle" tends to have a negative connotation, and some of us even avoid using it, but there is always a blessing to be found in every struggle. The good news is that we do not have to remain in bondage. Although we suffer the consequences for our thoughts and actions, we can transform unforeseen situations in our lives by the renewing of our minds. "Be not conformed to this world, but be transformed by the renewing of your mind that you may prove what is that good, and acceptable and perfect will of God" (Romans 12:2).

God traveled with Jacob day and night and protected him constantly, but he had done wrong to his brother Esau, and according to the law of cause and effect he had to reap what he had sown. Consequently, Jacob had to pay his dues. This law was enacted in many ways:

1. He became a fugitive, fleeing from his country and his family,
2. He suffered guilt and mental anguish as a result of his conniving ways,
3. He had to wait extra time for Rachael's hand in marriage.

Charles Fillmore writes in *Keep a True Lent*

> "The true over-comer is qualifying himself to become a member of this super race. It is well for such a one to cultivate the childlike spirit and let go of all striving even for spiritual things. In the realization of protecting, providing love, all the strain of fear and anxiety will be removed, and life in abundance will then find easy entrance into the consciousness, bringing strength and health and eternal youth and life."

Overcoming experiences involves a mental process and is seldom achieved in an instant. Sometimes our efforts may even seem futile, as if no progress is being made, but the more we persevere, the more assistance we will receive from the Christ of our being, and the more successful we will become. It takes unceasing discipline in the form of strength, courage, and faith and allows us the privilege to take responsibility and thus prove our allegiance to heaven. David fasted and prayed constantly; Jacob wrestled with himself until he found release, and Job argued with his counterparts until he received wisdom from within.

Jacob's struggle represents the struggle of humanity to express and experience spiritual fulfillment and ultimate freedom. By going through the process Jacob first had to let go of the past by engaging in a mental cleansing. Next, he had to affirm the non-power of the past over him, and then he had to replace his adverse thoughts by affirming the truth about himself.

Like Jacob, when we continue in the relentless search to attain spiritual fulfillment, we become strengthened, more conscious, and willing to take responsibility. We then become empowered and joyful in the awareness that God does not punish anyone, nor does He hold anyone in bondage. There is always a way out, with God. "All things work together for good . . ." (Romans 8:28).

33

Looking Up

The important message in the story of resurrection is hope. No matter what faces us we can attain victory by simply denying negation and focusing on the indwelling presence of Christ. The resurrection signals new beginnings, new opportunities, new growth, and new mercies. It reminds us that despite what is happening in our lives, there is hope. All we need to do to overcome limitation is to employ a change in consciousness, or look up to a new awareness in truth. Jesus showed us how to achieve this by His death and subsequent resurrection. In John 11:25 Jesus reminds us, "I am the resurrection, and the life: he that believeth in me, though he were dead, yet shall he live."

We experience resurrection daily in our lives. Each time we overcome a negative habit or change a negative thought pattern we rise up in consciousness with Christ. Charles Fillmore says

> "The resurrection happens within us each time we rise to Jesus' realization of the perpetual indwelling life that connects us with the Father. A new flood of life comes to all who open up their minds and their bodies to the living word of God."

In order to experience the resurrected self, however, we need to be connected to the divine source; not just connected, but we also need to activate that connection with regular periods of communion with God. In order to get electricity in our homes for instance, we first go to the electric company, apply for a connection, and pay an initial fee, but although there is a connection, no energy will be transmitted until the switch is turned on.

In a likewise manner, in order to accomplish our goals, we need to activate that switch to the divine Presence within us by doing our spiritual work. God is the one and only true source from which all our blessings come, and like the vine and the branches we are connected, but ultimately we need to act, or turn on the switch to our divine nature with the reading of God's Word and with regular periods of prayer and meditation.

A resurrection, as demonstrated by Jesus, involves a process that the soul employs in an effort to purify itself, and the process involves a sequence of events. It begins with the period referred to as Lent, a forty day and forty night period when Jesus was tempted in the wilderness. Next is the trial of Jesus prior to the crucifixion, the betrayal of Jesus by Judas, Peter's denial of Jesus, Jesus' triumphant entry into Jerusalem, and the events during and after the crucifixion. This all culminates with the resurrection. Each event is historically relevant and metaphysically significant from an evolutionary standpoint, as without them there would be no resurrection and subsequently no uplifting of humanity.

Challenges come with trials and persecutions, and overcoming them involves a willingness to take responsibility. According to the Gospels, on the morning of the resurrection, Mary Magdalene went to the tomb of Jesus only to discover an empty tomb. Prior to the crucifixion, Jesus had told them that He would rise after the third day, but they had forgotten. In her astonishment she summoned Peter and the other disciple whom Jesus loved—supposedly John—to witness what had happened. Both Peter and John witnessed what had happened, but according to the scripture only the one that loved Jesus—John—believed.

Mary, who was very connected to Jesus spiritually, stayed on at the scene, her eyes wet with tears. Her intuitive spirit must have warned her that she would eventually behold the Master, but she was looking in the wrong direction—in the grave! Suddenly, she saw two angels, one at the head and one at the feet where Jesus had laid. "Why are you weeping?" the angels asked. "They have taken away my Lord, and I don't know where to find Him," she replied.

Suddenly, something within her compelled her to look up when she saw someone whom she thought to be the gardener. "Why are you crying?" he asked. Mary replied, "If you know where they have laid Him, please let me know so that I can find Him."

Mary was totally unprepared for what came next. When she heard her name called in the most intimate way, there was no mistaking the speaker. She then claimed Jesus as her redeemer, exclaiming, *"Rabboni!"* meaning "Master." When we have an intimate relationship with God, He will call us by name and we will experience His presence and power in our lives always. "Fear not: for I have redeemed thee by thy name, for thou at mine" (Isaiah 43:1).

Jesus is always calling his beloved by name, but to be a beloved of Jesus we have to be truly conscious of His love and promises for us by always "looking up". No matter what faces us in the material world, when we look up, or take our eyes off negation, there is always a brighter picture.

The direction of our gaze is of utmost importance. To look down is to dwell in negation and if we concentrate on negation, negation will increase. Lot's wife looked back and she became a pillar of salt.

To look up is to expect Good. If we chose to concentrate on God, then God's good will multiply in our lives. Abraham lifted up his eyes and saw God's abundant and unlimited Good, from all directions. Moses changed the direction of his gaze and turned aside, and when he looked he saw God through a burning bush and discovered his divine potential. After looking down into the grave Mary saw evidence that Jesus had been there, but it wasn't until she was prompted to kook up that she recognized her Master. "In the morning will I direct my prayer unto Thee, and will look up" (Psalm 5:3).

There is a story about a new convert to Christ who had a very strange dream in which he was trapped down in a very deep well in the night. He looked up and saw a single star shining far above him. The star seemed to have had a very profound effect on him as it shone its silvery light upon him and he felt uplifted. He looked down and then he began to go down. He looked up again and he began to go up. He looked down once more and he began to go down. He found that by simply keeping his eyes on the star he rose out of the well until his feet stood firmly on the ground. We never know what awaits us when we look up.

The three people who had firsthand experience of the resurrection were Mary, John, and Peter. Significantly, "to look up" means to change our limited awareness of seeing and being, incorporating the intuitive or feeling nature of Mary, the believing quality of faith that Peter represents, and the harmonizing quality of love represented by the disciple John.

Often during times of adversity we are so engrossed in our trials that we fail to recognize that our good is within our reach, and instead of looking up, we continue to dwell in the darkness of negation.

Because Mary was so engrossed in the death of Jesus, she did not recognize Him right there beside her. Yet no matter how engrossed we are in the dark, there is always hope, as God is always calling us by name. The tomb may appear dark, but there is always an opportunity to resurrect our selves. All we need to do is just to look up in faith.

Charles Fillmore writes, "Many Christians who continue to think about the crucified Jesus are still looking in the tomb for Him. They are trusting in death to save them instead of looking up to the risen glorified Christ who is life wholeness and truth."

To look up is to take our eyes off the challenge and look toward the solution instead. The solution lies right within us, not far off in the sky or in some distant place. The Christ presence is right where we least expect it—within us. The light may appear to come from above, but it is all around us and within us. We are forever connected.

34

A Change of Consciousness

We are what we think.
All that we are arises with our thoughts.
With our thoughts we make the world.
Speak or act with an impure mind, and trouble will follow you
As the wheel follows the ox that draws the cart.

We are what we think. All that we are arises with our thoughts.
With our thoughts we make the world.
Speak or act with a pure mind
And happiness will follow you as your shadow, unshakable.

Buddha

"The next step in human evolution is to transcend thought. This is now our urgent task. It doesn't mean not to think anymore, but simply not to be completely identified with thought, possessed by thought."

Eckhart Tolle

Life constitutes a series of challenges that result in ultimate growth and development of the soul. Challenges appear in all shapes and forms, invariably initiating emotional pain and discomfort, but the truth is when we view them with an attitude of non-resistance, they become our stepping stones and lead us into new awareness.

Sometimes failure, making mistakes and messing things up once in a while is not so much of a bad thing. This is what life is all about—doing, being, successful, failing, making mistakes and trying again and somehow our creativity seems to spring from trying to mend broken pieces.

I proved this reality some time ago when I left my house unattended for quite some time. Because of work deadlines and other important duties I had little time to put my house in order. As a consequence things were completely out of place and before I knew it I felt lost in my own home. As this was quite unlike my true nature I found it hard to concentrate and instead of achieving what I hoped to achieve I found myself completely behind my schedule and to effect some type of normalcy I had to surrender and dedicate an entire day to the cleaning of my house.

Apart from the fact that this was a refreshing break from my routine, I felt completely relaxed and free, and in my effort to restore order I recovered a missing item, which proved to be a tremendous help to complete my assignment. I also discovered new and practical ways to reduce the limited space I had previously created by throwing out what was not needed and by shifting and rearranging the rest.

Nature also has a way of teaching us many things. As I lived in Kansas City, Missouri, some time ago, I experienced a very severe ice storm during the winter that had a great effect on our lives for many days. Fortunately, there were no loss of lives, but activities were curtailed to a minimum and many people were greatly inconvenienced.

It was a very beautiful sight to behold, however, as every trunk, branch, and stem of every tree was laden with the most intricately carved ice that glistened in the sunlight like diamonds. Yet at the same time it was a very sad experience, as late at night one could hear the crashing sound of the tree limbs as they eventually gave way to the weight of the ice.

Not long afterward came the spring, and within a couple of months one could witness a very drastic change, as there was evidence all around of new life, which signaled new beginnings and new consciousness.

As I meditated on this experience, I realized that every death signals a new birth, and when we fail to take responsibility, nature has way of ensuring that it is done for us with natural disasters, in this case with a snow storm. In this way a natural pruning had taken effect for the process of life to be continued, but there was another side to the equation. Not only did people learn to survive after the storm, but people also learned to communicate more with each other and give a helping hand to those adversely affected by the storm. Overall, it was a time of community.

Our lives are no different. When we fail to take care of our bodies with nurturing foods, exercise, and rest we suffer the consequences of ill health. When we neglect our spiritual responsibilities, chaos happens in our lives and propels us to take action. Ultimately, all things will work together for good.

Challenges often come as a signal that a change is in progress. A change in consciousness happens, because we subconsciously had a desire for it. In other words, whenever the student is ready the teacher will appear. Myrtle Fillmore once said

> "All of us sooner or later come to the place in our development where we are no longer satisfied to go on living the old life, without the knowledge of our oneness with God, the Source of our being. Sometimes when we reach that point in our soul's progress, we do not at first know just what is taking place. We may become restless and dissatisfied. We may go through

> experiences that we do not understand. We may even be tempted to think that our good has gone from us. But just as sure as there is a God, the one Presence and one Power, we shall find that all is well and we are but going from one room, as it were, into another larger and lighter room."

Everything works in divine order and nothing happens before the right time. Similarly, the change we desire does not take place outside of us, but within our consciousness. As it is within, so it is without. There is a story about a little boy who constantly asked his father to buy him a duck. One day to his surprise, the father bought him three little duck eggs instead. The little boy cherished the eggs. He attended to them daily; he covered them and kept them warm. Each day he would look at the little duck eggs in pure delight. One day when he returned from school, instead of his eggs he saw broken shells. What had happened to his eggs? He asked his father. Lovingly, his father led him to the backyard and proudly showed him the three little ducks that had come from the eggs.

What an amazing story! How interesting to note that it is not the outer part of us that is important, but what lies within us. Our outer layers are subject to old age, decay, and even death, but the inner part of us will never die.

Charles Fillmore refers to the process of change as "Chemicalization," which he describes as "a condition in the mind, being brought about by the conflict that takes place when a high spiritual realization contacts an old error state of consciousness."

This process helps us to receive new insights and ultimately experience conscious oneness with the Spirit of God. Whenever there is a burning desire within us, we usually go to God in prayer with the hope that God's light will reveal that which we desire. In John 3:1-9 Nicodemus a Pharisee seemed to have experienced a divine stirring from within him when he went to Jesus in the night for clarification. Even though Nicodemus never asked Jesus a question, Jesus told him, "Except a man be born again, he cannot see the kingdom of God". (John 3:3). Jesus further explained to Nicodemus who was still obviously in the dark, that to be born again is to be born of water and of the Spirit.

According to Charles Fillmore in *The Metaphysical Bible Dictionary,* a Pharisee's consciousness represents, "thoughts that arise out of the subconscious, binding man to external forms of religion, without giving him understanding of their real meaning." In the Revealing Word 'Water' he says represents cleansing, while 'Spirit' represents the moving force of God in the universe. So to enter into the kingdom of God one has to cleanse the mind by denying negation; and to be born of Spirit is to acknowledge the presence and power of God as our sufficiency in all things.

Because of misconceptions and ignorance about our true identity in relation to God and the world we live in, most of us display Pharisee consciousness from time to time, becoming self-righteous, self—centered, and egotistical, and fixed in our religious beliefs. There is no virtue in our devotion to the law or to religious beliefs or rituals. Some people for instance believe that merely attending church or having a water baptism are sufficient to offer them salvation,but although these things act as a conduit to foster our spirituality, it ultimately takes a deep surrender of self to bring us to that point of spiritual awareness.

Jesus specified that one has to be born not just of water, but also of the Spirit as well. As we struggle in the process to find ourselves and experience salvation, we need to change the Pharisee mentality within us by denying error (cleansing) and affirming Truth or the goodness of God (Spirit). When we die to our old ways of thinking and being, the light from within begins to emerge and the truth is revealed.

A subsequent release of the old is generally not easy for most people, so arriving at a new consciousness can be an individual experience as well as a gradual process. Nevertheless, the ultimate experience for every person is the inner realization of the presence of God within. This inner realization takes place for those who are prepared mentally, physically, and spiritually. When we consent to be used by the universal process, our hearts will open like a flower and great things will be revealed to us. "And when the spirit of truth is come it will guide you into all truth" (John 16:13).

The Bible is the story of mankind, and every adventure in the Bible depicts different stages in our evolutionary journey. Our human experiences help to mold and shape us so that we may abound in hope, ultimately experiencing the fullness of life. The death of the old self is a continuous process. "I die daily" (1 Cor. 15:31).

Our spiritual work should take precedence over all earthly things, and all things will be added unto us. When we practice the truth constantly, trust God, and surrender to His will and purpose for our lives in due season, we will be victorious. The result consequently depends on the preparation. So it is within, so it is without. The little boy who wanted a duck exercised patience and took care of the little eggs diligently, not really expecting any result, and he was rewarded with an increase of *three* little ducks!

Likewise, it is important that we diligently attend to our spiritual life, and when the time is right we too will reap the rewards. We ought to nourish our souls with good food, exercise, daily prayer and meditation, and right living, and we too will reap the fruits of the Spirit: love, joy, peace, longsuffering, gentleness, goodness, faith, meekness, temperance.

Job suffered many tragedies in the Bible and could not reconcile his dilemmas. His friends were of no help, as they offered no spiritual alternatives. Job thought he was doing everything right in the sight of God, but for some strange reason he could not make a spiritual connection with the Divine Presence. Being self-righteous, Job struggled with his humanity, asking God why the righteous would suffer. After relentlessly searching for an answer Job could find no resolve, and he lamented in chapter 23:8-10

> "Behold, I go forward, but he is not there; and backward, but I cannot perceive him: On the left hand, where he doth work, but I cannot behold him: he hideth himself on the right hand, that I cannot see him: But he knoweth the way I take: when he hath tried me, I shall come forth as gold."

No matter where we are in consciousness, the ups and downs will always surface, so we ought to face our fears and try to find that solid place within to anchor ourselves. The truth is God is always with us, but in order to find Him, we have to search for Him with all our hearts.

When Job exhausted his human reasoning and found no answers to his woes, he finally surrendered to the presence and power of God within him and in that moment of surrender the truth finally dawned on him, and he experienced God's light and peace in its entirety.

Job's new enlightenment was worth all the discomfort and pain he previously experienced. He persevered in trials and overcame his mental struggle, and now he could now see with the eyes of spirit! In his newfound joy Job declared "I heard of thee by the hearing of the ear: but now mine eye seeth thee" (Job 42:5).

Job's patience eventually paid big dividends. Not only did he get to know God much more intimately, but he also received material wealth and success three times as much as he did before.

How happy and relieved Job must have been that he endured the many trials that he faced! Had he not been through these severe challenges he might not have had the opportunity to prove that God is omnipresent, omnipotent and omniscient.

The more we advance in truth, the more challenges we seem to face, and we sometimes even feel like we have made no progress at all. Emily Cady says in *Lessons in Truth* says

> "When these transition periods come in which God would lead us higher, should we get frightened or discouraged, we would only miss the lesson that He would teach and so postpone the day of receiving our fullest and highest gift. In our ignorance and fear, we are thus hanging on to the old grain of wheat that we can see, not daring to let it into the ground and die, lest there be no resurrection, no newness of life, nothing bigger and grander to come of it."

1 Peter 4:12-13 says

> "Beloved, think it not strange concerning the fiery trial which is to try you, as though some strange thing happened unto you. But rejoice, inasmuch as ye are partakers of Christ's sufferings; that, when his glory shall be revealed, ye may be glad also with exceeding joy."

After the breakup of my marriage I encountered many trying experiences, and my search for the truth intensified. Because of willfulness, I had strayed away from my good, but like the prodigal son I managed to find my way back home to my center through a wonderful organization called Unity of Jamaica.

Here at this blessed place I found the answer to all my restlessness. Gradually, my vision became clearer, and a promise of hope and healing beckoned. I became convincingly assured that I was headed in the right direction toward self-growth.

There was something magical in the air the moment I entered the sanctuary. I had a feeling of complete belonging, and I knew instantly that I had found my right spiritual home. I had my first experience with a guided meditation, and the experience had me entranced as I became open and receptive, completely surrendering to the experience.

After a few minutes of releasing my thoughts and relaxing my physical body, I felt a warm glow within me. I literally felt unburdened and uplifted in spirit. I flowed in unison with the rhythm of my heart and experienced a freedom I had never before known. In that moment, time stood still and my experience was a pure unadulterated peace. My experience was so ecstatic that I wanted to remain in that space forever, but the soft, gentle, comforting voice of the minister interrupted my mental solace as he invited us to return to the here and now. Feeling spiritually fed and nourished, I reluctantly opened my eyes, knowing with surety that my life was about to change, my healing at hand.

Having been awakened to this new sense of being, I became delirious with my spiritual practice. I was determined to relive this experience over and over again, and I pledged to devote more time each day in prayer and meditation.

I was in love with God and excited about my new life. I loved my new church home and my newfound family who welcomed me into the fold with warmth and encouragement. Their love and support were enormous, and for the first time in my life I felt a deep sense of peace.

A new chapter of my life had begun, and I looked courageously ahead in great anticipation of many blessings. I was ready to explore the truth and open myself to this new experience, and I looked forward to learning many worthwhile lessons in truth. I was willing to discover my real self and find a new meaning to life.

There were moments of doubts and apprehension, however, when a few people seemed to have doubted my validity. Nevertheless, I learned to ignore the voice of negativity and focused instead on the power and presence of God within each individual. I subsequently found strength and courage to persevere, finally overcoming this feeling of alienation.

Prayer and meditation were my defense, and soon the consternation and rejection I felt quickly dissipated. I continued on my path with a strong resolve never to be intimidated or discouraged, and soon after releasing judgmental thoughts I was accepted by the group.

I began to vigorously apply myself to the study of Truth, and soon I began to learn the truth about myself in relation to God. I learned that as a child of God, I have the power of God within me to create my world of good; that my thoughts and my actions have consequences, and the quality of my world therefore depend upon the type of thoughts I entertain.

In my quest to discover the presence and power of God within me and to understand and live the principles of truth, I began to question my old beliefs that were ingrained in me since childhood. My desire to learn and grow became evident, and my reasoning ability gradually grew stronger and stronger.

It wasn't long before the truth began to unravel and my rational mind began to reason. If God is good and everything that God made is good, then humankind—being made in God's image and likeness—must also be good. And if all things work together for good as we read in Romans 8:28, and if all things were made by God as John 1:3 also tells us, then God must be in every experience, whether we call them good or bad.

I further rationalized from the Bible that God is the source from which everything comes, the source of all power, all authority, and all strength. I concluded that God must therefore be everywhere equally present, within us and without us, in every cell, particle, nerve, tissue or fiber of being, and that He is capable of restoring all things to newness of life and purpose.

The more I began to explore the depth of my being, the more open and receptive I became and the more I began to experience God in every aspect of my life. With my new understanding and reasoning ability the Bible finally began to make sense to me, and my life began to take on a new dimension. How wonderful and comforting it was to know that God is pure love, and that the unconditional love of God frees us from all mistakes of the past or present whenever we seek it. How freeing it was to know that God wants us to experience His goodness in our lives, and that whatever He has is ours. "Son, thou art ever with me, and all that I have is thine."

In order to experience God in all situations, we only need to spend quality time with Him through prayer and meditation and by further practicing the truth. As I began to practice the presence of God, my life became pregnant with possibilities, and amazing things began to happen to me one after the other. I felt as though I had found the pearl of great price. I was walking on holy ground, and Unity of Jamaica became my haven. Here I was spiritually nourished, and I felt like a new creature.

I began to read the Bible more vigorously and to contemplate its teachings, and I asked God to enlighten me and open my awareness to the truth. My understanding of biblical teachings gradually took on a new dimension. I realized that the Bible was actually the story of mankind and reflected hidden and infinite parts of me. This was certainly a rewarding experience, as previously the stories of the Bible seemed very remote and impersonally related. Now the Bible seemed alive, and I was hopeful that with time the light of interpretation would be revealed as I applied myself to the truth.

I began to relate to the characters in the Bible from a collective, individual, past, as well as from a present perspective. Like Job we all have been victimized by some sort of tragedy; like the Israelites we all yearn for the Promised Land; like Simon Peter, who tried to walk on the water, our faith wavers at times; and like David, even the best of us miss the mark and fall short.

At first some metaphysical Bible interpretations by Charles Fillmore seemed farfetched, but the more I opened up my awareness, the more they made sense. I tried not to be too gullible, however, but rather I prayed for a divine understanding. I soon found myself finding my own interpretations, and whatever I was unable to discern I left alone. Gradually, my understanding was increased and the lessons continued to unfold.

The most important element of my journey was to understand the concept of the Christ within as stated in Colossians 1:27. "To whom God would make known what is the riches of the glory of this mystery among the Gentiles; which is Christ in you, the hope of glory." The "Christ within," according to Charles Fillmore in *The Revealing Word,* is "The spiritual nucleus within each person. Each man has within him the Christ idea, which is a state of perfection exemplified by Jesus. All men can attain this perfection by rightful living."

Further study of the Truth also helped me to differentiate between Jesus and the Christ. I discovered that Jesus was a divine human being who lived in a time, place, and culture that expressed human struggles and tragedies, but He nevertheless demonstrated to humankind how we too can experience the love, peace, joy, and light of God at any place or time. Jesus is the way shower in that He demonstrated mastery over self and all aspects of earthly life, and went on to achieve Christ consciousness through a life of purity, love, and power, and we too can do the same. "The things that I do you can do also and greater things than these can you do" (John 14:12).

Charles Fillmore says in *The Revealing Word*

> "Christ is the divine man. Jesus is the name that represents an individual expression of the Christ idea. The Christ abides in each person as potential and perfection. To abide in Christ is to live in the perfection of God mind, the thought of God, the living Christ."

Although each individual is different from a personality standpoint, we nevertheless all share the individuality of the Christ. It is comforting to know that in realty we can never be separated from our Christ Self except through our very minds. "And a man's foes shall be hey of his own household" (Matthew 10:36).

God's presence is within us, without us, and in all situations and circumstances. When we give in to fear, we automatically stop our creativity and the ultimate awakening of our souls. In his book *Stillness Speaks*, Eckhart Tolle says

> "In each human being there is a dimension of consciousness far deeper than thought. It is the very essence of who you are. We may call it presence, awareness, the unconditioned consciousness. In ancient teachings, it is the Christ within, or your Buddha nature."

We experience a false sense of separation whenever we live in sense consciousness, but the good news is that we can always change our thinking at any moment and be reconnected with the Christ of our being. To become conscious is to change our attitudes and beliefs through which the quality of life, as well as the quality of our interaction with others, is determined.

Jesus said in Matthew 16:24, "If any man should come after me, let him deny himself, take up his cross and follow me." To take up one's cross and follow Him is to deny one's belief in lack or limitation, and affirm the truth that as heirs and joint heirs of God we have the potential to live life abundantly. It is comforting to know that the Christ within is constant and unconditional, equally without and within each individual.

In his book *The Twelve Powers of Man*, Charles Fillmore says that each of these powers is represented by spiritual centers in the body, and they are all expressed and developed under the guidance of Divine Mind. These twelve faculties are realized when man is developing from personal consciousness to spiritual consciousness, and they are likened unto the twelve disciples who Jesus called to Him after receiving his soul development. Charles Fillmore describes this awakening as the first and second coming of Christ spoken of in the scriptures.

Identifying with the Christ presence within through prayer and meditation was the ultimate experience of spiritual fulfillment and joy in the Lord for me. I became observant as I endeavored to put my divine faculties of faith, love, understanding, wisdom, power, imagination, order, judgment, strength, zeal or enthusiasm, renunciation, and life to work. As a result of my new awareness, I looked forward to each new day with renewed courage and faith. I became in love with life and enthusiastic about the future, and I looked forward to new discoveries, new insights, new mercies, and a greater awareness in truth.

Life is centered on individual consciousness, and it has been proven that whatever we concentrate on expands. "For as he thinketh in his heart, so is he" (Proverbs 23:7). We were all meant to succeed, but success in life requires action. When we chose to focus our attention on God or good and not on material things, new doors of opportunity will open up for us.

Consequently, what is ours is ours by divine appointment, and no one can take it away from us. "I have set before you an open door and no man can shut it" (Rev. 3:8).

Centered in this awareness, I place myself and all those for whom I pray in the all-encompassing love of God.

I come into your presence giving praise and mighty thanks for all your goodness and tender mercies. I bless You and honor You for Your love, which hath created and sustained me from day to day.

Attuned to you, dear God, I accept my divine potential. I am your child, made in Your image and likeness, ready to receive my good. You are the inner wisdom I seek, the true light that guides me along my life's path. Through Your healing grace I am transformed by the renewing of my mind.

All that I could ever need or want comes to me through Your loving provision. You know the desires of my heart; You know what is best for me. My thoughts are centered and in tune with spirit. I make wise choices and I am blessed.

In this awareness, dear God, I feel the power of Your divine presence continually blessing me. I speak the word of love, wholeness, harmony, peace, prosperity, success, and spiritual fulfillment for myself, my friends, my family, my loved ones, and for all mankind. I rely on Your power to adjust and prosper my life. With Your help, dear God, my inner world is in order, and a pattern of order is expressed in my life.

Thank You God, for Your guiding, comforting, and protecting presence; for hearing me always, and for hearing me now. I pray this in the name and through the power of Jesus the Christ. Amen

35

Finding the Key

> "When you close your doors and make darkness within, remember never to say that you are alone for you are not alone; nay, God is within, and your genius is within, and what need have they of light to see what you are doing?"
>
> Epictetus

Opportunities are always knocking at our doors, but we have to be in tune with the spirit of God in order to hear the knock, and be willing and ready to open the door. "Behold I stand at the door and knock: if any man hear my voice, and open the door, I will come in to him, and will sup with him, and he with me" (Rev. 3:20).

The kingdom of God—an abundance of every good thing—is inherent in each of us, but ultimately we have to seek it and live it in thought, word, and deed. The more we practice the principles of Truth, the more successes we will achieve in life.

In Luke 17:21 when the Pharisees questioned Jesus about when the kingdom of God should come, Jesus told them, "The kingdom of God cometh not with observation: Neither shall they say, Lo here! or, lo there! for, behold, the kingdom of God is within you." In other words, all the good that that we desire is already within us. There is no need to toil, sweat, beg, or plead. It is not about using the intellect to achieve. It is about tuning in to the mind of God through which we receive divine ideas.

We were all meant to have abundance, and the key to unlocking the door is to discover and claim our divine potential. When Jesus asked his disciples whom they believed Him to be, they all had different answers. Simon Peter was the most insightful, however, when he replied, "Thou art the Christ, the Son of the living God." Jesus commended Peter for his amazing insight, saying to him

> "For flesh and blood hath not revealed it unto thee, but my Father which is in heaven . . . And I will give unto thee the keys of the kingdom of heaven: and whatsoever thou shalt bind on earth shall be bound I heaven: and whatsoever thou shalt loose on earth shall be loosed in heaven" (Matthew 16:17, 19).

Jesus then renamed him Peter, meaning the "rock," further implying that on this rock he would build his church.

The consciousness of the presence of God within us is what we need to demonstrate Good. This is our birthright. We are right in the midst of it at all times. We do not have to go searching for it. By looking within, accepting who we are, and claiming our divine inheritance we can find the key that unlocks the door to our good.

In 2 Kings 4:17, Elijah reminded a widow that one could achieve abundant success using what is available. With a son to maintain and bills piling up after her husband's death, she became financially destitute. In a state of panic she went to the prophet Elijah for help. "What do you have in your house?" Elijah asked her. "Not a thing," the woman replied, "save a pot of oil."

The first thing Elijah instructed her to do was to borrow some vessels from her neighbors. Next she was then advised to fill them with the oil. Lastly she was told to sell the oil which was collected, pay her debts and live off the rest of money she collected. The widow sent her son to work borrowing many vessels from the neighbors and filling them all with oil and to her amazement the 'little oil' she thought she had completely fill every vessel that was burrowed from her neighbors, with not a drop remaining.

This demonstration by Elijah was more than a miracle. It was a divine outworking of God's law. God's substance can never be depleted unless to the one who believes in lack or limitation. God's substance is freely available to all, but we must believe, and not just believe but we must also put our creativity to work.

The truth is that God is able to do all things in and through us, and there is no limit to God's good. The fact that the oil stopped after the last vessel was filled seems to convey the extent of the widow's consciousness. Elijah did not specify how many vessels she was to burrow . . . She burrowed just the amount of vessels that her consciousness could accommodate. If she had a house full of vessels, the oil would have filled them all. This reinforces the truth that as we believe so do we achieve.

As always the truth cannot be over emphasized that we all have the ability to change our limited beliefs and demonstrate God's abundant good by simply changing our thinking, accepting our divine potential, and putting divine ideas to work.

Metaphysically, a widow is portrayed as one who believes in lack. The house in which the widow lived represents consciousness. The death of her husband represents a change in the thinking process. Oil represents spiritual substance that is always available. Neighbors represent thoughts arising out of the subconscious signifying a message of Truth, Vessels represent our capacity to comprehend and our ability to measure and appreciate life, love and Truth and Son represents a state of consciousness in which the truth is realized above error.

Metaphysically, this story tells us that the kingdom of God within us is a limitless source of abundant and never ending Good. Any belief in lack can be quickly overturned by changing one's thinking process, believing in one's divine potential and by putting one's creativity to the test.

We have been given free will, but we have the ability to choose the higher road. We do not have to accept limitation. Because we have been given the gift of free choice, our thoughts are sometimes governed by our self-will, the consequence of which is often a feeling of lack. In truth, we cannot be separated from our Christ-nature, which is opulent, rich, and free. When we return to our Christ-center within, focus on our divine capabilities, and apply ourselves to the principles of truth, we are bound to succeed in our endeavors.

Although we may study truth to the utmost degree, nothing in our lives will actually change until we give ourselves permission to change and nothing will change until our awareness changes.

How to Initiate Change

1. Know who you are

God is Spirit; therefore, in our true state we are also spirit. Spirit is the source of everything; therefore, we are one with it. When we are aware of spirit and spend time with it, we will experience it.

To actualize the creative process we have to still the mind. When we still the mind, we know ourselves as pure consciousness. This happens when we align with the Spirit of God through nature, prayer, and meditation. Deepak Chopra says in his book *The Seven Spiritual Laws of Success*, "We are gods in embryo . . . connected to the source that creates everything. As our awareness of this fact expands, awareness itself shifts and new states of awareness become possible and accessible."

2. Expect good

Desire is not a bad thing. Unless we desire something, we will not get it. When we desire something it is actually the Higher Power knocking at our door, reminding us that we can have it. Nothing in the world can keep us from going forward once we know with authority that within us is the power of progress. If we lack the consciousness that we have the power to succeed, then we surely will experience stumbling blocks in our way.

God created us free and independent of limiting thoughts and beliefs, and the universe supports us in whatever we desire. We should always be aware of God's presence within us and know that our good is already supplied. All we need to do is to take a stand and expect only good. God's light, perfection, and life are all ours. In Him we live. He lives in us. We ought to find that Presence and live in it. God's limitless resources are at our command.

3. Entertain good thoughts

Every thought and every act has consequences, and we reap whatever we sow. If our thoughts are constantly negative, then it follows that our lives will also be negative. There is a story about a sales representative whose sales constantly amounted to the same amount—$11,791 each month. After being questioned, the young man complained that he worked in one of the most difficult areas in which to work.

The manager devised a plan and subsequently exchanged the area in which the man worked for much more lucrative areas. At the end of the month, the manager was astounded. The agent's sales for the month amounted to the same amount—$11,791.

It is obvious that this was the extent of this young man's consciousness. He had put a limit to his earnings, and no matter where he worked, his earnings would amount to the same.

Even though there may be equal opportunities for all, some people are able to excel while others don't simply because of their limitations. Some people sit and wait for some stroke of luck to land on their doorstep, while others are active in their search to attain it.

4. Live in the moment

The universe flows in divine order and so do our lives. There is a commonality of the experience of seasons applicable to both the universe and to the lives of humankind. The universe unfolds in a pattern, bringing spring, summer, autumn, and winter. Likewise humankind unfolds, growing from infancy to adolescence to adulthood. We will always experience ups and downs, but they are only uncomfortable so long as we view them as indispensable. Tough times do not last, but tough people do. If we are not happy with our lives as they are right now, we need to trust the divine plan; it is ever capable of unfolding in perfect, divine order. To everything there is a season, and a time to every purpose under the heaven (Ecc. 3:1). We should let go of our rigid grasp on life and live one moment at a time, changing what we can, and leaving the rest to God.

5. Develop the habit of Giving

Giving and receiving is a natural part of our being. They are different aspects of the flow of energy. We should be willing to give that which we seek. This will keep abundance and energy flowing through our lives. When we hold back and try to hoard, we invite stagnation and energy becomes blocked.

We should be careful of our intention for giving. We should never give to receive, as we have nothing to gain from this. If we would like to see our blessings multiplied, we should give freely and joyfully, as God loves a cheerful giver.

There are many other aspects of giving besides monetary giving such as caring, affection, attention, appreciation, and love. Affection is touching, and touching has the capacity to heal the one who is touched, as well as the one who touches. When we pay attention by listening with our entire being, energy is also circulated. When we show appreciation and reach out to give a helping hand to others, we live in harmony with the universe, and energy is circulated throughout our lives.

6. Never Give up

Author Ralph Marston states “Success is not the absence of failure. Success is what happens when you chose to move on beyond failure. Frustration and disappointment are painful for a very positive reason. The pain pushes you in the direction of achievements.”

Some time ago when I worked as a sales representative, I called a particular client to initiate an order, and I was told to call back the following day. After calling back the next day, I was promised a return call within the next two hours. Two days after not hearing from her, I called once more, and again I was redirected and told to call back in a few hours.

I waited until the next day, and was once again asked to call back the following day. This routine continued; I was asked to call back again and again and again. I was now at the point of frustration and just about ready to quit, but my resilient spirit and determination got the better of me. I was determined to win, and soon after persevering for almost two months I received my order!

7. Bless what you have

There is something mysterious about being thankful. It somehow raises our spirits and sets the tone for increase. We can never thank God enough when we consider how many blessings we have received each day. When we praise God and give Him thanks for what we have, no matter how small, He will increase that mite.

This was demonstrated in the feeding of the five thousand, as well as the story of the widow and the oil. Although the fish and the loaves seemed insufficient to feed the crowd Jesus gave God thanks for what was visible, knowing that there was no limit to God's inexhaustible supply. Everyone was astonished after Jesus acknowledged and gave God thanks, when five fish and two loaves of bread fed over five thousand people. Likewise the widow learnt how to multiply what she had on hand by believing in the inexhaustible supply of God within her, and also by putting her creativity to work.

Sometimes we tend to give thanks only for what we can see, but we should also learn to give thanks in advance even for what we hope to have. A farmer who always had bountiful crops was asked how he accounted for them. He explained that whenever he ploughed a field he blessed each furrow. When he planted a seed, he blessed each grain that went into the ground. When he went home at night, he blessed his whole farm and put it lovingly into God's Hand, thanking Him for the crop to come.

8. Surrender to the process

To surrender is to become still and trust in God's omnipresence, omnipotence, and omniscience. It is all right to have desires but we should not be too attached one way or the other to the outcome by constantly looking over our shoulder for the result. To become fixed on results is to doubt God. God works in the silence and everything in the universe unfolds in silence. Our responsibility therefore is to trust the divine spirit within and become one with it. The universal process is working with us always. When we surrender to the unknown, we enter into a field of infinite possibilities. Things happen beyond our wildest imaginations, as opportunities and surprise unexpectedly arise from deep within.

Consequently, in order to unlock the door to our good, we first need to turn our attention to our own indwelling Christ Spirit, and God, who is always willing, will give abundantly of Himself without measure.

In her book *God Will See You Through,* Mary Kupferle writes

> "Take time to be quiet, to be still and contemplate the truth that God's love is right there with you and His light is shining throughout your mind revealing all that you need to see and know. Listen within and let God's wisdom gently turn your thoughts over and over until the questions become answers and the doubts become newborn faith."

I invite you now to become still for a while and become aware of this moment. Mentally list all your desires. Know that all your desires are God's desires for you. Now, surrender them to the cosmic power of the universe. Know that according to your belief it is done.

36

Learning to Take Responsibility

"To resurrect, to rise into the sky, you must first meet the devil head on. If you keep looking for him in others, you will not find him. If you don't believe in him, you haven't bothered to look inside your own mind."

Paul Ferrini

"The good or ill of a man lies within his own will."

Epictetus

Affirmative Statements

The Father and I are one
When one door closes another door opens
Every exit is an entry somewhere else
All things work together for good
Whatever you see in others is a reflection of yourself
You reap what you sow
You cannot escape from yourself
Life is what you make it
The universe is on your side
The only thing that you keep is what you give away
The thing that you are unwilling to let go of will become your cross
It doesn't take a lot of strength to hold on; it takes a lot of strength to let go

Most of our distresses, disappointments, and sorrows in life are due to our belief in the myth of separation. The more willing we are to take responsibility however, the easier it becomes to effect the changes we need for healing of the mind, body and spirit.

We are all made in the image and likeness of God, but we also have human tendencies. When we become willing participants to acknowledge our faults and our misconceptions about our-selves, who we are and where we are in consciousness, we are ready to take responsibility. Nothing will change in the outer world unless we first acknowledge where we are in consciousness, embrace the little self, and let life unfold.

Taking responsibility is about changing our limited way of thinking and being without projecting our imperfections and inadequacies unto others. Committing to change is a big part of taking responsibility and change involves discomfort, patience and the unconditional acceptance of self and others. As we become bombarded with cares of the world, rather than facing our shadows, we tend to avoid them, projecting our feelings of insecurity onto others and engaging in various types of outer distractions. Unfortunately, holding others responsible for our experiences only serves to hinder our progress and hold ourselves in bondage.

To take responsibility is to acknowledge our powerlessness. It is to let go of the ego and know that we of selves are nothing. God is in charge. He is the only power and presence in our lives and in the world. "All things were made by Him; and without Him was not anything made that was made. (John 1:3).

One of the biggest obstacles which block our spiritual realization is reluctance in facing our shadows. In taking responsibility and facing our shadows our lives are transformed as we seek release from self-imposed bondage. We learn to make peace with the past, resolving past issues, hurts, and disappointments, and connecting the missing pieces that kept us from demonstrating our true worth.

Taking responsibility can be viewed as a healing process, which produces inner growth and outer transformation. Healing first begins after there is an acknowledgment that feeling wounded, hurt, and feelings of mistrust happen only because we feel disconnected from our divine self.

There are many lessons to be learned in life, and we are never too old to learn them. Sometimes taking responsibility is delayed because of the ego, and action is taken only after we have exhausted all options and human resources. To take responsibility is to acknowledge our shortcomings without blame or guilt, and to be willing to do whatever it takes to transform them.

Both victim and victimizer, light and the darkness are aspects of the little self, and we take responsibility by simply embracing them both. By embracing the darkness, we experience the light, liberating the self and ultimately the world.

Healing of mind, body, and spirit is the ultimate aim for most people. However, maintaining one's healing is a continuous process, which requires a high level of responsibility and commitment, self-discipline and humility. Consequently, healing is only temporary for some people because they have not learnt to take the responsibility required to maintain a consciousness of the Christ presence within them.

Finding time each day for prayer and meditation will assist us in taking responsibility and finding meaning for our lives. When we go to God in prayer with sincerity and humility and surrender all our cares, our world will be transformed, and everything will unfold in the right perspective. Daily communion with the Divine Presence will instill within us our self worth and ultimate call to action. We ultimately learn to accept responsibility, also realizing that no one can do the work for us.

Taking responsibility is being aware of each breath that we take knowing that the breath is what connects us to the Almighty. It is to trust the process and acknowledge that each moment is a blessed moment filled with golden opportunities. When we begin to pay attention to our thoughts, words, and actions, everything flows in unison with the divine.

The "I am" is a very powerful tool. The key to Jesus' power was His constant affirmation and realization of the "I Am." Jesus demonstrated His divinity by the power of His word and He went on to prove the innate powers of the mind and body by constantly affirming "I am": "I am the bread of life": "I am the light of the world": "I am the true vine": "I am the good shepherd": "I am the door of the sheep": "I am the resurrection and the life": "I am the way, the truth and the life."

Jesus told us in John 14:12, "He that believeth on me, the works that I do shall he shall do also; and greater works than these shall he do; because I go unto my Father . . ." To take responsibility therefore is to claim our divine inheritance by speaking boldly in the name "I am". "If you shall ask anything in my name, I will do it" (John 14:14).

In the book *The Revealing Word,* Charles Fillmore writes "The 'I am' is Spiritual identity; the real or Christ Mind of each individual . . . the "I am" is the metaphysical name of the spiritual self, as distinguished from the human self." Consequently, we take the name of the Lord in vain whenever we attach limitation or negativity to the "I am." Thou shalt not take the name of the Lord thy God in vain; for the Lord will not hold him guiltless that taketh His name in vain" (Exodus 20:7).

Finally, to take responsibility is to nourish the soul with adequate exercise, rest, and food; to find time for play and relaxation; to connect with nature and to let go and let God. When we connect with the beloved within us, the beloved without us will materialize. As we learn to take responsibility, we ultimately become more fruitful; and every seed we sow takes root and grows.

37

A Seven-Day Contract with God (Working with the Law of Mind)

Day # 1

> "Wilt Thou be made whole?"
>
> John 5:6

Affirmation: "Using my imagination I see myself as God sees me; healthy and whole in mind, body, and spirit."

The more I affirm this statement and believe it, the more my subconscious mind accepts it as a reality. I am a child of God, made in His image and after His likeness. Therefore, I have all the divine attributes of the divine mind.

By taking myself out of the way and surrendering to my Christ self, I am able to feel the presence of God permeating, cleansing, revitalizing, and refreshing my entire being. In the stillness of my soul a paradigm shift takes place, and the still small voice reassures me, "Lo, I am with you always."

Day # 2

> "Thou salt also decree a thing, and it shall be established unto thee: and the light shall shine upon thy ways."
>
> Job 22:28

Affirmation: "I expect only good and my good comes to me now."

God is instant, constant, and unchanging good. I am made in His image and likeness. Therefore, I am also constant and unchanging good. I live in this awareness that the Christ presence within aligns me with my God-self. All things work for good, so I behold good in everything. I do not strive to achieve good. I am good.

I have no desire except to feel God's presence in my life. When I acknowledge God's presence and power within me, my life flows in divine order and my cup is filled to overflowing. I let go and let God work in and through me to bring forth His manifest blessings. I claim my good with gratitude, and I enjoy the fruits of the spirit that are always available to me. I give thanks that the presence of God within me is ever-renewing, all-providing, and ever-protecting. All my needs are met. I am prospered and blessed in every area of my life. I am whole and free.

Day # 3

> "God is in the midst of her; she shall not be moved;
> God shall help her, and that right early,"
>
> Psalm 46:5

Affirmation: "I am calm and centered in the Christ presence. Nothing can disturb the calm peace of my soul."

As I go about my daily routine, little annoyances come in my way, and at times I may get easily distracted. Temptations do come from every angle, but I keep remembering my contract with God, and I know that with God as my protector I have the power within me to rise above all limiting thoughts and beliefs. No matter where I am in consciousness, I can never be separated from God's protecting presence. He is my rock, my shield, and my hiding place. I stay connected to God through prayer, and all feelings of doubt, anxiety, and worry fade away.

Day # 4

> "Thy word is a lamp unto my feet, and a light unto my path."
>
> Psalm 119:105

Affirmation: "The light of the Christ fills me with all that I need to live fully. I am confident, happy, and successful in all my endeavors."

I start my day today knowing that with God as my silent partner nothing can hinder me from achieving my good. The light of God is my dwelling place. God's Word is a lamp unto my feet and a light unto my path. Feeling deeply anchored in this light of God frees me from all tension and stress. God within me is my anchor, so I keep my mind stayed on Him and I accomplish all my tasks with ease and confidence. It is a wonderful experience to live in the kingdom of God. I feel safe, comforted, alive, enthusiastic, successful, and free.

Day # 5

> "I can do all things through Christ which strengtheneth me."
>
> Philippians 4:13

Affirmation: "The presence of God within me is a limitless source of faith, strength, and power."

Something wonderful is happening to me today. I am empowered with the understanding that God is with me always, and there is nothing to fear. Because God loves me, I have within me all that I need to face everything in life. He has fully prepared me for life's entire journey as His love, life, guidance, wisdom, strength, peace, and power flow through me generously and freely.

God within me is a powerhouse of unlimited good, an unending source of faith, strength, and power. I therefore cannot fail. God loves me just as I am. He guided me through every experience in life. I am victorious, an over-comer and a beloved child of God.

Day # 6

> "Then shall thy light break forth as the morning, and thine health shall spring fort speedily."
>
> Isaiah 58:8

Affirmation: "God is my health; I can't be sick."

Today I give thanks for God's breath of life. I bless and honor my body and its functions for being the temple of God. I nourish my mind and body with the proper nutrients, adequate rest, and exercise. Any form of restlessness or discomfort in me is instantly converted into strength and wholeness, and a new surge of life now wells up within me. I am totally transformed into new ways of thinking and being.

I relax my body now and allow God's love to flow gently from my heart and radiate throughout my entire being. The spirit of God within me is a source of ever-renewing faith and strength. I am sustained by God's presence. I am free of tension, stress, doubts, and fear. Praise God!

Day # 7

> "In Him was life: and the life was the light of men."
>
> John 1:4

Affirmation: "God's life within awakens me. I am alive, alert, and enthusiastic."

This is the day that the Lord has made. I rejoice and give thanks for it. I am conscious of the changes that are now taking place in my life, and I embrace these changes because I trust the process. I open myself to receive a divine flow of knowledge and wisdom. Divine inspiration now floods my subconscious mind, and I feel empowered by the Holy Spirit within.

My mind is poised and my heart is serene, for I know that the spirit of God works in and through all to bring forth great possibilities in my life. I feel wonderful! I am energetic, confident, and blessed. I am free and unlimited, open to all possibilities. I am thankful for life, for God's grace, for divine understanding, and for my growing ability to discern the truth. Thank you, God!

38

The Abundance of the Universe

Living life with the right attitude is no doubt the prerequisite to enjoying the abundant life outlined by the Master, Teacher, and Way-shower Jesus the Christ. Where there is right intention, good character, unselfish motives, and a rich Christ consciousness, energy flows, and the abundance of the universe take effect in our lives.

The abundance of the universe manifests in many different ways, but in order to realize it, one has to be in tune with God and be cognizant of one's blessings. Every human being is a child of God, and just as an earthly father provides for his children, even more so will our heavenly Father provide for our spiritual and physical needs. God is infinite and boundless wealth, and as His children we are heirs to it all!

We are heirs of God; therefore we were all meant to be successful. Success is knocking at our doors each and every day, but we need to act; we need to open the door. Success, therefore, comes with the price of assertiveness, alertness, self-discipline, willingness, and most of all faith in believing that with God all things are possible.

Because God is good, He would never create conditions of hunger, thirst, desires, or needs that cannot be satisfied. God created humankind in His own image and after His likeness. Mankind, therefore, has the potential to co-create good with God as principle. God is the source of all good things, and because all He has is ours, the demand and the supply must therefore be equal.

God wants us to have an abundance of every good thing. The fact that we desire or want something means that it was there for us in the first place. We are His heirs, but we experience lack only because we believe in the myth of separation from God or from our good. We always have a choice either to believe in our divine potential and experience abundance, or to doubt our divine capabilities and experience lack.

Regardless of where we are in consciousness, the Father is always with us, and whatever the Father hath is ours. Therefore, we can never be separated from our good except in thought. The realization of our good can only be experienced through the conscious awareness of God, who is within us and without us. As soon as the prodigal son reconnected with his father, he was instantly reinstated in his rightful place as heir to his father's abundance.

God's kingdom is not limited in any way, but we find Him only when we diligently seek Him. He will freely give to us the desires of our hearts. Jesus tells us in Matthew 7:7-8

> "Ask, and it shall be given you; seek, and ye shall find; knock, and it shall be opened unto you: For every one that asketh receiveth; and he that seeketh findeth; and to him that knocketh, it shall be opened."

God is all, and all is good. He is our sufficiency in all things. He is both physical and spiritual. He is our help in every need. He is in essence everything that we desire. When we understand the laws of the mind in relation to God, we will realize that the principle Jesus used in feeding the five thousand is the same principle we ought to use in demonstrating our own good from healing to supply.

For us to have abundance in our lives we first have to have consciousness of abundance. With God the sky is the limit, but we have to work in partnership with the Divine presence. We have to believe that there is indeed abundance; not somewhere far away and out of reach, but within our very grasp. Next we need to seek it, not by toiling and sweating, but by being open and receptive to divine guidance from within and acting on it. "Lift up now thine eyes, and look from the place where thou art northward, and southward, and eastward, and westward: For all the land which thou seest, to thee will I give it, and to thy seed for-ever" (Gen. 13:14-15).

To "*lift up our eyes and see*" is to raise our consciousness and believe that nothing is too difficult for us to achieve though God. The kingdom of God is already within us, and the sky is the limit; but we must have the right consciousness to get there by trusting and being innovative and humble in spirit.

It has been told that some time ago during the Great Depression a gentleman owned a huge sheep-rearing field in Texas. Unfortunately, because of this depression, the gentleman struggled to take care of his bills and his family. In fact, he nearly lost his property. Things were so bad that he had to rely on government subsidy.

Then one day, things changed drastically when it was discovered that his land had an output of thousands of gallons of oil. As he had signed an agreement when he purchased the land, he consequently had full rights to the property. Having been forced to live like a pauper, the gentleman was suddenly and instantly turned into a millionaire!

Many of us wish that we would strike gold in a similar fashion, and some of us might see it as remotely farfetched, but we were all meant to have abundance. It is right within our reach, but we have to act. We too can strike gold, not necessarily by purchasing a sheep rearing property, but by accepting and claiming our divine inheritance.

Because of His belief in the omnipresence of God, Jesus was successful in all walks of life, and the more successful He was, the more He stayed connected to God in prayer. Jesus knew that He had an inexhaustible supply of every good thing within him, and wealth, health, and prosperity were therefore within His very grasp. Jesus never took God's goodness for granted, however, and He demonstrated this by doing the work, raising His consciousness to achieve, giving thanks in advance, and then claiming His desired good.

God's abundance is everywhere, equally present, and equally distributed. In order to demonstrate God's abundance, however, we have to be fully conscious, devoting our lives to the divine presence within us, giving thanks always in advance for our needs to be met, and by claiming our desired good by speaking the Word. Using five loaves and two fish, Jesus showed us how to have a consciousness of abundance in the face of apparent lack, and demonstrated how the potency of thought and constant acknowledgment of God can work outstandingly in the miracle of the feeding of the five thousand people in the Gospels of Matthew, Mark, Luke, and John.

It was near the Jewish festival of Passover, a very busy time in Jerusalem. Jesus wanted to be alone with His disciples, but the crowd would not allow that. They had heard of the many miracles that Jesus had done, so they wanted to share in the experience. Although Jesus wanted to be alone, His compassionate spirit gave in to the needs of the people, and so He availed Himself to the needy crowd.

People of all description gathered together to see Jesus. They were eager to listen to Him, and so Jesus sat down to teach them. He healed the sick and taught the people about the kingdom of heaven. Evening came and the people stayed. *This was worth it*, they thought. They would never be the same again. It therefore didn't matter that they were in the desert and they had no shelter nor food.

The disciples became concerned, however. "Send the people away so that they may buy food in the town as they go home," they told Jesus. But Jesus would not hear of that. "We must feed them before turning them away," Jesus said. "Where can we buy bread for them to eat?" The disciples reasoned that buying two hundred pennyworth of bread would hardly be sufficient for each one to have even a small piece, as there were five thousand men besides the women and children present. "They had no idea that they would have journeyed so far in the desert," they declared. But Jesus knew what the disciples did not know. He knew that God's substance is always available when you work with the divine law.

As fate would have it, one small boy saved the day. He had not forgotten his lunch basket. In it there were five small loaves of barley bread and two small fish. He willingly offered his lunch to share with the multitudes of people in the desert.

The disciples watched in awe. They were curious. How was Jesus going to share five small loaves of bread and two fish with over five thousand people? "This is going to be interesting," they must have thought.

Jesus knew that God answers even before we call, and while we yet speak God hears (Isaiah 65:24), so next Jesus acknowledged God as omnipotent, omnipresent, and omniscient, after which He looked up to heaven, blessed the food, and gave thanks in advance for the manifestation. With a sure conviction of God's omnipresence and opulence, Jesus then broke the loaves and divided the fish among all the people, and miraculously not only did they all eat, but all were filled and there were also twelve basketfuls remaining.

There are certain principles involved in this story that help to unlock the door to uncover our consciousness of good.

1. Acknowledge God as absolute Good, everywhere equally present.

If we are made in God's image and after His likeness (Genesis 1:26), then we also have the potential to be good. Also, wherever we are God is. God is all and all is God (John 1: 3). Therefore, God is divine substance, and we also have the potential to manifest divine substance.

2. Establish Order in all things

Life flows much better when centered on purpose. God is not the author of confusion (1 Cor. 14:33), so before we go to God, we need to set our priorities right. First we get ourselves centered by getting rid of outer distractions and focusing our attention on God within us. In this awareness we expect only the highest good. Jesus first initiated order by asking that the people be seated in groups of fifty. When there is order in our minds, then we can begin to claim what is rightfully ours—the abundance of God's kingdom.

3. Learn to connect with God through Prayer

Prayer is an activity of the mind, so our minds are the connecting link to God. When we focus our attention on God with prayer and meditation, all our needs will be supplied (Matthew 6:33). Jesus first acknowledged God in prayer before claiming His good.

4. Acknowledge the Gift in Giving

It is in giving that we receive. Even in the face of adversity, it is important to give. Jesus likened the kingdom to a little child, and it is interesting to note that a small boy in this story had such a powerful consciousness and lesson to teach in the act of generosity. This is certainly the consciousness of the divine presence within. We all can learn so much from little children that God is opulent, absolute source of all Good things. We become as little children when we live in this awareness. Children have no fear of losing. They know that their parents will always take care of their needs.

5. Look beyond the Appearances

Jesus looked beyond the physical appearance of two loaves of bread and five fish. There is always abundance in the Father's house, but what we see is normally what we will get. If we can envision abundance, that is what we will manifest. If we envision scarcity or lack, that's what we will demonstrate. Ideally, we have to reach for what we want first by seeing it with our imagination.

It is good to note that Jesus did not place His attention on the food that was available. He placed His attention on the power and presence of God. He knew that God's substance is inexhaustible, so instead of seeing two fish and five loaves He looked beyond the appearances and lifted His vision to a higher frequency. Hence, He saw God's provision as an unlimited amount and sufficient for everyone.

6. Whatever you bless blesses you in return

To bless something is to invoke good upon it. This is a spiritual principle that never ceases to bring an increase. When we bless finances, our health, our children, our relationships, our vehicles, our home, and the food that we eat, we somehow bless the Giver of all good things—God the good, omnipotent—who in return increases our good magnificently.

The working of this miracle by Jesus shows us how the seemingly impossible can become possible. Five thousand men, women, and children were all fed with five loaves of bread and two fish. Inexhaustible mind-substance is available at all times to everyone. Spiritual substance, which comes from the opulence of God's kingdom, is never depleted, but we have to learn how to take hold of it using our consciousness.

This limitless and unfailing resource is always ready to give of itself. It has no choice in the matter; it must give, for that is the nature of God.

7. Learn to Conserve. Do not squander God's abundance

Another important factor in demonstrating God's abundance is to be conservative of God's substance; to not squander or take it for granted. Although God's substance is inexhaustible, we should never waste or squander divine substance. This shows a lack of appreciation, and whatever we squander we will end up wanting. Jesus wanted to get this message across, so He advised the people present to gatherer together the twelve baskets of leftovers that remained.

The True Gift

This miracle excited the people. When our needs are met, we become joyful and expectant of more blessings. As a result of this miracle, the people wanted Jesus to become their king. Jesus had a different agenda, however. His mission was not to rule an earthly kingdom; His mission was to do the will of the Father; to seek and to save that which was lost. He therefore sent the people away and went up unto the mountaintop alone to pray.

Whenever we acknowledge God in every experience both good and bad, abundant blessings will unfold. God's abundance is available to all who seek it, but we should not sit around in an attitude of complacency. Although there are certain measures of life's blessings like sunlight, rain, the air that we breathe, and many other essential gifts freely given to all regardless of what we have done or left undone, we definitely need to live a Christ-centered life in order for us to experience God's abundance. To experience His abundance is to live in the kingdom of God, and to live in the kingdom of God is to seek Him always, to be obedient to His Word, and to trust in His divine will of good for us despite daily the trials and tribulations in life.

God's abundance is not necessarily about the outer demonstration of material possessions; it is about moving from sense consciousness to spiritual consciousness with an inner sense of contentment, confidence, and appreciation. Most of all, it is about God delivering in the appearance of lack and obvious need.

The principle that Jesus used to manifest divine substance applies to all aspects of our lives, but we should never seek God only for our desires to be fulfilled. In Luke 4:3-4 the Devil knew that Jesus was hungry so he tempted Jesus, "If you truly are the Son of God, command this stone that it may be made bread." Jesus answered him, "Man shall not live by bread alone, but by every word of God." The realization of the Christ spirit within us is more important than food or clothing. When we have the consciousness of God, we do not have to fish for food, clothes, or shelter. Having a consciousness of God as our all sufficiency is, in essence, everything that we need. "Follow me and I will make you fishers of men" (Matthew 4:19).

God's supply is opulent and unlimited and materializes in many shapes and forms. There is no stereotype ways in which it manifests in our lives. All it takes is a conscious belief in God's omnipotence, omnipresence, and omniscience. When there is complete surrender of self, God who is always willing, will to give us all which is perfect and good. "Every good gift and every perfect gift is from above and cometh down from the Father of lights with whom there is no variableness, neither shadow of turning" (James 1:17).

The Lord Will Provide

The more I invited the Presence of God into my experience, the more I learned to surrender to Him for the perfect plan of my life to unfold according to His perfect will and purpose. Yes, I had many desires and many anxious moments, but through it all I learned that learning to let go and let God was the main object of my existence. Many times I tried and failed, but I never stopped trying, as I knew deep within that God wanted me to find that anchor.

As I became more ingrained in the practice of truth principles, acknowledging God in all things became my mainstay, and God's abundance never failed to manifest in my life time and time again. Following the footsteps of Jesus comes with trials and errors, but the more we try, the more we will succeed. Sometimes things happen in our lives that at the onset may appear frightening and overwhelming, but they usually work for good in the end.

This reality became evident just prior to receiving my ministerial training, when for some unknown reason I lost interest in my successful garment manufacturing business. My lack of interest unfortunately resulted in a decline in sales that further led to the closure of my business. Unfortunately, I had many financial obligations to fulfill and I had no idea how I would survive. As my financial resources grew more and more exhausted, I began to experience a crisis that took a toll on my health. I tried everything I could possibly do to recover from my financial dilemma, but to no avail. Prayer was my only defense.

I knew from the depth of my soul that God would provide, but I must admit that at times I had my doubts. Not knowing how or when God would come to my aid, I held on to my faith with a great conviction that He would supply all my needs. One morning after my daily ritual of prayer and meditation, as I reflected on my financial dilemma, I began to daydream. As I drifted off into oblivion, I visualized a package with money mysteriously arriving at my door. I humored myself and brought myself back to reality, dismissing this idea as being ridiculous.

Despite my financial situation that morning, I was in a jubilant mood. With my thoughts centered on God as my all sufficiency, I felt very hopeful. Putting my needs aside for a moment, I went for my usual morning walk feeling strangely uplifted and light. I began to sing songs of praise and thanksgiving when suddenly something on the ground caught my attention. I stooped down to examine it and to my amazement it was a Jamaican $500.00 bill! I was astounded. Not long ago I had envisioned this miracle, and now it was really happening after all. How great is our God!

God had shown me that the abundance of His kingdom is within my very reach. There is no lack in God! The amount I received that morning was hardly enough to take care of my needs in that moment, but it was a definite reminder that the Lord will provide. I continued my morning walk in joy affirming, "God is my instant constant and abundant supply. In Him there is no lack."

Although I continued with my spiritual practices and tried to exercise my faith, my financial situation continued to be of grave concern, as I found it difficult to fulfill my monthly obligations. Deep within me, however, I knew that God would see me through, so I kept on affirming, "God is my supply." I acknowledged God as the giver of all good things and opened myself to the riches of His kingdom, praying constantly, thanking Him in advance for His abundance in my life. I knew that God wants the best for His children, and that He always provides. My responsibility was now to be patient and wait.

Having grown up in a very tightly knit family, my siblings and I learnt to support each other in times of need, as well to share each other's joys as well as our sorrows. I was moved to tears when quite unexpectedly one day my sister offered me a significant interest free loan repayable at my own convenience. I acknowledged my blessings as this generous offer was the answer to my dilemma. Not long afterwards I began to benefit greatly from the return and I once again proved that "God is "my instant, constant and unfailing supply". I blessed my sister and thanked God for using her to bless me.

During the beginning stages of Unity on the Rock Prayer Ministry when our finances appeared low, God never failed to provide for our needs through many trials and hardships.

Having had to relocate due to the sale of the apartment in which I lived, I prayed asking God to provide me with a safe, comfortable, attractive and affordable apartment. Soon after, I was divinely guided to a specific location, where one studio apartment was available. Having lived in a two bedroom apartment previously, a studio apartment seemed quite inadequate and I began to have second thoughts. The Holy Spirit seemed to have intervened however, and I was prompted to take a look.

Surprisingly, the apartment was quite spacious with a view of the ocean, and most of all, it was affordable, and significantly less than what I had been paying before. I decided to take it without a moment's hesitation. My financial situation was still of great concern, having not had a salary for almost two years, so I welcomed this apartment, which was virtually half the price of the previous one. This was definitely a divine intervention, and it was obvious that God was actually preparing me for further blessings.

I moved into the apartment with mixed feelings, secretly wondering how comfortable I would be in such a smaller space. The apartment was airy and full of light, but I had to add a lot of finishing touches to make it more comfortable. Eventually, it was transformed it into a little haven, and I left many things unpacked, knowing that God would provide me with a larger yet affordable apartment at the right time.

As I became familiar with my surroundings, one day I noticed the absence of the office manager. I later learned that she was no longer employed, and they were looking for a replacement. On impulse I jokingly offered my services, completely unattached to the result, not remotely believing that I would be considered. Getting the job would be wonderful I confessed, as the reality of the situation was that I really needed an extra source of income. In fact, financially it would be greatly beneficial.

Things began to unfold much sooner than I expected. My request for part time employment was considered and soon after the president of the homeowners association agreed to interview me. The interview was short and informal, and I was gratified when I was offered the job at a moment's notice.

I began working the following week for three hours per day, Monday through Friday, and although I had no prior experience as a condominium office manager, I adjusted quite easily. The president of the association was kind and understanding and she availed herself to helping me with my transition. My coworkers were also helpful, and we soon became a harmonious team. I felt elated, happy, and thankful for yet another blessing. My remuneration was handy, and I wondered how I would have managed without it.

As the manager of the apartment complex, I had many privileges. One of them was to meet the owners and to become aware of the availability of the other units. It was certainly a new experience, and I served with joy and gratitude. Another blessing soon materialized when I was prompted by the Holy Spirit to pursue my interest in purchasing a one-bedroom unit. Although I did not have a clue how this would be possible, I decided to probe the possibility anyway.

Judging from the average costs of the units, I did some mental calculations and reasoned that a ten percent down payment should not be too difficult to achieve. In fact, that would be the biggest hurdle, as the monthly payments would almost amount to my present rental. So my main concern would be to find the deposit and qualify for the mortgage loan. With faith in God to guide and help me, I was convinced that I could make it happen.

As fate would have it, I learned that a one-bedroom unit was up for sale at a very competitive price. Knowing that I was not in an immediate position to purchase, I prayed for divine order and promptly called the owner who lived off island, expressing my interest in renting with an option to purchase.

The owner of the apartment conceded to my request, and I was subsequently given six months in which to start with the sales proceedings. Not knowing how I would achieve my goal, I was happy for the six-month period, during which time I was convinced I could find a way mentally, emotionally, and physically to pull through it.

The lease and option to purchase agreements were executed with the help of my employer, who is an attorney, and I wasted no time in moving into the apartment in faith. I prayed, thanking God for this abundant blessing, and I envisioned myself as the new owner, affirming my ownership day and night.

My next step was to qualify for a loan from the bank. In my curiosity to know the requirements, I decided to see the bank officer beforehand, who willingly gave me the specifics, most of which at the time seemed quite out of my reach. I wondered how would I be able to accomplish this, but I took it into prayer and meditation and made an appointment to meet with her in the following three months. In the meantime, I nevertheless kept seeing myself qualifying for the loan at the appointed time.

I called everyone I knew who I thought could help me qualify, but it was always a hard luck story. Unfortunately, everyone was experiencing a financial challenge at that particular time. That did not stop me, however. “I must find a way. I will find a way. God is my source,” I kept affirming day and night.

Finally, I called my sister in Jamaica and asked her for a loan. She agreed without reservation, and within a month the funds were transferred to my bank account. I was grateful for her generosity, but unfortunately I still did not qualify for the loan, as my salary was inadequate. The managed told me that the only way I could qualify was to increase my deposit. So the reality of the situation was that I needed more funds.

There were times that it seemed quite unrealistic, but although it looked far-fetched, I knew and affirmed daily, "With God all things are possible." Despite doubts and anxieties that constantly plagued me, I believed with all my heart that I would be victorious. This became a true test of faith, however, as I had virtually exhausted all my options. Once again I had to resort to my inner reserve and practice deep abiding faith, reminding myself that "The lord is my shepherd, I shall not want."

As the time drew near, I became restless and sometimes despondent, but my resilient spirit would not be thwarted. Where would I get the remaining funds? Only God knew. I curtailed my spending habits to a minimum, and saved every dollar that I could put my hands on, accumulating extra funds from facilitating workshops, performing marriages, and selling recorded radio talks. Miraculously, there was money coming into my account from virtually every angle, and before I knew it my account soared way over the required deposit. I felt confident and victorious.

The final hurdle was to submit my application and wait for an approval from the bank. I surrendered knowing that God, who started a good work in me, would bring it to completion. I must admit, however, that as I approached the final furlong I had many trying moments, as impatience and doubts surfaced over and over again.

I can never forget the feeling of exuberance I had when I received a message on my wireless phone. "Ms. Linton, please come to the bank to sign your commitment letter." I was overjoyed. This meant that my application was accepted. I quickly responded and went to the bank to sign the commitment letter, wondering to myself if this was really happening. I went home that day feeling very elated and extremely humbled. I was overjoyed and relieved, and I gave God thanks for this wonderful demonstration of His goodness. Gradually, everything quickly fell in place, and before I knew it, it was time for the appraisal.

The closing date arrived, and when I was awarded custody of the apartment, I gave way to tears of joy. I gave thanks to God from the bottom of my heart, knowing and affirming that without Him this would not have been possible at all. All things are truly possible to those who believe, and the principle never ceases to work when you exercise it. God is good all the time. God is opulent and unlimited supply, and when our intention is good, all things are possible. When we acknowledge Him and trust Him, He will grant us our desires, but we must step out in faith and act.

It is good to trust God always, no matter what is happening in our lives, and lean not on our own understanding. In all our ways we should acknowledge Him and He will direct our path (Proverbs 3:5-6). "The kingdom of God is within us" (Luke 17:21). God is mind, and the wealth of mind is revealed in divine ideas. Divine ideas are therefore man's inheritance, but we gain access to these ideas only by seeking first the kingdom of God and its righteousness. Divine substance is therefore instantly available to all who seek it. Charles Fillmore says in Dynamics for Living, "Divine ideas are man's inheritance. They are pregnant with possibility."

Once more, as my needs became real, I continued to place my faith in God and waited for His answer with a feeling of surrender, knowing that He never slumbers or sleeps. The kingdom of God within is a sphere of divine ideas, and when one is connected to that inlet through prayer and meditation, outstanding results unfold.

Whenever we open ourselves by trusting God and surrendering to the process, He will make a way for us, and His goodness will be revealed. God, who is always on our side, will open doors that seem humanly impossible to open, removing seeming obstacles making the way of success possible.

In the creation story in the book of Genesis, the process took a period of seven days; the first six involving various degrees of mental work, culminating on the seventh day with a period of rest. The beginning of creation started with a decree: "*Let there be Light*," and there was light. According to Unity teachings, "Let there be" represents the Mind; the six days of work represent ideas, and the period of culmination or fulfillment represents the expression. The seventh day represents the involution.

From a metaphysical perspective this means that to create our abundance we first need to turn to our indwelling Spirit for inspiration or ideas. God is always giving us of Himself. The ideas we receive then take form in our soul or consciousness before becoming manifest in the outer world. Nothing is complete without surrendering to God. After the work is complete, we hand it over to God. It is God who gives the increase.

With God, the sky is the limit. As we continue on our spiritual path, let us maintain balance in our lives by devoting adequate time and attention to every aspect of our being. As children of God we have unlimited access to the abundance of the universe. We should keep employing a positive attitude, entertaining the highest and best thoughts expecting only good, and we will experience the bounty of God's inheritance.

Daily Affirmations

Faith draws my good from the invisible into the visible.
Everything I conceive and now believe I will achieve!
I say yes to my good!
I expect my good to come, and I am ready to receive it!
I know that a power greater than myself—the Supreme Being, God—is responding to me in a personal way.
I receive the best because I expect the best.
The good that I seek is even now seeking me.

When my faith falls short and I fail to experience good, I turn to God in prayer. During quiet moments with God I renew my understanding of my divine nature, and I am reminded of my spiritual inheritance.

Turning within now to that quiet place of rest, I acknowledge God within me as my instant, abundant, and inexhaustible supply, my never-ending source of all good. Wherever I am, God is, and all that God hath is readily available to me. I am a child of God. I am whole and free. I accept my divine inheritance. In His presence I am strong, peaceful, confident, healthy, secure, and wise. Knowing this truth brings me peace. With joy in my heart I give thanks for the fullness of life. My cup is full to overflowing. Thank you, God. Amen.

39

Giving is Receiving

> "He which soweth sparingly shall reap also sparingly; and he which soweth bountifully shall reap also bountifully. Every man according as he purposeth in his heart, so let him give; not grudgingly, or of necessity: for God loveth a cheerful giver. And God is able to make all grace abound toward you; that ye, always having all sufficiency in all things, may abound to every good work."
>
> 2 Corinthians 9:6-8

God gives freely to His children all the abundance in the universe and as His children God also expects us to give. Giving is a part of our nature. Just as breathing is important to life, so is giving important to our existence. Giving and receiving are opposite ends of the same stick. One cannot exist without the other. When one outweighs the other there is imbalance in our lives that results in illnesses and limitation. In his book *A Path with Heart*, Jack Kornfield writes, "Compassionate generosity is the foundation of true spiritual life, because it is the practice of letting go. An act of generosity opens our body, heart, and spirit, and brings us closer to freedom."

The purpose of giving is not to impress or placate God. God first gave to us, and our gifts are unlimited blessings. Everything we have received comes from God, and when we give, we give back to God only a small portion of what we have received.

In the creation story in the book of Genesis, God provided for our every need in abundance, and using a creative process He showed us how to create abundance. After bringing forth all things into manifestation, God then made humankind in His own image and likeness, blessed us and gave us dominion over everything He made. God then made one request. "Be fruitful, and multiply and replenish the earth." In other words, we need to maintain the flow of life by sowing and reaping, giving and receiving, touching other's lives by acts of kindness, and living life fully. When we give of ourselves fully and freely to life, life in return gives back to us much more bountifully.

Although there is an abundance of every good thing in the universe—instant, unlimited, and freely available to all—accessing it involves action; we need to sow so that we can reap. "Cast thy bread upon the waters; for thou shalt find it after many days" (Ecclesiastes 3:11). Whenever we sow our seeds freely and bountifully we demonstrate our faith in the omnipresent God, and the return is also free and bountiful.

If we do withhold our hand, there won't be a harvest. A free flow of exchange is the essence of life, and hoarding is counter-productive and leads only to stagnation. The quickest way to receive is from the abundance of the universe; to let go of our attachment to things or people. Someone once said, "If you want something, give it away."

We do not have to rob or covet others of what they have, nor do we have to fight or hoard to achieve good. Abraham was very trusting, and throughout his life he lived according to his faith, demonstrating that it is more blessed to give than to receive. In the book of Genesis, when God called Abraham to demonstrate his faith, he did what God asked of him willingly. As a result, Abraham was greatly blessed.

The first rule in giving and receiving is to acknowledge that the giver of the gift and the gift are one. God is the giver and God is the gift. Both Abraham and his nephew Lot were very rich in cattle, but a time came when there was a disagreement between their herdsmen. To make peace between them, Abraham offered Lot his choice of land and Lot chose the more fertile land, which Abraham accepted.

Abraham was not attached to materiality, and he acknowledged God as his only source. Abraham was content with what he had. Once he had the consciousness of God, Abraham had everything. After he parted company with Lot, God told Abraham

> "Lift up now thine eyes and look from the place where thou art northward, and southward, and eastward, and westward: For all the land which thou seest, to thee will I give it, and to thy seed forever. And I will make thy seed as the dust of the earth: so that if a man can number the dust of the earth, then shall thy seed also be numbered. Arise, walk through the land, in the length of it and in the breath of it; for I will give it unto thee." (Genesis 13:14-17).

The lesson here is loud and clear. Seek God first and all things are added unto you (Matthew 6:33).

The story of Ruth and Naomi is another that sets the tone for the principle of giving and receiving. As there was a famine in Bethlehem, Naomi, her husband, and her two sons went to Bethlehem in search of food. After arriving in Moab, her sons met and married two Moabite women, but soon after disaster unfortunately struck. Naomi's husband died, as well as her two sons.

Quite broken and destitute, Naomi decided to return to Bethlehem to be reunited with her kin. She broke the news to her daughters-in-law who decided to go along with her to Bethlehem. Naomi, who didn't want to disrupt their lifestyle, tried to discourage them. Orpah conceded, but Ruth remained loyal. She made it clear to Naomi that not only would she be with her whenever she went, but also she would endure all things with her.

Naomi and Ruth went to Bethlehem, and Naomi was reunited with her family. Ruth was instantly liked and accepted by Ruth's family, and it wasn't long before Ruth sought employment to support herself as well as her mother-in-law. With a stroke of luck, or with God's blessing, Ruth found employment with Naomi's rich relative, Boaz.

Soon Ruth proved her worth. Boaz was impressed with her good qualities and later asked her to marry him. Ruth accepted and married one of the richest men in Bethlehem, prospering not just herself, but her mother-in-law as well.

Later on in the marriage Ruth conceived and had a son Obed. Obed fathered Jesse, who became the father of King David. This rich union made Ruth the great grandmother of King David, from whose line Jesus the Christ came.

Because of Ruth's unconditional love and giving, she was consequently blessed and became a blessing to all mankind. Out of love, compassion, and kindness came Jesus the Christ.

It is always a blessing to think of others rather than focusing our attention on ourselves. Abraham, God's faithful servant, thought of Lot rather than himself, and he was blessed with posterity beyond measure. Ruth also thought of Naomi and not herself, and apart from receiving unlimited blessings, she blessed all mankind with the birth of Jesus.

Giving and receiving come in many different forms. We give and receive of our time, talent and treasure and they are all reciprocated. In her book, *Who's The Matter With Me?*, author Alice Steadman says "We are constantly giving of our time and life for another—but if it's done in love, our life force is generously renewed. That is why those whose "time" is filled can always find "time" to help you. God is timeless."

One of my most profound blessings came to me quite unexpectedly after volunteering as Sunday school superintendent at my home church in Jamaica. Being asked to sacrifice my Sunday morning worship experiences at the church for teaching and directing Sunday school was a big stretch, and I was a bit hesitant at the beginning. After a few days of contemplation and meditation, however, I willingly decided to let go of my reliance on and attachment to Sunday morning church experiences. I decided that the time had come for me to give back some of what I had learned.

After my initial commitment, I dedicated myself fully to serving others, and I immersed myself passionately in my new role, giving freely of my time, guiding, teaching, helping, and supporting kids of all ages. I looked forward to my new role and spent most of my time at the Sunday school. I served with gladness and gave willingly of my time, talent, and treasure. I was filled to overflowing with an immense feeling of joy.

Soon after, my love for the kids intensified and so did my blessings. Most of all, my divine purpose was revealed, which ultimately propelled me into the direction of ministry. It was quite interesting to notice that instead of falling behind spiritually, as was my initial fear, I actually progressed enormously, as I was forced to go deeper within to answer questions that came from inquiring minds. This was surely a wonderful and rewarding exchange of giving and receiving, and made quite an interesting observation that the children also had a lot to teach me.

Not that I ever anticipated any particular return, but the big dividends came when I was accepted in the ministerial program at Unity Village in Missouri. Not only was I accepted, but I was also awarded a scholarship with an adequate monthly stipend, as well as free accommodation. To top it all, I received an additional salary working part-time as a prayer associate at the prayer ministry for the duration of my ministerial training.

We should never give to impress God neither should we give for the purpose of receiving. "But when thou doest arms, let not thy left hand know what thy right hand doeth" (Matthew 6:3). We should never give grudgingly or sparingly, but give freely and generously in faith knowing that we can never out-give the universe. God loves a cheerful giver, and He always provides. "While the earth remaineth, seedtime and harvest, and cold and heat, and summer and winter, and day and night shall not cease" (Gen. 8:22).

40

Thanksgiving

"It is a good thing to give thanks unto the Lord,
And to sing praises unto thy name, O most High:
To shew forth thy loving kindness in the morning,
And thy faithfulness every night, upon an instrument of ten strings,
And upon the psaltery; upon the harp with a solemn sound.
For thou, Lord, hast made me glad through thy work:
I will triumph in the works of thy hands.
O Lord, how great are thy works! And thy thoughts are very deep."

(Psalms 92:1-5)

"Praise and thanksgiving is a spiritual tonic, which uplifts and inspires the consciousness, restores and energizes the physical body, attracts abundant wealth, and helps us adjust our lives in divine order."

Rev. Mary Mae Oesch

Expressing thankfulness to people who have blessed us is like connecting heart to heart with them. Both the giver and the receiver are blessed. No matter how menial the favor, it is always good to respond thankfully, as God is ultimately the source from whom all gifts come.

However, expressing thankfulness to others who have wronged us, is not so easy, but in most instances thanksgiving aligns us with the Christ consciousness, which brings us peace and actually increases our blessings. As the Son of God, Jesus had the power to do great things on Earth, but He never failed to give God the glory for each victory. He demonstrated the power of thanksgiving many times first by praying and giving thanks in advance for the desired manifestation, and it never failed that the supply always followed the demand.

Mary Kupferle says in her book *God Will See You Through*

> "Thankfulness is a builder and a strengthener. Thankfulness is a healer, a multiplier of the good, and dissolver of the negative. Thankfulness is a lifter and a life-giver. Thankfulness is a fortifier and a comforter. Thankfulness is an attracting power for blessings, a lightener of any load or burden, an ingredient of Spirit that produces miracles in the life of anyone in any situation."

During my tenure at ministerial school I made an interesting observation: things always seem lighter and easier when I constantly say "Thank you, God." My roommate Leiris and I both had fun trying to outdo each other in saying thank you. I never took any act of kindness for granted, no matter how simple it appeared. As I rode with her in her car each day, I never failed to thank her for the ride, and it was always amusing that her response was always to thank me for thanking her. Since then saying "thank you" has become a habit for me, and what a blessing it has been! It actually frees my spirit and gives me a feeling of inner peace and contentment.

Everything works in our lives for a good purpose, so we should learn to give God thanks in every situation. "In everything give thanks, for this is the will of God in Christ Jesus concerning you" (1 Thess. 5:18). Sometime ago on a return flight from Atlanta, Georgia to my home in St. Croix, I learned a great lesson; that God is always busily at work in even the most heartbreaking and unpleasant happenings in our lives.

On checking in at the airline ticket counter I was charged a fee for excess weight, which I paid willingly, acknowledging that I had to reap what I had sown, as this was a result of my overindulgent shopping spree. Unfortunately, my misfortune didn't end there. When I arrived at the boarding gate my hand luggage was considered too large to fit in the space provided on the airplane, and so not only was it taken away from me to be checked, but I was also charged another fee for extra luggage.

This time my reaction was quite indifferent. The inhumane way in which it was handled seemed to have put a damper on my entire trip, and I instantly sank into despair, feeling nothing short of self-pity. Had I been advised of this at the ticket counter, I could have checked an extra piece of luggage and saved myself the cost of being charged twice. Being charged twice for excess luggage on the same trip was mere punishment! *I am a Godly person. Why didn't God intervene?* I thought. What had I done to deserve this? After a brief period of mental persecution, I eventually found the strength to let it go and surrendered to the all-ness of God. *There must be some good in this,* I consoled myself afterward, and with this change of thought I decided to relax and enjoy my flight.

As I gradually relaxed I began to see the bigger picture. *What about the numerous blessings I received during my trip? Why don't I focus on the blessings I received instead of a little misfortune?* I reminded myself. I began to recapitulate the reunion with my siblings (some of whom I had not seen for a long time) the successful workshop I presented, the help and support from my family, the many financial gifts I received, and most of all, the opportunity to speak at a very successful church in Georgia. Gradually, I began to develop a new perspective; I acknowledged my blessings and affirmed that nothing and no one can take away my good, as God's storehouse of good cannot be depleted. I then blessed the situation and thanked God for His goodness in my life.

My itinerary took me through Miami, Florida, and as I landed at the airport I began to see the good in my apparent misfortune as I walked toward the boarding gate to St. Croix. The arrival gate was quite a distance away from my next boarding gate, and walking in high heels and carrying a laden pocketbook and a laptop computer over my shoulder for almost fifteen minutes was barely endurable. I could hardly imagine how I could have carried an extra piece of luggage (which incidentally had dysfunctional wheels), without literally torturing myself. I suddenly realized the blessing in being relieved of my hand luggage at the departure gate, and the idea of being overcharged for extra luggage became quite inconsequential. Filled with relief, I could only thank God for always being on my side, and for His grace and mercy that are always instantly available to me. Once again I affirmed, "All things work together for good to them that love God, to them who are called according to His purpose" (Romans 8:28).

The story of the Apostle Paul's conversion to Christianity after his brutal slayings of Christians and his subsequent devotion to the movement of Christianity speaks volumes in reminding us of God's omnipresence, His unconditional love, and His Goodness. After his conversion Paul became a devout Christian, a true martyr and believer in Christ, having suffered immense trials and persecutions himself during his missionary journeys. Not only did he persevere in all difficulties, but he also encouraged others, brought them to believe in Christ and continued to give thanks always.

During his second missionary journey Paul and Silas were accused of causing trouble in the city by teaching customs that were unlawful for the Romans. As a result, the majority of the people turned against them and the magistrate ordered that they be stripped of their clothes, beaten, and placed in prison with their feet chained.

At midnight in the presence of all the other prisoners, Paul and Silas began to pray when suddenly there was a great earthquake that shook the building so violently that it opened all the locks and doors of the prison, loosening the prisoner's chains. The guard in charge of the prison gates was petrified. If the prisoners escaped, he would be accused of assisting them. Paul reassured him that a miracle had taken place, but they were all still there. The guard was greatly relieved and inspired, and expressed his desire to experience this wonderful working miracle in his life. Paul told him about the goodness of God, and that the way to salvation was to believe in the Lord Jesus Christ.

God must have chosen Paul because he saw "divine potential" within him and knew that Paul was able to utilize the divine energy within him in a positive way. God's divine purpose was evidenced later that night when the prison guard being impressed with Paul's miracle of escape brought them to his home, washed and dressed their wounds after which, he and his entire household were baptized and saved. They all rejoiced and gave God thanks.

The next morning after the magistrates discovered their Roman heritage they ordered their silent release. Paul refused, however, demanding that the magistrates themselves come to release them. The magistrates who feared for their lives asked forgiveness and begged them to depart from the city.

Paul continued on his missionary journey traveling from city to city, and although he met with all manner of opposition and criticism, he continued to give thanks to God nevertheless, constantly proving that God's goodness would always be revealed.

Paul found himself in trouble once again in Jerusalem when he was accused of false teaching. He was dragged out of the temple, but as they were about to kill him, the captain who was informed of the incident rushed over to the temple and saved him. The captain then arrested him, however, and after having him chained, he asked what Paul had done.

Paul was once again accused of being an Egyptian causing an uproar, and leading four thousand murderers into the wilderness. He tried to defend himself, telling them that he was "a Jew of Tarsus, a city of Cilicia, and a citizen of no mean city". He tried to share the experiences of his journey with them, but unfortunately they did not want to hear about his journey. They had another agenda; they wanted him put to death.

Paul was bound with thongs, but the captain and the other offenders later fled the scene after discovering his Roman heritage. After the great dispute he was then unbound and brought into the castle to appear before a council. The following night the Lord appeared unto Paul and told him that he needed to testify in His name the way he had in Jerusalem.

Paul's enemies still wanted him dead, so they plotted to kill him, but Paul was not afraid. He had God on his side and he trusted God. He was later warned of the plot to kill him and after confronting them, he was later sent to Caesarea to appear before Felix, the Roman administrator of affairs.

The trouble never ceased. Paul was later accused by Ananias, the high priest, of being a ringleader of terrible violence all over and a nuisance to all! Paul tried to defend himself but he was kept in prison until the hearing, and guarded by a centurion, who was told to allow him some freedom, but to keep him away from his acquaintances.

Paul remained in custody for two years, after which time Porcius Festus relieved Felix. Festus continued to question Paul, but Paul continued to defend himself from the false accusations of the Jews and later made an appeal to Caesar. All during these trying times instead of thinking of himself and his misfortune Paul continued his Christian fellowship, encouraging others to live joyfully and peacefully in Christ.

Paul's conversion to Christianity after the persecution of the saints worked in a positive way, humbling him, filling him with a new sense of being and a deep and sincere passion for Christ and he wanted others to share his experience. As he once again told his story about his new-found vocation, and expressed his joy and fulfillment as a Christian to King Agrippa and his sister Bernice, Paul wished that everyone would have a similar experience of experiencing joy in the Lord. Agrippa was almost persuaded by his testimony, and the King, the Governor, and Bernice, all eventually agreed that Paul was innocent and not deserving of death or of chains.

Paul's experiences are very encouraging to those of us who are on the path to spiritual attainment. He encourages us to give thanks always and persevere during our challenges, as it never fails that good always overcomes evil. We may never know how, when, or in what form our blessings will come, but it is certain that they will. Paul had a definite purpose to fulfill. He was single-eyed and focused on the truth and despite all the obstacles that faced him he persevered with his missionary work, writing letters full of joy and encouragement to the congregation of Christian churches.

Instead of focusing on himself and the difficulties that he encountered, he thought of others and he praised God! As a result of Paul's relentless spirit, his deep abiding faith, his humility, his thankful spirit, and his genuine desire to serve, God never failed him.

Sometimes we fail to give thanks to God during our trials because we focus our attention on ourselves and not on the power of God within us, and we fail to see the bigger picture. Sometimes we take our good for granted and leave God out, even thinking that we are our own providence, but the sooner we realize that we can accomplish nothing on our own, the sooner we will be able to give thanks to God and realize our blessings in all things.

Giving thanks is a part of our nature, and a thankful spirit amounts to healing of mind, body, and spirit, and abundant good in all areas of our lives. In order to maintain one's healing, one has to live in the awareness of the Father and give thanks always. In Luke chapter 17, as Jesus passed through the midst of Samaria and Galilee on His way to Jerusalem, ten lepers stopped Him and requested healing. After healing them Jesus advised them to show themselves to the high priest.

Unfortunately, only one of them returned to thank Jesus. "Were there not ten cleansed?" He asked. "Where are the nine?" Jesus then told the one who returned that his faith had made him whole.

The one who returned to thank Jesus was aware of his divinity, obviously conscious of the truth that in order to maintain his healing, he needed to keep in the flow with the act of thanksgiving.

It is quite questionable as to whether or not the other nine lepers had really been healed, as to complete the healing process seemed to have required a final act of thanksgiving, which they had failed to do.

It is interesting to note, according to this story, that the one leper who returned to give thanks was a Samaritan, whose race was considered inferior by the Jews. Jesus did not consider anyone inferior, however, and He obviously wanted to demonstrate that there was good in Samaria, as well as in any other place, when He chose to go through Samaria in John 4:15-26.

In his *Metaphysical Bible Dictionary,* Charles Fillmore defines Samaria as intellectual perception that signifies a mixed state of consciousness. Consequently, it is in acknowledging our humanity that we are able to transform it and realize our good. We should therefore give thanks in all things, not just for the things that our limited senses perceive as a blessing, but in everything, even those things we do not consider a blessing. When we give thanks in all things, it is without doubt that blessings will continue abound.

Epilogue

The secret of living a victorious life is to "surrender" to the Christ Spirit within, and Jesus gave us specific instructions on how to accomplish this in John 1:43—"Follow me."

To follow Jesus does not mean that we have to literally be born in a stable, ride on a donkey, or keep the company of beggars, thieves, and culprits. Following Jesus does not even mean that we have to deny ourselves material comfort, or live in dire conditions.

To follow Jesus is to strive for the consciousness that Jesus represents, maintaining an attitude of non-resistance; holding on to our faith and looking beyond the appearances of lack, adversity, ill health, evil, and disharmony; being able to demonstrate in times of need; being forgiving, peaceful, and calm in times of trouble; being compassionate; unaffected by the demands of society; being humble, kind, and considerate; loving even those who use us and wrongfully persecute us; and finally, giving thanks always and putting God first in everything.

Jesus lived a very simply life yet He was able to demonstrate in abundance . . . from healing to supply. The ordinary circumstances of His life clearly portray that victory takes place when one displays lowliness of being. Jesus' desire was to do the will of the Father, and His agenda on earth was to demonstrate the kingdom of God within and exemplify the ideal life of a righteous person, even in dire circumstances.

Jesus was a master of everything, and He told us that we also have the divine capabilities within us, showing us how we may overcome weaknesses and limitations by denying flawed thinking and by affirming Good. Jesus told us that we could also do the things He did.

Unfortunately, living the perfected life is not always easy, as in our humanity we all fall short at times, encountering many trials and tribulations, failing miserably time and time again. Hence, it is not always easy to emulate these outstanding qualities of the master Jesus. Although we were made in God's image and after His likeness, we nevertheless have a choice either to remain in mental bondage or to free ourselves by starting with what we have. We may be able to demonstrate just one or two of these wonderful qualities of Jesus, but the more we try the more we will succeed. We ultimately facilitate our own healing by surrendering, or letting go of the lesser self so that the greater Self, the Christ within, can be realized.

No one is ever the same when it comes to encountering and surrendering to Jesus, the Christ Spirit within. The rich young ruler in Mark 10:17-31 found it difficult to demonstrate eternal life not because Jesus failed to effect a change within him, but because of his reluctance to surrender his ego, or his material attachment to the Christ of his being. Consequently, he went away very sorrowful. The truth is that we cannot follow Jesus and remain in a world of materiality. "No man can serve two masters: for either he will hate the one and love the other; or else he will hold to the one, and despise the other. Ye cannot serve God and mammon" (Matthew 6:24).

Jesus offers us living water, but He will not do the work for us. Through His death and resurrection we have been empowered with the realization of our divinity. We have the power to cast out demons, to tread on serpents, and to heal the sick (Luke 10:19-20). All we need to do to achieve this consciousness is to acknowledge our own powerlessness, take up the cross, or cross out dependency on outer things, and finally surrender the little self to the Christ of our being.

There are also many states of consciousness to be experienced as we struggle to maintain our divine nature. We go through many ups and downs, but God understands all our cares, all our burdens, all our humanity and He will comfort us and bless us in whatever state we are in.

> "Let not your heart be troubled: ye believe in God, believe also in me. In my Father's house are many mansions: if it were not so, I would have told you. I go to prepare a place for you. And if I go and prepare a place for you, I will come again, and receive you unto myself; that where I am, there ye may be also" (John 14:1-3).

Ultimately, a certain degree of preparedness is necessary to experience and express our divine nature. A story is told about a bus that was bound for heaven. On the bus were passengers destined for both heaven and hell. The stop for hell was first, and the people bound for hell were dropped off. One man who was bound for hell decided to stay on the bus, as he wanted to go to heaven.

When the bus stopped for heaven, the man decided to stay in heaven with the heaven-bound. While in heaven he became hungry. He looked around and he saw an apple tree with a single ripe apple on it. He reached up and tried to pick the apple, which was right within his grasp, but no amount of pulling would release the apple.

A little child suddenly appeared and effortlessly stretched and touched the apple that instantly dropped into his hand. As children often do, the little child bit into the apple a couple of times and then threw the rest of it to the ground. In his hunger the man reached down, picked up what was remaining of the apple, and bit into it. Unfortunately, all his teeth suddenly began to rot and dropped out of his mouth.

On the grass were children of all ages bouncing about and playing heartily. The man tried to walk across the grass, but the grass pierced his feet so deeply that it left him with unbearable cuts and bruises and he could go no further. It was obvious that this man could not fit into heaven, because he had not prepared himself and therefore lacked the consciousness of heaven.

As long as we live, we will be faced with trials and persecution, and our faith will be severely tested. No matter what faces us, Jesus never fails. He has made ample provisions for us in times of need and adversity. Before His crucifixion, He prepared His disciples for what lay ahead. As He would no longer be with them in the physical form, He cautioned them of the challenges that they might face in His absence. "They shall put you out of the synagogues; yea, the time cometh, that whosoever killeth you will think that he doeth God service" (John 16:2).

He encouraged them to persevere despite the many challenges that they would face, as they would eventually reap their rewards. "Verily, verily, I say unto you, that ye shall weep and lament, but the world shall rejoice: and ye shall be sorrowful, but your sorrow shall be turned into joy" (John 16:20).

The work is continuous, and no matter how diligent we are in our spiritual practices, we will sometimes seem to be susceptible to temptations. Yet, God, who is always near, will always steer us in the right direction. God will not suffer us to be tempted above which we are able (1 Corinthians 10:13).

No matter what we are facing, we can rest assured that within us is a reservoir of unlimited possibilities. "For God hath not given us a spirit of fear; but of power, and of love, and of a sound mind" (2 Timothy 1:7).

We are made in the image and likeness of God and in times of weakness God will work in and through us to accomplish all good. "I can do all things through Christ which strengtheneth me" (Philippians 4:13). Whenever our faith gets dim and we feel like all is lost, God will come to our rescue and see us through all our difficulties. "He which hath begun a good work in you will perform it until the day of Jesus Christ" (Philippians 1:6).

Our aim should be to become spiritually aware. The more spiritually aware we become, the more we will experience the fruits of the spirit: love, joy, peace, longsuffering, gentleness, goodness, faith, meekness, and temperance (Galatians 5:22-23), and the more we experience the fruits of the spirit, the more we will become aware of divine opportunities each day; the opportunity to love, to assist someone in need, to give a helping hand to a friend, to smile with a stranger, and most of all, to give thanks to God always in all things.

"I now bring my awareness to this moment. I breathe easily and notice any sensations in my body. I become aware of any tension or pain that I may have been fighting. I do not try to change them; I notice them with kind attention. In each area of struggle I discover, I give my body permission to relax and allow my heart to soften. I refrain from struggle or fight. I let go of the battle, because the battle is not mine. It is the Lord's. I breathe quietly. Gently now like a stream unobstructed, I flow with the love of God. I am now in the dwelling place of God, the secret place of the Most High God. The presence of God is within me now as life. I let go and let God.

In this awareness my mind is poised and my heart serene, for I know that the Spirit of God works in and through me to bring forth great possibilities in my life. God, You are the answer I seek to all my desires, hopes, and dreams. When I am tired, You give me rest; when I feel that I can't go on, Your grace is sufficient for me; when I am worried, I know I can cast all my cares on You; when I can't figure things out, I know You will direct my steps; when I can't manage, I know You will supply all my needs; when things seem impossible, I know that with You all things are possible. I am aware of Your promise: "Son, thou art ever with me and all that I have is thine."

Almighty God, with joy in my heart, I give You thanks now for the fullness of life. Your goodness flows through me as a nourishing river of gladness and thanksgiving. I am assured that You are always with me, and that You will never leave me or forsake me. I know that Your will for me is absolute good. I am grateful, dear God, that my blessings are a constant reality. My gratitude comes from an overflowing heart. Thank You, God, for your love that heals in every way. Amen.

Brief Glossary

Consciousness	a sense of knowing
Sense consciousness	a mental state in which a person believes and acts through the senses
Adam consciousness	the first movement of mind in relation to life and substance
Christ consciousness	the perfect mind that is in Christ Jesus
Pharisee consciousness	a selfish and unprofitable state of mind
Demonstrate	to bring forth; to reveal
Demonstration	outward expression
Divine Mind	God
Illumination	the light of Christ
Indwelling Christ	the spiritual identity of each individual
Manifestation	the materialization of an idea
Meditation	focusing the mind on God
Metaphysical	beyond the physical
Negation	a belief that is contrary to the laws of God
New birth	a new awareness
Perfected state	a feeling of oneness with the Divine presence within
Principle	basic law
Reality	absolute truth
Realization	the dawning of the Truth in consciousness
The silence	a still and relaxed state of being wherein there is silent communion with God

Self --------------------------------the Christ idea within
Spirit ------------------------------the movement of God in the universe
Subconscious mind----------memory
Substance ----------------------the underlying reality of all things according to the Divine mind
Truth ------------------------------that which is perfect and good in the mind of God

Selected Bibliography

*The Bible quotations used in this book are from the King James Edition.
*The doctrine in this book is attributed to Unity School of Christianity.
*All Unity literature used in this book is in public domain and used with permission of Unity; www.unity.org

Anonymous	*The Cloud of Unknowing*, Edited by William Johnston Doubleday, 1973
Butterworth, Eric	*Discover the Power Within You,* HarperSan Francisco 1968
Brumet, Robert	*Finding Yourself in Transition,* Unity Books 1996
Cady, Emile	*Lessons in Truth,* Unity Books
Chopra, Deepak	*The Seven Spiritual Laws of Success,* Amber Allen Publishers, 1993
Dillaway, Newton	*Consent,* Unity Books, 1947
Dossey, Larry, MD	*Healing Words,* Harper San Francisco,1994
Emerson, Ralph Waldo	*Self Reliance,* Peter Pauper Press, 1967
Ferrini, Paul	*The Silence of the Heart,* Heartways Press, 1996
Fillmore, Connie	*Keys to the Kingdom,* UnitySchool of Christianity

Fillmore, Charles	*Dynamics for Living,* Unity School of Christianity *Keep a True Lent,*Unity School of Christianity
	The Revealing Word, Unity Books, 1959
	*The Twelve Powers of Man,*Unity Classic Library *Mysteries of Genesis,* Unity School of Christianity
Fillmore, Myrtle	*Healing Letters,* Unity School of Christianity
Gaither, Jim	*The Essential Charles Fillmore,* Unity Books, 1999
	The Metaphysical Bible Dictionary, Unity School, 1931
Gomes, Peter J.	Sermons, Biblical Wisdom for Daily Living, Avon
	Books Inc. 1998
Kornfield, Jack	*A Path with Heart,* Bantam Books, 1993
Kornfield, Jack & Feldman, Christina	*Soul Food, Harper SanFrancisco 1996*
Kupferle, Mary	*God Will See You Through,* Unity School of Christianity, 1983
Morgan, Robert J.	*Nelson's Complete Book of Stories, Illustrations, &* Quotes, Thomas Nelson Publishers, 1952
Myss, Carolyn. PhD	*Anatomy of the Spirit*, Crown Publishers, 1996
Rowland, May	*Dare to Believe,* Unity Books
Ruiz, Don Miguel Ruiz	*Beyond Fear,* Council Oaks Books, 1997

Sanders J. Oswald — *Spiritual Maturity,* Moody Press, 1962

Sand Turner, Elizabeth — *Let There Be Light,* Unity Classic Library, 1996

Steadman, Alice — *Who's The Matter With Me?* E.S Press Inc. 1966

Underhill, Evelyn — *Mysticism,* E.P. Dutton & Co. Inc., 1961

Unity Movement Advisory Council *A Unity View of New Age and New Thought,* Unity School of Christianity

Walsh, Neale Donald — *The Little Soul and the Sun,* Hampton Roads Publishing Co., 1998

Whitney, Frank B. — *Mightier Than Circumstances,* Unity Books, 1935